W9-CPG-796

FREE WRITING!
A Group Approach

Exercises, Examples,
Fourteen Points of View,
A Poem, and Footnotes

by

Joseph Brown, Jean Colburn, Patricia Cumming, Nancy Dworsky,
Peter Elbow, Sandy Kaye, Seth Racusen, Robert Rathbone,
Steve Reuys, Lee Rudolph, Stewart Andrew Silling, Ken Skier,
Gary Woods, and David Wray

FREE WRITING!

A Group Approach

Toward a New and Simple Method
of Learning and Teaching Writing

HAYDEN BOOK COMPANY, INC.
Rochelle Park, New Jersey

808.042
F 853

161875

Library of Congress Cataloging in Publication Data

Main entry under title:

Free writing!

    1.   English language—Rhetoric—Study and teaching.
2.   Group work in education. I. Brown, Joseph S.
PE1404.F7   808'.042   76-48127
ISBN   0-8104-5982-5
ISBN   0-8104-5981-7 pbk.

Copyright © 1977 by HAYDEN BOOK COMPANY, INC. All rights reserved.
No part of this book may be reprinted, or reproduced, or utilized in any
form or by any electronic, mechanical, or other means, now known or
hereafter invented, including photocopying and recording, or in any information storage and retrieval system, without permission in writing from
the Publisher.

Printed in the United States of America

1	2	3	4	5	6	7	8	9	PRINTING
77	78	79	80	81	82	83	84	85	YEAR

Preface

This is a book for teachers about how to teach writing. Maybe. That is, it's written by people who have been trying to teach writing and have been writing themselves. We have worked together, with each other and with our students, over a number of years. We think we know how people can learn to write better. This is a book for people who are interested in learning to write better. Their own learning and others' learning.

Perhaps the most basic thing that we have come to know is that writing is something that you have to do to learn it. Learning about it is virtually useless when it comes to the doing. It may be a little like reading a manual on how to tune your automobile; somehow it all looks different when you get into the car's innards, and the tuning is something else again.

So this book starts out defeating itself [unless, maybe, it's a book for students to bug their teachers with (with which to bug their teachers)]. It tells the reader about how to teach and learn writing. But here and there throughout the book there are *instructions* about what a reader is supposed to *do*. Readers are accustomed to reading such things. Even our editor judged the effectiveness of these exercises by reading the instructions. Even one of our authors declared that she would simply read such instructions.

Nevertheless, the reading of these exercises will not help anyone learn to write, or learn to teach writing. You have to do the exercises. And you have to respond to the text. (Read this book only with a pencil in hand!) And if you're going to teach writing, you also have to do it yourself. Nothing we have learned, nothing we can tell you about, has any value at all outside the doing of it.

After you've done it, let us know what happened.

A few words about personal pronouns. We have followed our individual preferences in using s/he, he/she, she/he, he, she, etc. The resulting variety of usages forces awareness of crumbling conventions. We like such confusion; we think it reflects a reality in our lives and in the present culture.

Since we are numerous and often disagree (in footnotes and elsewhere), it might be best to start like a Russian novel, with a list of characters and initials:

1. *JOSEPH BROWN* [JB] has taught at Harvard and at Wesleyan, and is now at MIT. He is a consultant in the Humanities to the Detroit Institute of Technology. He is co-editor with the late Dorothy Van Ghent of an anthology called *Continental Literature*, and has published short stories.

2. *JEAN COLBURN* [JC] was born in Chillicothe, Ohio. She has degrees from Washington State, Northwestern, and Wayne State. A resident of Detroit off and on for 15 years, she has taught at Wayne State and since 1969 at the Detroit Institute of Technology where, in 1971, she became part of a group which established an experimental program. Since 1972 she has been director of the program.

3. *PATRICIA CUMMING* [PC] has taught at Converse College (Spartanburg, S.C.), the Boston Center for Adult Education, University of Massa-

chusetts-Boston, the Beacon Hill Free School, and MIT. She was among the founders of the Theatre Company of Boston, and her second book of poems, *Letter from an Outlying Province*, has just been issued by Alice James Books.

4. *NANCY DWORSKY* [ND] has published poetry and articles, and is co-author of a book on an 18th century mathematician, Sophie Germain. At MIT she teaches writing and literature and was an originator of an experimental freshman program, "Concourse," which unifies teaching in the sciences and the humanities.

5. *PETER ELBOW* [PE] has taught at MIT and is now at Evergreen State College in Olympia, Washington. He is the author of numerous articles on teaching and of the books, *Writing Without Teachers* and *Oppositions in Chaucer*.

6. *SANDY KAYE* [SK] was a member of the California Committee on the Open Door College. He has taught at Diablo Valley Junior College, in Concord, California, and at Northeastern University. Since 1966, he has taught writing and literature at MIT, and directed the writing and literature seminars in the Sloan Fellows Executive Training Programs. He runs a Writing Workshop at the Cambridge Center for Adult Education, and, with several of the other authors of this book, is currently involved in planning a community Writing Center.

7. *SETH RACUSEN* [SR].

8. *ROBERT RATHBONE* [RR] teaches technical writing at MIT and is the author of *Communicating Technical Information* (Addison-Wesley). He has consulted and lectured on technical writing at engineering firms all over the country.

9. *STEVE REUYS* [SWR] has taught writing at MIT and reading at the University of Massachusetts-Boston. He has worked at the Education Warehouse in Cambridge and with sixth-graders as a teacher aide in the St. Louis Public Schools.

10. *LEE RUDOLPH* [LR] has a hard time free writing: he was taught penmanship in Cleveland in a very oppressive way, was always told he held the pencil badly, and still gets cramps in his hand. Luckily he learned to typewrite. Now he is a mathematician, teaching at Brown University. He is the author of *Calculus of Elementary Functions* (with H. Abelson and L. Fellman) and *Curses & Songs & Poems*.

11. *STEWART ANDREW SILLING* [SAS] is the son of an Arkansas sharecropper. By the time he was 10, he'd watched his Ma and Pa work themselves to death out there, so he boarded a big old Greyhound bound for Boston. And that's where he is today, sitting in his garret, writing absurd lies that make people feel sorry for him.

12. *KEN SKIER* [KS], a 1974 graduate of MIT, received MIT's first Enabling Grant in Creative Writing in 1973, an Eloranta Research Fellowship (to experiment with the writing process) in 1974, and (with Seth Racusen) MIT's first Dean Irwin Sizer Award "for the Most Significant Contribution to MIT Education, for work in establishing the MIT Writing Program," in 1975. He has taught introductory and elective writing subjects at MIT, and is currently writing a handbook dealing with the writing process.

13. *GARY WOODS* [GW] is now at Harvard Medical School, where he is attempting to convince the administration to continue the pass-fail grading system. He is on probation as a conscientious objector.

14. *DAVID WRAY* [DW] has taught writing as a teaching assistant at MIT. He now conducts a writing workshop in "Concourse." He graduated in 1975 with a degree in Writing and Literature.

Contents

beginning

Thursday, 2:05

DAN WOLK

Sitting in building 14E, room 303, waiting for Pat and Ann(e) to come along to direct the show, though we know how the show is run. Is it that we're so used to being taught and not enough used to learning? People sit, not talking, and not needing to, some nervous in their silence, I writing about it. John starts something, but it's just conversation. Should I help out? No, it's not necessary. Some listen to John and Brian, others stare at the floor, Kathleen is writing as well. And Alan is reading. The conversation dies for a moment. Is there a bronzed Adonis to come resuscitate the young maiden? John makes a try. Why? Well, why not? Brian brings Paula (that is her name, isn't it?) into the conversation (5.41),[1] toolish. Nervous, self-conscious, but that's ok. And I sit here writing, as Kathleen does. Why? To avoid conversation? No, not in my case. My nature is production, not empty words about the weather, why a teacher hasn't arrived yet. I look up to see what's happening. Nothing. Alan is reading, Kathleen is writing. A door opens down the hall. Pat or Ann(e), potential savior? No. Oh, well, better luck next time. Fernando nervously tears the holes from a sheet of spiral-bound notebook paper and plays with it, for lack of anything else to do. Why? Why not? Here's Pat, apologetic. "Where's Anne?" she asks.

The class can begin.

---

1. A course in Organic Chemistry.

Beginning I

This book comes out of our experience teaching a series of writing and literature courses given in the Department of Humanities at the Massachusetts Institute of Technology. The place is important because literature is not taken for granted at MIT, though it has been required; both students who "like" it and teachers who believe in it often feel as if they must continually justify it to themselves and others. It is not really a question of the gap between the two cultures: literature, it is felt, is probably, even certainly, a good thing, but in some essential way it is not real—because not quantifiable—and hence not important.

There are, of course, many scientists who are deeply and creatively interested in the arts; but skepticism about them is expressed just often enough to remind us that we must explain our claims to truth. This can be wearing. Sometimes it makes us long for a place where some basic premises about the role of art in society are shared and taken for granted. Usually, though, it makes us aware of ourselves and what we are doing in relation to the needs, lives, and interests of our students. In any case, part of the scientific discipline is to question assumptions, and students trained in science who take a strong interest in literature often come to it with a careful and deliberate skepticism (though in some cases, also, the enthusiasm of converts). Further, they have had little training in, and in many cases less patience with, the traditional academic disciplines of literary study.

As teachers we have found this situation alternately, and sometimes all at once, exhilarating, frightening, challenging, and confusing. Those of us who are on the faculty of the Writing Program came from "good" English departments in major universities, and when we began to teach we thought we could proceed in the way that we had been taught: we would ask our students to read good books of imaginative literature (many of which had meant a great deal to us), and ask them to discuss these books in class and to write intelligent, original, analytic papers of the kind we had learned to write so well ourselves.

In these classes we found an occasional student who would do this for us, and even do it brilliantly,[1] but in general we discovered that this approach did not work. Many students read the books quickly and resentfully if at all; they refused to "discuss" them in class; and their papers were boring and awkward, full of poor sentences and unsupported generalizations.

These papers were impossible; and we believed that if this were so, it must be because the students could not write. It was not their fault, it was the fault of their high schools. If they *could* write, surely they would turn in interesting papers about the good books we had tried so hard to explain in

---

1. Cf. Nancy Dworsky's definition of a good student: one who makes us feel we are good teachers.

3

class. And everyone would feel better! They would get A's and we would feel justified. Clearly, it devolved upon us to Teach Them to Write.

These problems are not, of course, unique to MIT. A wide variety of needs, interests, and values exists in any college or university. Further, each department wants to believe that its discipline and subject matter are of unique, lasting, and universal importance to mankind—in particular to that portion of it confined (by chance, economic necessity, idealism, boredom, coercion or greed) within the college walls. And in most colleges it is still also true that a large and often unwilling segment of this population is exposed, by force if necessary, to the "idea of the humanities," and more particularly to that fraction of it dealing with literature and writing (even if subsumed under categories like "communications skills").

In our situation, the relentless pressure of so many unmotivated students in our classes led us to change our teaching; and what we learned from them is not, we believe, only applicable to highly qualified students in a technological institution. Many of us have taught or, having left MIT, are teaching in other institutions, experimental or otherwise, where students are not so highly selected. The problems we encountered before coming to MIT have led us to look for the solutions we found here; and these solutions, in turn, have been useful in other places and with other students. We have had, in each of our freshman classes, at least two or three foreign students with real difficulties in English; the way of teaching we describe in this book, while not always in and of itself sufficient to teach them English, has proved of real benefit to many.

There was, though, one group of courses where none of the problems we had in our other classes applied. In these courses students read the course material, often with enormous interest, and almost always with patience and respect; they did the assignments; and they talked about them with interest, and sometimes passion. They related what they read to their own lives and problems and concerns; they talked with one another about these, and grew to know and trust one another, to feel sympathy and understanding.

These classes were the elective writing courses; the assignments were to write a certain amount, on any subject, during the term; the course material was (largely) the discussion of this writing—essays, stories, poems.

This is not to imply that even in the best of our classes this sort of energy was created all at once, always, or all by itself. Much of this book is concerned with how to set the stage so that it can happen—something we found out by trial and a good deal of error, and with a lot of help, criticism, advice, and good will from our students. Nevertheless, when it did happen, it was so exhilarating that we began to want it to happen in all our courses, even in our sections of the required freshman course. Even if the attempt failed, we thought it would be worthwhile.

So we devised a course which would be open to this kind of experience. The course has undergone many changes and vicissitudes (some of which will be described later on) and it has not always succeeded. Many students did not want to take it or any Humanities course, and it was far more important to them, in terms of their interests, commitments, and careers, to do well in the very demanding courses in math, chemistry, and physics they had to take. Our course is demanding too, though in a different way, and they resented it. They also had lives outside the classroom. Further, many of them did not particularly want to be writers (though they agreed, we suppose, as everyone does, that it is a good thing to write well). The course, borrowing what we thought was the essential and energizing principle from the elective courses, revolved around the students' own writing, which was distributed and/or read aloud to the class.

Nevertheless, whatever happened in the class sessions, one thing occurred: the writing improved, sometimes astonishingly. The classes improved, too, but later. The difficulties of teaching the course made those of us who were teaching it meet and keep meeting—at first to give the different sections a certain coherence, but later and more importantly (during the arid stretches where nothing we tried seemed to go well), to give each other courage and suggestions, often born out of despair. Finally, one of the students, Don Kollish, suggested that we ask them to help us teach. And they did. Out of this group of people in this situation comes this book.

We would like to thank all our students for their help. We would also like to thank Nathalie Rogers Fuchs and Paul Crowley, from Greenhouse, who led a group that several of us participated in for most of one week. We began the group because we thought we should "study the group process." We did not end it with any clear intellectual formulations. But one result of those meetings is "A Proposal for a Pilot Writing Program at MIT" and this book.

Susan Longaker and Robert Boynton provided patience, wisdom, moral support, and help when we needed it most.

And finally, we would like to thank the Department of Humanities for providing summer funds for two summers.

Beginning II: Free Writing

PATRICIA CUMMING

Free writing is a basic and very simple exercise; one of those, like touching your toes with alternate hands or diaphragmatic breathing, that everyone ought to do every day because it is easy (it only takes ten minutes), and its moral, spiritual, and physical benefits are incalculable. It helps you to know yourself; it can free you from the mundane or show you that you are hopelessly enmeshed in it. It is better than aspirin for tension, and has no counter indications. It helps when you are depressed; and sometimes you find out what you were concerned about. These are the instructions we give classes, friends, ourselves:

> Write for ten minutes. Do not stop writing. Do not worry about spelling, punctuation, complete sentences, grammar. If you can't think of anything to say, write "I can't think of anything to say," over and over again until you do think of something. Do not read over what you have written (at least not for a while).

Free writing is not only a way of finding out what one is thinking but also how, in what rhythms, words, phrases; it is a way for people who are locked into textbook language or other people's thoughts to find their own.[1]

For people whose training has served mainly to make them more and more self-conscious about their writing, it can be enormously liberating and exhilarating; suddenly they find that thoughts and feelings they had never believed they could express, appear, often movingly and coherently, on paper. Some of the best writing I have seen has been done when I stopped "teaching" and asked a class to write for ten minutes.

It is important, especially at first, that people should have an accepting audience for their free writing. I have told lots of people about free writing, urged them to do it, but they don't, or they try it once or twice and don't learn anything from it. Somehow it remains too personal and private; it can be too easily dismissed (though it is still good for getting started when all

---

1. Oddly enough though, for people who are blocked and uneasy, sentence structure, grammar, and spelling improve in their free writing. They knew what it was all along. And it became available to them when they were free. For others, the rigidity of the sentence has to be broken down before they can find their own voices. [PC]

2. I think that if a person—especially one who has not done any free writing—anticipates that what he or she writes will be read by *any*body else, it is no longer free writing. Most blocked writers find their own internal critics intimidating enough: add to that the unknown threat of an unknown reader —or worse, a reader in a position of authority—and the thought, to say nothing

else fails). It is writing, yes, but not communication. The writer needs other people to accept what he or she has said.

Many of us use it quite extensively in classes, especially at the beginning of the term; some only occasionally. When we do it in class, the teacher writes too and usually asks students to hand their papers in.[2] It helps to give them some distance before they read them over (it often looks to them like bullshit at first); further, we want to preserve the idea that writing, even unfinished writing, is communication. But free writing is a special kind of communication; it is confidential, and remains the writer's own property exclusively, to be used or thrown away as s/he decides. We add:

> I'd like you to hand your papers in, with your names, but you don't have to if you've written something you don't want anyone to see. I will read your papers and hand them back, without comment, and I will never refer to anything in them or discuss them in the class or with you unless you specifically ask me. Of course, you may find you have written something you want other people to see, but that's your decision.

Sometimes it is very hard not to talk about someone's free writing; it may be so much better than his or her "papers," and you may very much want to say how good it is. And maybe you can if you are very careful to be general. But you have made a promise, and if you violate it, even with the best of intentions, the writing becomes much less interesting and honest. People edit; and the barriers are up again.

A class's free writing can change your perspective completely. I remember one class—bored, sleepy, apathetic; every topic that had come up died within two minutes; after struggling with them for most of the period I gave up, and said "Okay, this is a writing class. Write. For ten minutes."

They did. One girl, Catholic, thought she was pregnant. A boy had just stormed out of the house after fighting with his parents; he had said he would never go home again and wondered if he would. Another had an all night job. Another was broke and hungry; all he could write about was

---

of the experience, becomes far too frightening. It will be forced writing; and it will be fake. *However*, there's nothing wrong with a laissez-faire exchange of papers: those who wish to read what another has written can put their own free writing on a table. They pick up a paper from the table, and return it when read. No discussion, no immediate feedback. Usually only some students exchange papers. But others say they have been freed to do other writing; and some use their free writing as the first draft, or the inspiration piece, for a more formalized piece of writing—a story, a poem, a play. When a student doesn't hand in a piece of writing, I strongly encourage him or her to save it, "just in case you'd like to read it sometime. You don't have to show it to anyone. Just hang on to it." Some of them do. [KS]

food. A girl wrote a poem about being free. Two or three people even wrote about what we had just failed to discuss (they *were* thinking about it after all; they were just unwilling to speak that day), and several wrote about the class, why it didn't seem to be going well (but they wanted it to; they cared). I had written that it was a boring class, and besides it was all my fault.

*   *   *

KEN SKIER

On the other hand, free writing can be a most useful method for channeling excess energy. When students in my elective, evening writing class got too giddy—when, that is, *we* got too giddy, too happy, too high on being together again after another long lonely week Out There, and when jokes and general good times threatened to stretch throughout the class hours, I would ask what people wanted. I pointed out that we could continue what we were doing, or we could do something else. Any suggestions? Sometimes there were ("Let's go out." "Let's turn off the lights." "Let's get up a kitty for beer."). We'd discuss the alternatives. Sometimes we'd select one. Other times I'd say, "You go ahead; do what you want to do. I'm going to write." I would either say or imply, "You can write, too."

Within sixty seconds, what had been the loudest classroom on the hall would have become the quietest: all of us—or almost all of us—sitting, scratching our pens and pencils on our notebooks, looseleaf sheets, and yellow legal pads. The room remained charged, but the energy was no longer dissipating into the air: it was turning into words, stories, sequences of images and ideas on paper. We'd usually write for twenty minutes or so. When our eyes all met again, we'd talk. Sometimes those who wished to would read what they had written. Other times we'd go on to something else, but on a new level, a cooler, calmer level, more directed, ready to work, ready to write, ready to deal with our writing—to communicate with each other, constructively and creatively.

i

writing

Opening Dialogue

KEN SKIER

"What are we going to do in this course?"

"A number of things. A lot of what we do depends on you."

"What do you mean?"

"Well, what do you want to do?"

"Huh? *You're* the teacher."

"And you're the students; this course exists for you, not me."

"So?"

"So this course is called Writing and Experience. That's not very specific. It's not supposed to be. But two things are included in that description, implicitly. We deal with *your* writing here, and we discuss *your* experiences. Not Hemingway's. Not Faulkner's. Not Shakespeare's."

"Not at all?"

"Not unless you want to. I'm not going to impose them on you. There's a great deal to be learned from studying Shakespeare, Faulkner and Hemingway, but you won't learn unless you're ready for it, and you probably won't be receptive if the course and material are required. If you really want to do it, we'll do it."

"Well, where's the syllabus?"

"Syllabus?"

"You know—the schedule. Every course has one."

"Not this course."

"Huh?"

"The syllabus in this course is *you*,[1] and I can't put that down on paper; that's your responsibility. I may be part of it too, if you'd prefer that I participate. I'm not going to ask you to do anything I'm not willing to do, and I'm going to try to get this class to progress as much as possible as a *group*. Not 'Me, Teacher: You, Freshman' or even 'Me, Critic: You, Writer' or, worse, 'Me, Writer: You, Learning-to-Write-r'. This is a writing

---

1. This statement, so nakedly expressed, is a hard fact of life in learning how to write: we resist it, students and teachers alike, because it means looking in strange places for that intellectual continuity which is the life line of the teacher and the cry of the student. What provokes the resistance is the need to feel that there is a connection, sharply conceived and powerfully worked out, between what happens in class the first day and the knowledge we bear like a chalice before us out of the classroom on the final day. Reading lists are putative models of that continuity or structure; a series of illuminating lectures dramatizes the structure; orchestrated discussions imitate it. Any course which deprives us of that structure, particularly when it substitutes an amorphous, sometimes sentimental hypothesis labeled the experiential "you," is bound to antagonize everyone involved, let alone those colleagues outside the classroom who hear reports of mushy dialogues inside the classroom, in the form of sup-

workshop, a place where we can try to connect with each other and with ourselves as well. The way we try to do that is with words."

"What do you mean?"

"I mean we work with words—your words. *Your* English, the language you know and use and think and speak in. Maybe the language you feel in, if that's how you experience things. Your voice. You."

"But I took this course to learn how to write well. I don't want to write like I speak; that's incomprehensible."

"You're making sense to me now."

"Yeah, but—"

"Don't you want to be able to write, and have it come out the way you intended?"

"Sure. That's why I want to study people who knew how to do it. Like those guys you mentioned. I've read some of them."

"Much?"

"Only what I had to, in school. It was all right."

"But you didn't read any more?"

"Not when I didn't have to. I had better things to do."

"But you want to study them here?"

"Sure."

"Why?"

"Huh? Because—well, because they wrote well."

"But you don't want to read them!"

"Yeah, well, you know how it is."[2]

"Sure. I haven't read much of them, either, and what I did I didn't enjoy unless I read it out of class."

"So what are you saying?"

"That there are better ways to learn to write."

"But those guys were the best!"

"And you don't read them! You want your writing to be read, don't you?"

"I guess so. Why not? I mean, I have to be able to do it, and someone's going to have to read it."

---

portive rather than critical responses to "student" writing, and begin to fear for the deterioration of all standards. Sometimes they have every right to be afraid, since students will not stand still for lessons once they have been freed to learn. [JB]

2. At first I was bothered by this moment in the dialogue: no one, particularly a student, gives in so easily. But now I realize Ken Skier is after bigger game: learning to listen for the ambiguous signals a student emits as he struggles to discover how the teacher wants him to take the course, what he has to do to pass it. The teacher part of the author of this dialogue has learned how to speak to that ambiguity in his student self by treating it as a problem in logic, so that by the time everyone realizes it was only a strategy of freedom, no one minds the strategy itself. [JB]

"And you want it to say what you want it to say, don't you?"

"That goes without saying—right? That is, if you said what I thought you said."

"I did. I think. But what did I mean? I meant that the only way to improve is by working on *your* writing, *your* voice, and *your* experience, refining them as you revise them. Shakespeare knew Shakespeare, and Hemingway knew Hemingway, and they each wrote the way they wanted to, to say what they wanted to say."[3]

"But who wants to read about *my* experiences?"

"I do. And the class will. Because there's more to this course than your writing. There's you, as a human being. And the more we can understand each other, the better we can understand ourselves . . . which is about as much as you can get from any course. It'll help your writing, too."

"But what do you want me to write?"

"I don't want you to write anything—specific; don't you see? You're not supposed to be writing for me. Say what's important to you, as well as you can. We'll work on it when you've written it; not before."

"What good will that do? I don't know how to write. That's why I'm taking this course."

"I think you're taking this course because it satisfies the Freshman Humanities requirement, but I'd like to see you do something for yourself, in spite of that."[4,5]

"I want to learn how to write!"

"I know you do—or think you do. The thing is, you already know how to write; you just don't realize it. Over the course of this term I hope to help you realize it."

---

3. They also knew a lot of other people, of course, and they put them into their stories and plays, so, whether at war, in London, or an MIT workshop, the writer ends up discovering other experiences, as well as his own. It's a productive transaction, as the author points out later on in the dialogue. [JB]

4. By now it should be obvious that the teacher is *projecting* his own values onto the student, and the student, recognizing a steamroller when he sees one, has chosen to play along. Unknown to the teacher this student has already published two novels, and she taught a feminist literature course in her high school. [DW]

5. Dave, you and I—and my students—know that I don't conduct my classes that way; this chapter—this dialogue—is a distillation of many such conversations and discussions, with students both male and female. I ask them why they're taking the class. Mostly they say it's the most interesting course that meets the requirement. I'd like to get rid of the requirement. Recently we did, to a large extent. But even a requirement is no reason for students to take a course that they don't want to take. And if they're going to be there, for whatever reason, I'd like them to get something out of it. Mostly, they agree. This conversation, being a compression of many, many conversations and discussions, comes on much stronger, and quicker, than its real-life—or at least, academic-world—counterpart. Those dialogues take many hours, in toto—not ten minutes. [KS]

6. Sure this isn't an introduction? [ND]

"How?"

"By getting you to write—regularly and at will.[6] Pick up a piece of paper and a pen and put down words. That's all there is to it, though there are countless variations on the theme."

"But I can't write unless I've got something to say. I have to be in the right mood. And I have to have the time."

"That may be true—for you. But not everyone writes the same way. That's one of the things I hope you'll experiment with this term: different ways of writing. That means different styles; it also means different writing *processes*. There are lots of ways of putting words on paper. One of them —which I'd like you to try—is called automatic writing."[7,8]

"But I'm not a machine! How do you expect me to write like one?"

"I don't. But if you do it right, this is far from a mechanical process. It's also called free writing, if that sounds better to you. And it doesn't care about what you've got to say, or what mood you're in or how much time you've got. All it involves is writing continually for ten minutes, without stopping to plan ahead or read over what you've written. You've just got to keep the pen moving; write nonsense if you have to."

"But how good can that be?"[9]

"Objectively, you mean? As a piece of 'good' writing? Probably not very. But you'd be surprised—fairly often that simple exercise produces superb pieces of prose."

"And when it doesn't?"

"Even when it doesn't it only takes ten minutes. And it can do two valuable things: get you into the habit of writing, and help put you in touch with what you're thinking about, with what matters to you at the moment."

---

7. Free writing and automatic writing are two different things. Automatic writing has historically been attributed to spirits, and usually occurs with the writer's hand under hypnotic anaesthesia. [DW]

8. So did this chapter. [KS]

9. This is an important question. It is, as they say in the lit crit game, a textual (and contextual) crux. The answer to it is at the heart of this book. Behind it lie twelve years of the student's intellectual life, which has been defined for him as the pursuit of an unattainable perfection in the guise of standards whose validity he must learn to accept. The first tentative grope toward freedom is *not* to deny those standards. Rather, we learn to ignore their grip on us while we discover what we have to say, what we believe, what we deem important, without being overwhelmed by the whispering judgments of all those people who brought us to the edge of learning and then informed us that though we must, inevitably, fall, one or two of us—the really "good" writers or scientists or managers—would make it to the top of the mountain. As a result, most of us stop writing or playing or experimenting with the unknown and the uncertain. Patsy Cumming talks about the process in "I Can't Write" and "Responding to Writing." Sandy Kaye speaks of it in "Why Write." It's implicit in Nancy Dworsky's devastating attack on the system in "Writing as an Agon."

We're not rejecting judgment, then. We're not proposing chaos. Rather, we learn to see into the terrible heart of Lear's cry: "None does offend, none—I say none!" precisely because we still recognize certain values: clarity,

"But how can it matter to anyone if I just write it down?"

"It doesn't have to matter to anyone—it matters to you![10,11,12] And if it matters to you it'll mean something; it'll be real. That's why I won't give you a specific assignment, unless you force me to. I can think of hundreds of things to tell you to write about, and you'd do it, and hand it in, and we'd go over it, but it would be false. You'd be writing it because I told you to, and you'd be writing it for me. Hemingway didn't write for a teacher—he never even went to college—and neither did Shakespeare. If you want to emulate the masters, why not start there?"

"Where?"

"With writing for you, with what matters to you."

"Then what is the course for, and you, and the class? Am I supposed to do this all on my own?"

"No. And I'm glad you brought that up, because I've been misleading you, in a way. The class serves a very definite purpose, and so do I, and it's important. But it's not important until after you've written something. Anything—just something you've written that matters to you, that you care about. That's the only assignment I'll give you: make it honest. Write a piece that *means* something to you. It doesn't have to be "finished," but if you don't care even a little about it you're wasting our time: yours, mine, and the class's—and I don't want to see it. Just care a little, and you'll be fine."

"But what does the class do; what do you do?"

"We read what you write."

"And that's it?"

"Not entirely. But it's the most important thing we'll ever do for you."

"What good is that? Anybody can read my stuff."

"Oh?"

"I just have to ask them."

"Then you're exceptionally lucky, and the class and I might be superfluous. But we might serve a purpose. You see, we don't just read it and leave it. We read your writing regularly, and you know it, and you get feedback. You get to see how your writing affects us, which parts work and which don't, and you get to see it regularly, whenever you write, and you're going to write every week."

---

subtlety, ambiguity, discrimination. We merely propose that writers and readers come at them from another direction, which turns out to be a state of mind: an ease, a confidence, about doing "bad" work on the way to discovering what is "good." An opinion, a standard, begins to get verified when more than one person freely shares it. In class, we discover the wheel every term: the wheels differ in size, color, texture, but the shape (and its value) persists, like a dream, a book, an emotion, an idea. [JB]

10. That's questionable—or at least not self-evident—since anything written at another's command stands a good chance of boring the writer. (I've been bored by my own free writing whenever I'm bored with myself—and that's not infrequent.) [ND]

"You were making this sound like such a free class, but you said that just like my tenth grade teacher."

"Look—*you're* the one who wants to write better. *I'm* not going to make you write, or force you to hand in what you write. But I can't help you unless you do those things. Neither can the class. You've got to work at it. If you wanted to swim better you'd have to go down to the pool. You could watch movies of Mark Spitz at the 1972 Olympics, but it wouldn't make much difference. You'd have to go down to the pool, and force yourself to swim laps, and swallow water, and burn your eyes with chlorine, and tire out your muscles treading water and kicking. And you'd have to do it regularly—every week at the bare minimum. Someone like Spitz practiced for most of every day."

"So now I'm in training?"

"Only if you want to be. But if you want to be able to write, you're going to have to sit down and write."

"I think I'd rather learn to swim."

"Touché."

"Thanks, Coach."

"Look, I'm only your 'coach' if you want me to be. I can maybe tell you some things about style, and suggest various experiments or techniques if you're interested. I can even direct you to authors—*published* authors —who've done some of the things you're trying to do, and whose works might prove helpful. But I am first and foremost your reader, and secondly, your resource. Somewhere in back of that—way the hell behind that— you'll find your teacher. Think of me as a more experienced member of your writing group; that's all."

"You mean you won't correct my papers?"

"Take the writing you do badly and turn it into good writing?"

"Exactly."

"No."

"No?"

"No, I won't do that. I won't impose my own impressions and evaluations on you. Not unless you want them—and even then you're going to have to ask me, in no uncertain terms, to suggest changes which might make the piece more effective, for me as a reader."[13,14]

---

11. If absolutely nothing interests you, Nancy, don't write. I wouldn't force you. How could I? But anything that interests you is going to be in your head (or heart, if you want to get sentimental). And if it's in your head, or your heart, it'll come out through your hand, when you free write. [KS]

12. I don't think it will necessarily bore the writer once it dawns on him that he doesn't have to show it to anyone. And the boredom, if it does come, has nothing to do with the idea of coercion: rather, we dread to face the possibility that we really have nothing to say. Once faced, we discover the fear was groundless. Usually. [JB]

13. I don't know why Ken keeps offering to give in to students on important matters if they *really* want him to. Either his principles are good (and I

"But you don't want my writing to get better?"

"Better, yes. Just like mine—no. If you expect me to say what writing is good and what is bad, you're going to be disappointed. I won't make judgments like that, and I hope you and your classmates won't either. Such judgments rarely, if ever, improve someone's writing—at best they make the writer write the way his critic wants him to, and in any case they stifle him. They put a harness on his creative process, and blinders on his imagination."

"Then you won't tell me what you think of my writing?"

"I'll tell you what I think, and I'll tell you what I feel. But I won't say it's good and I won't say it's bad. I'll tell you all you want to know about how it affected me."

"But you won't correct it?"

"No! To 'correct' a piece of writing—especially a personal piece of writing, which is usually the truest kind—is implicitly to say that there is a right way to write, and one or more wrong ways. I won't do that; there are far too many 'right' ways to write—so many different ways—that I would be pompous and oppressive beyond my capabilities to tell you that you're wrong, and that I know what's right."

"Then what will you do?"

"I'll tell you how your piece of writing affected *me*. As one reader. I won't say something is 'good' or 'bad,' but I'll tell you if it worked or if it didn't—for me. But there are others in the class, and you should weigh their opinions as well as mine. And, at the limit, if you really want me to make changes, I'll take a copy of your writing and mark it up—making very clear to you that these are changes I'd make if I were writing it, and that would probably make the piece more effective *for me*. But that's the most you'll get: my own, *personal* response."

"So, that's the course?"

"That's the course."

"Well, teach—coach—I've got one more question."

"Yeah?"

"What do I do now?"

Find a piece of paper and write for ten minutes about whatever is in your head. Don't stop. Write "I have nothing to say. I have nothing to say . . .", if you have nothing to say. Use additional pages if you need them.

---

think they are) so he should stick *to them*, or they are questionable so he should drop them. [ND]

14. My underlying and overriding principle is to respond to student needs. If the student wants direction, I'll try to respond to that—but with suggestions, *not* requirements, assignments or "exercises." [KS]

I Can't Write

PATRICIA CUMMING

I can't write, I'm trying to begin, I can't think of anything to say. No—there's too much to say, but first I have to find a good title, a good first word, an arresting, unforgettable first sentence. And then everything has to be beautifully organized—how? I can't do this, it's too hard, too confusing, too frightening; I put up a good front most of the time, my friends believe me, I've hoodwinked my teachers (some of them; or they were kind); but if I write this badly I will, finally, be exposed; people will laugh, or they will feel sorry for me—and I will vanish.

I can't simply say what I want to say (whatever that is), I have to say it cogently, intelligently, brilliantly. I can't.[1]

Further, the people who are going to read this are as follows: my third grade English teacher who let no child out of class without making her or him cry at some time during the year; the professor who once wrote: "All these words display a commendable enthusiasm, perhaps, but when are you going to write the essay assigned in this course?"; my mother who said my paragraphs were too long; and my teacher who said they were too short.

So now I've stopped writing. I've rewritten the first page five times, and have not improved it much, though Strunk and White rattle around in my head, full of good advice. (Use active verbs. Eliminate unnecessary words [none of my words are necessary]. Keep sentences short. Avoid Latinate constructions.) And another, nameless person proclaims: "You must now write a transitional paragraph in which you state the main points of this essay in a clear, incisive, and well-organized fashion."

I have written one—I've written nine. They are all lousy: either condescending and didactic ("These are real problems, but they can be solved") or phony democratic ("We are all hung up in some of these ways"). On the other side of this paragraph or the next lies everything I want to say like a mowed growing field; but I am caught in a barbed wire fence of imperatives, and I have lost my voice, rhythms, self. I've lost any sense I may have once had of how I could speak to anyone who might read this. Those ghosts—I could never talk to them; no matter what I say, they will never understand. And so I had better put on the mask of the Rhetoric Handbook.

Only the words that come out of that mask are unreal or false or boring or dull—rhetoric indeed, and I can't stand them. I hate myself for writing them, I hate people who are going to read them, and whoever or whatever it is that is making me put myself through this.

---

1. I am reading this piece as a fleshing out of the student in Ken Skier's "Opening Dialogue": she is now able to articulate freely all her doubts about the teacher's "advice." [JB]

But.

The people who are going to read this first are not the people I remember. They are friends of mine; and if this seems silly or wrong they will try to help me put it right.[2] I *can* talk to them, and I ought to be able to write something they will understand.

At least I can try a first draft in time for the meeting. It would be awful if I were the only person who hadn't written anything.

The difference between people who feel they can't write and people who think that perhaps, sometimes, they can, does not lie in ease of composition. Writing is usually hard, for most people; and it is hardest for those who want to think of themselves as "writers" and do write and do get published. I once believed that the distinguishing mark of writers was that they could write (easily, fluently); I have learned, alas, that more often than not they feel they can't, and that most of them work longer, harder, and worry more (not less) about it than other people.[3]

But there is a difference between them and people who never finish anything, or finish it quickly and reluctantly and unhappily: and that is—hope. The hope that finally, out of all the fear and confusion, something written will come: something true and clear and one's own, something that one can read to oneself or other people without too much embarrassment and maybe, sometimes, with pride. People who can't write are people in whom that hope has been destroyed.

To restore hope to someone who believes s/he can't write, to give him back the belief that something s/he has written might be important or interesting to someone else, a group of real other people must be present to give their reactions. The simple fact of reading something to others changes the

---

2. I disappointed the author early on. She gave me her piece and I had nothing to say about it except how much I liked it. She waited weeks for me to criticize it, convinced, apparently, it was so bad that I couldn't bear to speak to her about its badness—I was being too kind. In fact, no one was saying anything and she got depressed thinking how bad it was. Like the rest of us, the author has trouble controlling hard judgments of herself: our teachers have done a good job: they don't have to be around anymore, telling us what's wrong with us. We know it now in our blood. [JB]

3. Some of them have systems, cards or notebooks, or special green paper. They haunt stationery stores, sure that somewhere the equipment exists which will finally enable everything to become clear and coherent the first time, and dispel those periods of overwhelming ineptitude. [PC]

4. This group should not, however, contain my third grade teacher. It should teach them to talk about writing in a different, less evaluative (and less hostile) way. [PC]

5. What in fact people said about this was that they liked the first part (people laughed when I read it), but unfortunately the balance seemed preachy. Nancy Dworsky said that she has to be careful about this in her writing, so she is sensitive to it. *I* did not think I was being preachy, and a number of people

character of writing entirely; it ceases to be a lonely exercise, written in a void, to and for a void, and becomes what writing really is—a communication from one person to others.[4] The person on the other side of the blank piece of paper becomes tangible; s/he will probably neither hate nor love you because of what you have written, but may feel closer to you even when the writing is not "finished"; in any case s/he will probably not cease to like or respect you because of it.

It's important to learn this; for some people it may be the most important thing they can learn, the elements of style notwithstanding. And it is hard to remember; you have to keep finding it out over and over again. I would have put off writing this for months if we did not have a scheduled meeting (deadlines help too); I *know* that the reality of reading it aloud and finding it flat or awkward, however dispiriting, will not be as horrifying as what I can conjure up in my own imagination. We are our own worst critics; for one thing no one else cares enough about what we write to criticize it with the intensity we possess; for another, most things seem less imperfect to readers than they do to the author because the audience is blessedly untroubled by the author's visions of what s/he really wanted to say (and how). The audience deals simply with what s/he did say.[5]

But sometimes people can't think of anything to say at all, at least not anything they are willing to put on paper. The walk across the room from chair to desk can seem like crossing the Sahara by bicycle or rounding Cape Horn in a 12-foot boat. And having arrived there, it is sometimes extremely difficult to stay. There are dishes to wash, phone calls to make—just this morning I weeded the strawberries and mulched the tomatoes, all very necessary. Then it was lunch time. This afternoon I cleaned out a closet. Now it's eight o'clock.

---

said that perhaps they were bored because they knew what I was saying and agreed with it, but that it had to be said. I felt mollified, but was still uneasy about Nancy's reaction—Peter Elbow, in *Writing Without Teachers*, says (p. 134): "I am always noticing how much I can usually learn from someone with some strong obsession or axe to grind . . . If someone has a hang-up about X and sees it in 50 percent of what he reads (which is actually typical when you start learning someone's real reactions), then you better take him seriously when he sees X in what you wrote. He is an expert on X and can detect it in very small quantities. Very small quantities are important because they affect other readers who can't see X."

So I cut out half of what follows and reorganized the rest. I don't know that I've changed the tone very much. I do feel strongly about what I have written; I am afraid that if I adulterate it, I will sound condescending or be manipulative, and I'd rather preach. Nancy says, about the next-to-final draft: "Somehow, I think I'd define 'preachy' as condescending and manipulative as well as didactic. Sincerity seems a whole other matter—what follows sounds sincere to me—not preachy." I'm glad it does now.

The real problem, though, is this: I like the first part best too, but I wonder if it sounds enough like a book. The second part sounds more like expository prose. [PC]

These things may not have been a total waste of time. For me at least it's pointless to try to write something if I feel angry or self-abusive. You need a clear day for writing, one when the light makes everything sharp, focused. What I did accomplish to day made me feel virtuous as well as guilty; all those pages I rewrote or couldn't cope with last night are coming clearer now. In fact, perhaps, some of the time I spent was a way of getting things straight in my mind, of listening to my own voice; and it was also good for the strawberries. Other times I do things that make me feel guilty and nothing but guilty—sleep, read magazines, fiddle, etc., and that, once started, gets worse, not better; it can go on for days. I have a friend who, when he procrastinates, manages to stay at his desk. He cleans drawers or rearranges files and answers letters, and seems to write a lot. I wish, though, writing, including not-writing, didn't take quite so much *time*.

Somehow, growing up, I lost both my fluency and my spontaneity when it came to writing—it was all those red penciled comments in the margins. Eventually those can be useful, when it comes to editing; but the real problem is to get something to edit—words—on paper.

There is a basic difference between the creative and the editorial process, although we often forget this and assume (wishfully, I think) that they are the same, or at least should somehow both operate at the same time, mixed exactly, so that reason tempers feeling without stifling it, and form and imagination interact: the whole emerging in perfectly balanced sentences.[6]

Editing can be agonizing, but it is at least a possible task, and one for which you can get some real help, from friends, classes, teachers, ex-teachers, typists, etc. Most books about writing are really books about editing; it

---

6. Sometimes it does, in my case in about 1 page out of 20. But I have to have written the other 19. Some people, who write slowly, do seem to be able to allow this to happen in their minds before they put anything down on paper (sometimes their work reads slowly too). Lawrence Kubie, in *Creativity and the Unconscious*, says that when this occurs it does so in a part of the mind he calls the preconscious; that is where creativity resides. I find this plausible, but it doesn't help me write. How can I *get* to my preconscious? I'm sure it would be splendid if I could. "A genius," James Thurber has said, "is someone who does not have to do all this hard work." [PC]

7. But we do disguise ourselves sometimes: as a way of getting hold of the material we wish to recreate for a reader; as a way of controlling that reader; and as a way of seeing what we're really like; which occasionally means coming at it sideways, slowly, a little evasively, but finally pouncing on the truth and making it real. It's what Kafka does when he takes the self which nakedly addressed his father in the famous letter and disguises it as a cockroach. He couldn't give the letter to his father, but he published *Metamorphosis* while he was alive, for everyone, including his father, to read. [JB]

8. This starts me off with some kind of bad feeling about the book. It makes me—as reader—feel some kind of distrust. It's pretending, and I don't believe it, pretending to be a free writing at a time of desperation. I believe you

is something that can be explained, and even accomplished, at least on those days when one is sanguine, objective, kind, coherent. But no one can help you when you can't think of anything to say or how to say it.

You can, however, do some free writing or Smarterbook exercises (see Appendix I). You may not say exactly what you thought you were going to say, but you will say something.

The strange thing about free writing is that it is almost always interesting (to me, though not always to the author), more interesting sometimes than the most carefully polished prose; even when it simply consists of "I can't think of anything to write" over and over again. When someone has to say that to me twenty-five times I know it must be terribly true, and s/he is saying it much more simply and more directly than in some of the "essays" I used to get from the freshmen, which meant the same thing, after all. Boring writing most often comes when people try to disguise themselves or write in someone else's voice—a teacher's, a book's, a television commentator's; they write the way they think someone else wants them to write, and their stifled anger or discomfort is obvious. It is like wearing someone else's clothes because one is afraid to wear one's own.[7]

I have been talking here mainly about people whose fluency has been dammed up by the kind of treatment they have received as they have been educated, but who must write because there are things they want to say or have. People who want to be, or are, writers, and who have written well, have problems of a different order of magnitude when they are blocked. While I once had hundreds of explanations for why this occurs, each one different depending on the person, I now feel they have the same common denominator, and that is fear. Of success, of failure (or both), of hurting or

---

get stuck, I believe maybe you even write those things down when you feel stuck. But I slide immediately into the stance of naive reader and say, "What is this? She's the writer, she's the teacher, she's publishing a whole fucking book —and a book of poems too—and she's trying to pretend she's as desperate as me. It's *her book*, it's published. Who's she trying to kid? She's trying to sneak a fast one over on me, buddy up to me and trick me in some way—pretending she's like me." It feels disingenuous. Makes me get my dukes up.

I think what bothers me is that in both "Opening Dialogue" and "I Can't Write" it is left ambiguous just what the exact relationship is between these words-on-paper and reality: what is the "mode of reality" of these words? And it bothers me that a book about writing of this sort should start out with that kind of ambiguity. I respond as though it were a hype.

I need somehow for you to acknowledge that you *have* come a long way with writing—that your desperation isn't the same as someone's who has never published or given pleasure to others with writing. This would be cured if you began by simply saying, "Yes, I have written this, that, and the other, managed to publish, managed to give my writing to others with pleasure, and gotten enormous pleasure out of identifying myself with writing, *nevertheless* I sometimes (or often) get very stuck, I promise, I really do, and once last year when I felt particularly stuck I actually wrote the following words and meant them." [PE]

losing someone one loves, of being oneself. Writers want to, feel they *must,* tell the truth. But at times that truth can seem so awful (even if it is said, or known, only to oneself) that it must not be spoken. The price of not saying it is to remain mute. Fear and imposture are the greatest enemies anyone who writes can have.[8,9]

---

9. I *could* say much of that (but won't). I understand why you don't believe me, but it makes me angry, just the same. I've taken the risk of dropping the mask of professional/teacher/writer and said what really happens to me.

And you say (smugly) you don't believe I'm afraid. *Feelings should never be responded to that way, never, never, never.*

> *Remember:* each person is the expert *on his/her feelings and point of view. Your job is to honor and respect his/her expertise on those feelings, assumptions and values, and to help him/her articulate, clarify and own them. (We can't change in ourselves what we don't own in ourselves.)*
>
> K. Morimoto, *Serving as a Discussion Leader*

Feelings are not intellectual constructs, to be treated with skepticism and doubt, they just are. And they are scarey. They may be more or less convincingly expressed, and this is (maybe) the point you are making, but I think you could have been more careful about how you made it. (**** ***!)

You and I differ, I think, profoundly, on what "feedback" should be. You want it all, redundant, hostile, and (therefore) "honest"; and I try to say what I think the writer can accept at that point, and no more, and no less. Often, I'm wrong. But I try to keep people from getting hurt in my classes; I think the courage to risk, to experiment, to be true, even if ill-conceived, is more important than anything else. Some writers want to be trodden on, to be *criticized* ("in blood: red ink," one student told me): there, I am authoritarian, I resist that, with whatever prestige I have. There's something else I try to teach, besides writing, and that is concern for other people, awareness of them. Trust, which is the base for a really fruitful class, is a fragile thing. It involves for both the writer and the respondent, listening, trying to know.

The point is, precisely, that however much you've written, the same dreadful uncertainties apply—Auden, hardly a shy or unprolific writer, once said that each time he finished a poem he wondered if he'd ever write again. Further, this was one of the first pieces written for this book, *none* of us had any confidence then. Of course, now it has been scrutinized and revised, I've written others, the book has been finished, and it's only taken me three weeks after the final manuscript was sent in to write this footnote. [PC]

Footnotes, Feedback, and Reality

PETER ELBOW

I'm bothered by the footnotes. On the reality level I feel them as pretending to be actual feedback—actual movies of the mind—actual sharing of empirical feedback: the book pretending to be a laboratory example of the kind of thing we are talking about. But I'm bothered because I don't think it really succeeds. What's here in the footnotes is too easy. I feel the real business of genuine feedback is much more risk laden: it involves really finding out everything. There's always a kind of hold-your-breath wondering each time you start a new feedback situation because you always wonder whether it will succeed. And of course some classes don't—really don't get to FULL feedback, because there *is* such genuine exposure and risk.

I feel the footnotes don't do justice to that reality. I respond by feeling: They have the form, the overtones, the smell of the thing, but they don't get the real thing. How do I as reader know that the writers really put in all the feedback? They might have left out the footnotes they don't like.[1] And even if these are ALL the reactions that people really wrote down, then they couldn't have written down a very large proportion of what was actually happening in their minds. In short, it feels too easy, gimmicky, cute. I don't believe it. They distract me in reading. If someone really has a full reaction—enough to interrupt me with, then I'd really like to see it worked out—not just a passing swipe.

I like the idea of trying to get the process of feedback actually in this book. It decreases the number of ways in which we are talking about something rather than doing it. But to really do it I think it would be necessary to take one piece and then give full movies of different minds reacting to it. And give them in all their complexity, and even redundancy, and, hopefully, instructive uncomfortableness. I think the unspoken message in the footnotes as they now stand is, "You can join in this new game of giving feedback if you just make occasional clever or smart-aleck comments." It's too easy.

But there is a desperate need for people to really see what it is. No one gets it from a description anyway, only by seeing it in action. I certainly can never make people conceive it until they do it.

I guess my general stance in writing and life has tended to be—still tends to be—"nice guy sincerity." But now I often feel it's hollow. What's making me suspicious of parts of our book is the very tone I so often adopt: lots of cues which say, "Trust me, I'm just a nice guy, just a bluff fellow, just trying to do my best, a little bit mixed up at times, sometimes I can't see what I'm doing, but believe me, the moment I have any feeling, I'll be sure to let you know just what it is. You can trust me. I'm sincere."

---

1. Authors did get to choose their footnotes. [PC]

I think that the kind of teaching we've been trying for in recent years —the kind of teaching we are talking about in this book—is precisely the kind of teaching that tempts us to drift into sincerity that doesn't ring quite true. I think lots of students nowadays are very suspicious of just the kind of sincerity I mimic above (and tend to embody). "Groan. Shit. Spare us this sincerity. What do we have to do to get a B here?" We aren't clear-eyed and unflinching enough to look squarely at what the hard realities are —the realities of different roles, different skills, money, power, for example. "Nice sincerity" can be a cover for us when we are timid about calling a spade a spade.

What Happens to Students in a Free Writing Class

SANDY KAYE

The history of free writing classes at MIT consists of the usual mixture of excitement, confusion, and resistance that accompanies any degree of innovation within an institution or a profession. Over the past several years, we have expended a good deal of energy explaining, defending, even protecting the work which has led to the theories and practices discussed in this book. But we have always been aware that our conviction that writing could be taught to more people more effectively was neither unique, nor original (we have learned much from Ken Macrorie's explorations, among others); and it is clear, now, that the widely-based revolution in teaching writing has helped to reaffirm the crucial importance of writing in the design of curricula at all levels of education.

Nevertheless, the most important aspect of our responsibility to be precise about what we do, and what we hope to accomplish, relates not to administrators, colleagues, or foundations, but to students; and I wish to address myself, here, to the task of making clear to potential students some of the kinds of experiences they can expect in a free writing course. What follows is a series of portraits, based in some measure on people in a class called "Rewriting," at MIT, in 1974, but typifying my own observations of some fifty or so writing classes in different environments over the past ten years.

Students reading this chapter can measure realistically, I think, some of their possibilities for learning, and some of the difficulties they may encounter in a free writing class. Naturally, in compiling these portraits, I do not speak for the other authors in this book, nor for their classes; we have differing ideas about the strengths and weaknesses in free writing classes. But the analysis of experience which follows, in the form of generalized portraits, exemplifies principles we all share about teaching writing. My hope is that this chapter will serve as a detailed form of catalogue copy for prospective students.

I. THE SEAFARER

There was a lack of long, sustained periods of involvement on every person's part, but I felt comfortable. I mean, there's a difference between a desire for approval, in seeking responses to a piece of writing, and a desire for 'useful' criticism. Sometimes you're up for it, and sometimes you couldn't care less. It's not a thing you can plan into a class.

Roland, *Notes*, "Rewriting" 5/8/74

The Seafarer is a mixture of ambitions, side-forays, intense hobbies, and long periods of absolute stillness, inability to work, or inclination to communicate—those long periods of brooding alone, on deck, looking out over the limitless, grey horizon. There are ports of call, and the brooding comes to an end for a short, exhilarating time; and then, the Seafarer is off again, sometimes without even being aware that the ship is slipping out to sea.

In a class of ten or twelve people, there may be two or three such folk. In the Spring of 1974, there was Roland—archetypal—and two extreme examples, Mario, who stayed on the bridge during the voyage; and Alan, who kept shuttling back and forth. But Roland is archetypal.

Seafarers have real doubts about whether they will ever write anything "good"—not in anyone else's eyes, but in their own. It's a solitary voyage. They have read almost anything (Roland has one of the world's great science fiction collections, and he is closing in on the leaders of the great comic book treasure hunt; Alan, of course, is one of his competitors), and will have derived some elaborate system of criteria for "good" that doesn't match anyone else's; but they will also have a passion for figuring out other people's writing—how it works, how it might be better. Roland's comments, in class—and remember, free writing classes are really surrogate audiences for readings aloud[1]—are equal portions of objectivity and subjectivity: analysis of the most practical and detailed sort, and sitting-alone-in-your-living room guffaws. If you say something foolish, he may shake his head violently, but he is equally lacking in condescension or respect. (One night a visitor delivered an eloquent analysis of a story, accompanied by a rising crescendo of snorts and headshakings from Roland, who then explained the flaw in the argument; but none of this was personal, or related to what *other* people might think of him for pointing out the flaw.)

The Seafarer has to get things right, or clear, in his own head; he keeps at it. It might be considered intellectual greed, except that I've never heard anyone complain about dullness or simple-mindedness in one of these Seafaring quests. It's as if the Seafarer goes on these journeys for himself, but *for* everyone else, too.

But as Roland said, you can't "plan" this into a course in writing: the Seafarer is a moody character; until he's ready to come back with the news, there's nothing you can do. So, just when everyone has begun to depend on the vitality of the Seafarer, he fails to show up, and doesn't answer if you leave a message. (You try to keep track in a loose way, to see if he's still in town, but even that is hard to pin down.) The Seafarer is related to the class only as it fits into his particular quest, or period of null before a quest. Other people come to every class, write regularly, listen carefully, talk about other people's work in a helpful way. The Seafarer disappears, and when he returns, he has treasures, and they're the main thing:

---

1. Not necessarily, though. There's a lot more than just reading in a free writing class. There's talking. And listening. Sometimes even writing. And there's a sense of "groupness"—however fragile—which simply isn't present at Open Readings. Reading aloud can be important, but is not essential, or in any sense sufficient. But then again, I've never been in your class, Sandy. Maybe those forty-five students wanted in because they knew what they'd find. [KS]

Roland comes up with a shocker: twenty-five or so pages of wild stuff: interior monologue, fantasy, wishing, dreaming, mad stuff to make a marvelous story; is it, yet? Now? Already? (Roland is seen as "stingy" in pretending to be zonked out, while all the time writing this stuff in hiding.) There are many good sections, set pieces like the "Professor's Questions"; the idea of the narrator talking to himself is done well: "God—get ahold of yourself, Narrator"; has many elements of a play. And, you can see Roland's philosophical background in it all.

Alternation of voices is weird: self-mockery vs. self-trumpeting; this may be a theme of the thing, rather than a drawback, though. Still, there's a feeling of: "When is it going to happen?" People are so fascinated they stop taking notes, etc., and listen.

Notes of the Meeting, 5/1/74

All the way through his reading of this wild, rough draft, Roland comments: "O, this is good," or "I can't read this crap, it's terrible!" Of course, no one knows what to say; Roland's out far, and alone; and while he can tell another guest, "Some styles need to be experienced for a time, before you can comment on them" (*Notes*, 5/15/74), he is still let down that people don't immediately catch up with him.

That's the way it will be, for some people: with all the talk about "feedback," and the class as "audience," if you are an essential Seafarer, you will end up giving a lot more criticism than you get. *Your* crucial need is not for criticism; you want the class to be the port in a storm; you come back, report to sympathetic shore friends who nod, or admire, or are befuddled, but who are interested. This may not sound like much; but if it is not enough, then you're probably not the Seafaring kind, and so, should move on to the next portrait, where you may find more of yourself and judge whether, or how, you can make use of a free writing class.

II. DR. LOGIC

I learned from tearing apart other people's stuff. Everything else in this place is macroscopic, not micro. People, listening, give off fewer visual clues here—they "soak," and Lecturers don't have any idea. That's what I've learned: how to read my own stuff with the eyes of the Reader.

Hunter, *Notes*, 5/8/74

In the beginning there were the words, and that was that. Nobody had any idea what Hunter was talking about, or trying to do. It wasn't that we suspected he was trying to pull the wool over our eyes; rather, he seemed one of those obscure cats who turn up every once in a while.

If it was Acid, then at least the subject was new, a new variety of Acid Jive—not about the empty rowboats down the main street of town, and all those who *should* be in it, and why they weren't—no, not that kind of thing at all, but much more a cross between Faulkner (a passion for diction and prose rhythm), and a camera running wild.

The confusing thing was that whenever Hunter came up to the surface (and incidentally revealed that he had been there all along) to comment on someone else's writing, his criticism was crystal clear, specific, and delivered —sometimes over a period of ten minutes or so—with airtight organization. This occurred once every other class, but it was so stunning that we came to call him Dr. Logic, a kind of extreme case of the second most familiar mode of behavior in an open writing class: the sort of person who works very hard to integrate everything—the writing, the remarks people make, the attitudes revealed in and around those remarks. Doctor Logic goes to class every time—in contrast with the Seafarer—and frequently stops the proceedings: "Wait a minute, I don't get it," or "I don't understand that," or variations on what might be considered the non-directive teacher's standard vocabulary. But Dr. Logic isn't looking for long-range gratitude or indirectly accomplished admiration. He just wants to understand—especially the very things that can't, ever, be understood. Not that he doesn't know *that*; but the good Doctor wants the best approximation at the given moment.

And somehow, the more energy he puts into analysis, the more creative he becomes in his own work. That's what makes it all, in his irritable, often impatient way, worthwhile.

Because the whole business is *for* him—as with the Seafarer—and if you happen to learn anything by listening in, or engaging in a twenty-minute dialogue with him, that's your good luck. Dr. Logic is on his own quest, too; and while the Seafarer may sail off into the horizon and not return, or return when the class is over, or show up with twenty-five exciting pages, Dr. Logic sticks at it, week by week, using this real sense of time passing to organize his learning.

Three weeks into the term, Hunter brings in two-and-a-half pages, mostly dialogue. He's been working them over, in his mind mostly, for a while. They're very clear, except for the usual first-draft confusions for a reader: "Who's talking here?" and "Why is X angry at Y to begin with?" But the overall clarity surprises everybody. (Is this the same guy who wrote the other inscrutable stuff?) Our second line of response is: "How come, given the real people he's trying to talk about, the writing is so dull?"

And that's exactly what's *in it*, for Dr. Logic. He needs to find out from people outside his own head what, or how much of the material he has bothered to put out makes any sense at all. Whereas the Seafarer simply dishes it out, "Take it or leave it; you probably won't get it anyway, and besides, I'm the best judge of that, but I have a sneaking suspicion I'm too hard on myself," Dr. Logic truly doesn't know what is going on in the empty space between his own mind as a writer and the reader's mind; and he'll exhaust himself trying to find out, sometimes going beyond everyone's endurance to get there.

Dr. Logic believes there are answers—not The Answer, but provisional answers, and without much self-consciousness, he pursues them.

When the class goes sour, he won't even notice, won't be concerned. Hell, we'll always be there for him anyway, no matter how we're all suffering with the lousy writing that's coming in, or the lousy criticism we're putting over on each other.[2] As far as Dr. Logic is concerned, *that* is a process that can be studied and understood, too; but one he's not interested in. And then, in the seventh week, after the doldrums have been outlasted, the good Doctor brings in his elaboration and re-write of those first few comprehensible pages. Each point of our criticism has been given some attention (as if, hell, we *are* his audience, now; he might as well try to reach us). The characters move away from sketches towards individuality; the psychology of male-female, and male-male relationships (the particular wars that the good Doctor is interested in) are made more distinct; and the chronology is straightened out. He's coming around to "normal" time because, if he wants to learn anything from us, he has to give us enough to go on. There's plenty more to do. He listens, writes down, stops the commentary to understand one thing or another, gets into a complicated argument with one or two people because what they're saying is so obviously bull, but he wants to be sure, doesn't want to lose a single scrap of feedback.

And that will be it, probably. Whatever else he does on that story will not come in during the term, might be sent to us through the mail except that the good Doctor knows that *that* is going too far; you can't ask it of harried academics and other students who either don't take the job of writing as seriously as he does or—he might be willing to admit without a smile —in the same way he does. He's gotten a lot of information on his own question of the "differences between how he visualized the activity of his characters, and how the Reader can get *into* it" (Hunter, *Notes*, 4/3/74); now he'll work at it some more, on his own.

Self-motivated, logical, impatient: these are the characteristics of a Dr. Logic; the class is his laboratory, a series of experiments, approximations; it's one way of learning, in a free writing class.

III. MINNESINGERS

I just like the fun of it.
Dan F., *Notes*, 5/8/74

Minnesingers can't help themselves. They write new stories every week, find different forms every other week, come up with new kinds of narration without even trying. Mainly, they're studying other things: Pre-

---

2. What I like most about this piece is the way SK never lets his palpable ability to set up a functioning free writing class get in the way of his self-awareness: always, in our heads, as he has continued to imply, ought to be the image of the Emperor parading his new clothes. In this way we remember who we are and acknowledge the limitations of our ideas even as we celebrate them. [JB]

Med, Physics, or Philosophy. Writing is an avocation,[3] the pressure's off, the words come toppling out with humor, or philosophy, or fantasy as the glue.

Since Minnesingers[4] go right along singing their songs, they aren't vulnerable to criticism in the familiar ways. If you say, "Holy God, this stuff is terrible," a Minnesinger will laugh—driving Dr. Logic to distraction —and say, "I know. I knew it while I was writing it, but I still wanted to see how it would come out. But I've got another thing, here, if you still want to listen—" Minnesingers (unless they are philosophy majors) are invariably good-humored. Sometimes (this is damned rare, lately) their writing is so funny that Dr. Logic cracks a smile; and always, they are back next week with something new.[5]

The Minnesinger is more down-to-earth than some of the other people in the class. He may even write a story about university life, or about some aspect of day-to-day existence ("After all," he'll say, "that's what I know most about"). This does not at all restrict him to realistic portrayals of the bullying that goes on in the laundry room in the basement of the dormitory, or to descriptions of the preparation of food in the cafeteria, because a Minnesinger's unquenchable avocational talent for finding stories is applied to an infinity of situations.

It does mean that the content of his stories drives the more lugubrious, or the more political, or the more sociologically oriented people up the wall. Early in the term, this leads to long battles about what is "appropriate" in a work of art. A politico says, "Stories should hold the line against bad stuff, like people watching T.V., or exploiting X, or dehumanizing Y—stuff that doesn't help people clear their heads." Someone else says that is the way people really are. The Minnesinger sits through it all, listening for a clue, smiling, unflappable, because in some way his inclination to write is beyond his control, and his investment in "being a writer" is humble but insistent. Dr. Logic feels the lack of "design," of "theory," behind a Minnesinger tale: "the contents of a character's psyche should be directly related to his place and time . . . and to the reader's expectations, as the story sets them up; and to the reader's abilities to *read* the story in

---

3. *Most* of the writers in our classes are also studying other things. It's the rare one for whom writing is other than an avocation, and usually he manages to conceal it. When writing is more than an avocation, it very often comes sauntering out as a vice, once secret, now decadently public. Such writing sometimes makes a class nervous. [JB]

4. Sandy, I gotta ask you: what does Minnesinger mean? Is that an allusion, or what? I never heard anything like it. Is it a small sewing machine? Come on, give! [KS]

5. One writer a few years ago asked in class why no one wrote funny pieces, everything so grim, disheartened. We concluded it was harder to make us laugh than weep. Not a profound insight, but we analyzed brilliantly the etiology of despair in college students. And then wrote some pornography which kept us smiling for a week. [JB]

the way the author intends him to" (Hunter, *Notes*, 2/27/74). This is a grand invitation to talk, to discuss, to debate; the Minnesinger nods, as if he realizes what Dr. Logic says is true, but can't see how it applies to the act of creation. He's waiting for specific advice on how to fix the story to make it funnier, how to make the Klein bottle of an ending even more potent and entertaining.

When the class goes to pieces, in Going-to-Pieces Week, the Minnesinger, like the good Dr. Logic, hardly notices; he's working too hard—all that biology, or the psychology course. But the stories keep coming out, like new teeth; and it is his story, in the midst of the bad times when everyone is wary of saying anything and the Seafarer has gone off to uncharted areas, that pulls us all out of the doldrums, because of course, he's done it again: the story gets us deeply into details, and that's for *him*, the writer; but it raises general questions, which are for *us*, the readers. The questions will be central, crucial: What is the relationship between structure and theme? how do we judge the appropriateness of that relationship? and how is the reader clued in to that appropriateness? What is the relationship between time passing, in the story, and changes in the social and political culture of the story? And, too, there are questions of design: each section of the story has to be vital in itself, but also tied in with the overall conception. We all get a sense of how chronological order is not even the most useful, let alone the only way of organizing a story.

All of this seems more the passion of the rest of us; the Minnesinger sits quietly, takes a few notes, but has an expression of bemused tolerance, as if he is already at work on his next one. After a few weeks, we see a somewhat more complicated story, with a tone of meditative self-irony. Where did *that* come from? Surely, he didn't just toss that off? And then, at the last of the "last classes," he brings in his latest, a story which has the full interplay of Narrator, the prism of the Narrator's memory, the characters the Narrator brings to the reader, *and* (as the Minnesinger puts it himself) what the Narrator "can admit to himself" (Dan. F., *Notes*, 5/15/74).

We try to figure out why it is that the Minnesinger's stuff has universal appeal—why it is that his stories "always call forth a lot of comment from everyone." The only resolution seems to be what Dan himself promises: "I'll send you some rewrites, from Palo Alto," where, of course, he's going to Medical School, his first love, and which is why, we theorize, he's free to do his singing for the "fun of it."

IV. COMPOSITES, AND THOSE WHO SUFFER

Of course, most of the people in any free writing class, whether or not they know anything about it beforehand, will enter into it with the vague purpose of getting some writing done. Some people behave in ways not so radically different from the generalized case studies presented above: people who can work pretty much on their own; who will get whatever scrap of information they can from the others in the class; who write because they can't not write; and who listen to what other people say because they are familiar with the drive to be heard.

Most people have elements of each of the three types: Seafarer, Dr. Logic, and Minnesinger. The balance among these elements will be related to each person's capacity, at a given moment in time, to do some work at writing.[6] But there are always those who suffer in free writing classes—some for valid reasons, others, not; and I think it's worth trying to clear up some of the confusion about why this is so.

The kinds of people I've talked about so far are people who, whatever their style of learning, will be able to get something done no matter what is said or not said in a class, or in a conference, or over a beer in the Student Center. Dr. Logic may want to take hold of somebody and shake the answers out, but he is also aware that that expectation is a structure he himself has created (a geometrical truth, not Truth). The Seafarer may shake his head in dismay at the paltry experience of the people in the class who have never been on the trips he has taken—who have never spent months out of touch with the day-to-day world, and then come back; but part of the reason why he goes out so far is to be able to bring back something fresh, and rare; and he agrees that a few lucky people don't need to go that route. The Minnesinger sings. So, these are people who have already committed themselves to doing it—not as a wish, or because the class will "make" them, but because they can't avoid it. I think it is very rare that someone who has not made this commitment,[7] on whatever level of consciousness, gets any real work done[8] in a free writing class; and not so rare at all for people with something like this commitment to get very little done. The impetus to write may be based on something as fragile as one long letter written to a friend, or a lover, or a parent, but there has to be the initial experience of having done it, and of wanting to do more. If you haven't

---

6. I don't fit in any of these categories, and neither do many of the women writers I know. And some men. The students you describe seem freer to use the class for their own purposes than I would be or ever will be in *any* institutional situation in this country, unless it were run by women, when I might allow myself to operate in the ways that you describe. Maybe. But it's hard to imagine. Not go to class? Prolong a discussion until *my* questions were answered? Not feel responsible for taking the class's criticism seriously, or for the class and its other members?

These are all portraits of rebels, people with an essentially private commitment. I recognize S. Kaye in most of them. But not myself, and people like me —docile, hard working, hopeful, scared. Wanting very much to *be* a writer, but not sure that I can ever sit down and make words appear (somehow) on a page; not sure that even if I can, they will mean something, or be true enough, or that anyone would read them without laughing or being bored. [PC]

7. Sandy, I just don't agree! Many—and sometimes most—of the people in my classes have no such commitment. Maybe this is more true of writing poetry than it is of fiction, but it happens with prose writers too. They come because they've always wanted to try it. Maybe they wrote a poem in the third grade. Maybe they were walking down the street and wrote half a stanza of a song and always hoped they would get around to finishing it, so they come to a writing class to see what that might involve. Sometimes the impulse is so slight

had that experience yet, wait until you do, *unless* you are very good-natured, confident, generous of spirit, and not too hard on yourself. There will be one or two people in every group who will discover that they weren't really up for writing this term, in this particular group of people.

A more difficult determination, and one made even more precarious by the open structure of free writing classes as compared to the more traditional structure (with the Professor at the head of the table and students along the two sides facing him), is the question of an attitude toward learning and teaching, and beyond that, I'm sure, of the kind of faith the individual has in his or her own integrity. The people who have the worst times in writing classes are those who believe that there is a professional charade which is intrinsic to all teaching, and that this charade will be abandoned at the appropriate moment. For them, the real genius of teaching lies in the orchestration of the revelatory moment when all pretenses at an open-ended process of learning are swept away in the one true critique which the instructor has been saving to deliver at the most telling moment.

There is this craving in almost everyone I have ever known, including the most free and open teachers. It is very strong in me, and I do not think I would be able to describe it or detect it with such clarity at the beginning of each new class if it were not a strong component of my own style of learning and teaching. But for most people (even those who expect one writing class to resolve what must be a life-long struggle over whether to "go on writing"), the wariness and suspicion that twelve or fifteen years of public education in America have produced toward any true *process* of learning can be allayed long enough, or balanced with work that is intense enough so that the class will be a useful experience. It is only those few

---

that it barely gets them through the door of the classroom—sometimes they come far enough in to find a chair, and sometimes they only settle on the floor, near the door. And then they wait. Wait to see what it's like, writing. But then there is a requirement that they write; especially at the beginning I always ask everyone to hand something in, no matter how casual or short; and then they get interested, find out what kinds of possibilities there might be for them. After a while, they try something else. Uncommitted, maybe to the very end of the term, but hopeful. These are the people who stop me in the halls, or in the middle of the yard, when it's sleeting, and the wind is blowing hard, and we're both late for class, to talk until they can tell me this (urgently): "I haven't done much writing since I took your class . . . but I should . . . I'm going to." There was no commitment until they took the class. And it didn't even happen there, it happened later. And maybe they will do more writing and maybe they won't. But it's become a possibility for them, for the rest of their lives. It's something they have, that and the writing they did do. Don't leave them out of your classes. [PC]

8. I think this is an important enough observation to be emphasized by a footnote. The crucial phrase is, of course, "real work." It's clear that a truly professional writer—more than teacher—has written that. We others often write here with our loyalty to teaching more apparent than our loyalty to writing. [ND]

people for whom the idea of liberation from all that chicanery and educational fascism is too threatening who really suffer in free writing classes. Their filter is not only subjective, it is murky with grievance: nothing can get through in any way in relation to what it is, and the whole value of a free writing class is squandered.[9,10]

The way to recognize this self-defeating stance toward learning is to listen to your own mind. If you find yourself deriding what people say at times, because it seems foolish—that's *not* it; you're all right; in fact, you may be a variety of Dr. Logic. But if you find yourself continually *not believing* what people say, then you are going to be in agony. All a free writing class can do is to give people a chance to talk to each other about writing; if you expect the class to make people better or worse than they are, or to provide an environment in which you can re-create others according to your own needs and vulnerabilities, then you will probably be disappointed. I have not found much that is comforting about free writing classes other than the excitement of being engaged in an authentic endeavor with disciplined people.

---

9. That's a beautiful paragraph. (An authoritative judgment.) [ND]

10. I don't think the whole value of the free writing class is squandered. I think that the experience of students who don't write, if they meet cooperation and good will rather than punishment, can be incredibily valuable. I speak from experience, having learned how to write despite not writing anything my freshman year. [DW]

Writing as Politics

STEVE REUYS

Writing as a means of expression, of exploration and discovery, of creation and renewal—all this seems most sensible and desirable. Writing helps the individual to become more of a person, to achieve his or her full potential as a feeling, thinking, communicating human being. What could be better than that? Not much, I hasten to answer. Of course, writing is not the only way to pursue these goals, but it is not expensive, not physically demanding, not overtly frowned upon by our society. And to the extent that it serves as one of the more accessible methods for many people (though not all, for illiteracy is not the imaginary problem some people conceive it to be in the United States), writing deserves to be promoted and used.

But something is being ignored here, one aspect of the whole problem that begins to come through with the admission that literacy is not the property of everyone in this country or, of course, the world. Operating in the upper and middle class strata, the type of society so well characterized by the institution of the university, this quest for personal growth is a magnificent one, a truly important one, and one that may help in the long run with the alleviation of the problems I am about to raise. But it is also a quest foreign to many people who occupy a rather different situation in life. They're not necessarily opposed to this sort of personal improvement; however, to a large extent it's a luxury they cannot afford, particularly when set against the stark day-by-day necessities of living, the struggle for existence in a world very different from the one inhabited by most of the writers and readers of this book. There is a political reality missing from this entire framework. It is a reality that cannot be ignored.

What I am trying to say is not that writing has no place in the lives of the poor and disadvantaged in this country, or that writing is hopelessly elitist and should be outlawed until after "the revolution." For one thing, these chapters have proposed writing as a personally liberating act, and the more self-liberation comes to the ranks of the powerful (and thus freedom from the economic, cultural, and moral discipline of our society), the better off will be the cause of equality and justice for others. So, even without any particular political applicability, writing could be helpful. But writing does have explicit political importance, and because of that, it deserves to be promoted beyond the walls of the college, into the mainstream of American life.

This juxtaposition of the university and the rest of society is well-demonstrated in a city like Cambridge. Proximate to the ivy walls and glittering names of MIT and Harvard lives another, very different segment of our population. Once the confines of the universities are left, one discovers a large community of poor, unemployed, uneducated persons, many of whom don't want to remain with those labels or the conditions they describe. This may involve working to improve either one's own position in the society or the situation of a larger group of people related by some common factor such as race, ethnicity, sex, residence, or employment. These are not necessarily distinct, separate orientations; effective political action is often able to fuse the needs of the individual and those of the group into an effort and a program that promotes the two together.

Although I was educated and am now teaching at one of these universities, the temptation to "change sides" is sometimes strong. I worked for a time at a place in Cambridge that helped with counseling and tutoring the city's often-unrecognized poorly educated majority. There I taught English grammar and reading comprehension to persons trying to acquire a high school equivalency certificate and wrote a handbook for teaching these skills using writing by the student as a primary material and method. And I have worked as a teacher's aide in a sixth-grade, almost all black public school classroom in St. Louis, Missouri. These experiences taught me many things, among them that writing can serve a number of purposes for the oppressed and disadvantaged in our society.

Specifically, writing is important and useful in four ways:

1. Writing can be truly invaluable in the process of education, for it provides personal learning materials to which the student can always relate effectively.
2. Writing promotes feelings of confidence and creativity within the student, particularly as they relate to dealing with our society.
3. Writing increases a person's effectiveness in communicating with this modern world and in functioning within it.
4. Writing can take on the explicitly political importance of the call to action, the inflammatory letter, the muckraking article, the impassioned outcry, the reasoned critique.

To begin with the matter of education. For many people, schools do not always furnish the most pleasant memories. It may be a time of struggle: first, trying to relate to the whole process, perceived as largely meaningless, in some way that might make survival, and even learning, possible; and when that fails, as it quite often does, trying to escape the process entirely. The problem is essentially the educational system's lack of concern for individualized learning and instruction, a problem that manifests itself in an authoritarian environment, the irrelevance of curricular materials, the disinterest of students.

A strong emphasis on writing by students can do something about this problem. By serving as the primary material in a curriculum, personal writing of the type recommended in this book allows for an individualization of learning not possible with standardized materials. Now, I don't mean to imply that the use of writing will itself produce a revolution in the schools; much, much more is needed. But writing is a start, as Herbert Kohl, among others, has perceived; his experiences with writing and a sixth grade class are described in his book *36 Children*.

How does writing make such a difference? With it, the curricular material can begin to bear an obvious and profound relation to each student's experience. It brings an important element of immediacy to the process of learning, an immediacy usually lacking in the classroom. The material has meaning; it has a context. Once it is seen by the student to have a bearing on his/her life, he or she may find the motivation so necessary to the learning process. It helps to remove the atmosphere of authority, of right and wrong answers, of imposed truth and imposed values. The student, through writing, takes an important part in the design and implementation of his/her own learning. Basically, it makes the process suitable to the student, rather than making the student conform to the process.

Schools often yield bad memories for still another reason: people may come away convinced that they are stupid and unimaginative and worthless. Some are told this quite bluntly; to others, the message is conveyed in more subtle ways, via tracking systems, teachers' expectations, and the like. Through these various routes, the infamous self-fulfilling prophecy is able to construct a vicious cycle: as the system pronounces students incapable of learning, these dictates are internalized by them; persuaded of this verdict's truth, they become reconciled to *not* learning, and thus seldom do; this reinforces the original judgment of their inability; and so on. Writing can break this circle by promoting interest and learning. Then, as the student actually *does* learn, the feelings of stupidity and incapacity are dispelled.

Also, writing can be an enormously uplifting experience, indicative of the creativity that lies within each person. And as the worth of a certain piece of writing, even with misspellings and poor punctuation, is recognized, the student realizes that he/she does have something worth saying, something that can capture attention, awaken interest, and evoke responses.

Thus, these self-deprecatory feelings can be overcome with the aid of writing. Admittedly, the world is worse for the amount of self-pride it contains. But until the present time, pride has been rather unevenly distributed. Richard Nixon has vastly too much; millions of other people have virtually none at all when it comes to relating to the official world. They feel powerless to influence the forces and people that control their lives, and in their cases a bit more self-confidence is certainly called for. Again, writing is no panacea, but it can help.

Now, confidence obviously helps when one is trying to get along with other persons and with institutions, but it's not all that is needed. Since our world dictates that an individual's interaction with society shall consist more of communication than anything resembling "action," being able to write effectively is of crucial importance.

Some societies, in other times and other places, have emphasized different ways of communicating—dance, music, the spoken word. But the modern Western world places a premium upon being able to handle, and handle well, the intricacies of written language. Without that ability, the person becomes a second-class citizen, largely cut off from the functionings of the society, from the most important down to the least. Thus, being able to write will increase one's chances of affecting the course of one's own life.

Unfortunately, a difficult problem arises from the seemingly simple pronouncements of the last paragraphs, namely whose "written language" is being spoken of. The people in this article, those on the fringes of social acceptability, on the bottom rungs of the economic ladder, are not the ones who make the rules of language on which people are tested and judged in our society, and usually the characteristics of their dialects are not harmonious with those of official Standard English. Thus, a debate is currently raging in linguistic circles around the question: should we, as teachers, stay within these rules and bolster the chances of our black or poor white students to play the game with the rest of the society and win, or should we ignore those rules not essential to communication, allow for natural and normal language differences, and hope to bury the linguistic chauvinism of the Standard English pushers?

Overall conclusions remain difficult; however, the answer for a particular situation may hinge on just who your students are and what they want from the class. One group may want the rules, hard and fast, and no fooling around with "creativity." Another might not care at all about formal rules of grammar as such and be looking instead for responses dealing only with the strength and the effectiveness of their writing. I told my Cambridge students working for a high school equivalency certificate that to pass they'd simply need to know the rules, but that there is nothing inherently superior about Standard English. (I might say here that it's easy for me to profess such fairness, but my own prejudices still sometimes surface when I hear people talking on the streets of Cambridge or Boston; these notions of inferiority are difficult to exorcise.) Meanwhile, the debate rages on, unresolved.

My final point has to do with some more explicitly political aspects of effective communication, of fluency in language, of writing ability. In some ways, things do not look good. "The pen is mightier than the sword" is an old cliché, and one which may have diminished in truth at about the same time as the sword disappeared from the battlefield. For instance, the last decade has seen strenuous debate over the value of verbal expression in affecting this country's policies in Southeast Asia. In general, grave doubts have been cast upon the worth of the word.

Paulo Freire, in *The Pedagogy of the Oppressed*, has discussed the value of language in political action, in liberation. In his view, what is needed is a "praxis," an effective working relationship, a cooperative give-and-take, a symbiosis, whatever one wants to call it, between the word and the action. One without the other is not sufficient. For this reason he has been promoting literacy among the poor of South America, and his arguments are certainly also applicable to the illiterate of the United States. His views seem correct; language is important.

But what of writing in particular, given a basic standard of literacy? Is there any political value in emphasizing writing as a further step beyond the basic ability to read and write? The answer is 'yes," for the more capable we become at either or both of these skills, the more effective we are likely to be in political action. This means developing perceptivity, the powers of critical analysis, and the knack of spotting propaganda. And it means developing the powers of writing.

By aiming at different audiences, writing can serve three basic functions in this regard. First, it can appeal to the world at large in an attempt to influence, to convert. As was said, the validity and value of this seem to be in question now, but a history of muckraking journalism, Tom Paine's pamphlets, the writings of Marx and Mao and Lenin, and countless other examples makes it unlikely that writing will be dismissed as a tool of exposure and argument.

Second, writing allows for an open forum on policy and practice by appealing not to an unconvinced public, but rather to those actually participating in the struggle. Such a forum is a basic requirement for true participatory government, or participatory liberation. Only so much can be done through speech, only so many people can be reached, only so much can be said. The rest must be done through writing.

And third, writing can aid the individual by heightening his or her political awareness. Our relationship to other persons, to power, and to the society and country in which we live are all political aspects of our existence that can be explored, revealed, and understood through writing.

In general, the more effectively people can write, and the more people who can do this, the stronger will be their struggle for liberation. I should state that the term "liberation" is meant here in a rather broad sense. Wherever people are oppressed, wherever their lives are being controlled by persons and forces that have no right to be in such positions of power, wherever people are not developing their full potential as humans, there "liberation" is needed. It's a rather open-ended definition, but this breadth is intentional, and thus, it may even include the college student. But the point to remember is that the plight of millions of other people throughout the world is a much more conventional, much more explicit political one, and the one toward which I've been primarily addressing my considerations on the value of writing.

In a sense I have followed a progression, one that began with the process of education, then went to a form of psychological development, then to communication, and finally ended with political action and liberation. As if embodying its political message, this article has moved through stages representative of a political orientation: learning from the world, preparing to meet the world, addressing the world, and changing the world. The direction is obviously not an inwardly personal one. Perhaps the emphasis is too far away from that, because I deeply believe in the value and importance of personal growth. But there is this other side which needs representation: the matter of how writing can help those who need help in dealing with the world. In some sense that is all of us, but again I'm now restricting my scope to those people under the more changeable forces of political and economic oppression, not the interminable powers of fate and death and sorrow that form the basis of our literature. The world this article has addressed is the world of imperialist countries and greedy landlords, huge corporations and inhumane courts, fascist dictatorships and brutal cops. If writing can help change these, and thus improve people's individual and collective lives, it will have done a great service. If it seems like a long road, one which maybe we've traveled, on and off, for thousands of years, you're probably right; I guess we just have to keep walking.

POSTSCRIPT

I sometimes have second thoughts about this piece. I wonder about things like: "Who am I to speak for the needs of people of whom I know so frighteningly little?" "Is this just more ivory tower academic theorizing?" "Am I using the very real plight of millions of people for my own concern and gain—namely, a chapter in this book?" "Are my arguments totally facetious—can writing ever be as powerful as I make it seem?" "Do I support writing because it's not personally threatening?" "Is my position a convenient reconciliation of two leanings in my own life—toward the arts and toward political action?" I wonder about these questions a lot and sometimes they bother me a lot, but then sometimes I also think of several of the people I've known or have heard about.

Eric and Jerome and some of the other St. Louis sixth-graders who liked writing stories and seemed to welcome it as a change from the usual classroom routine of memorizing grammar and learning proper letter form. Joy, a rather bright Cambridge high school dropout who, convinced long ago that she was stupid, was pleased to find that she could write things that would interest me. The long distance phone operators who are told they may get better jobs if they learn to write more effectively. A woman in Sandy Kaye's adult school class who works with a tenants' organizing group and wants to be able to write good articles for their newsletter.

These people aren't answers to my questions. But they, and, I suppose, millions like them are good reasons for having written this piece. My doubts haven't disappeared, but I can live with them.

Why Write? / Why Teach Writing?

SANDY KAYE

In the old days, people used to say: "But tell me, can you really teach writing?" Now that almost everyone is clamoring for somebody to *do* it, we have to admit that the old question was really no question at all, but rather a thwarted hope preserved in despair and petrified as resignation. "Can you teach writing?" has always been a phony question; the real question behind it is: "Can you learn writing?"

Almost everyone remembers a terrible English class, or a helpful English teacher, or a lab assistant whose comments on the writing in a lab report made all the difference—not just for that one lab, but for a lifetime of professional writing. People have either been turned away from or attracted to writing *by* someone else; and that is where the confusion about teaching and learning arises. Learning is an intimate experience, charged with the energy and excitement that "intimacy" usually implies. If the dominant figure in the learning process is a respected teacher, a parent, a lover, a supervisor, the message sticks: "Yes, I'm listening, say more"; "No, it's not time for you to speak, you're a fool for trying." A few lucky people can recall the letter, or the poem, or the memo, or the paper in school when they first realized that it was all right, that they had as much right to speak as anyone else,[1] that if they wanted to work at it they could do it pretty well. But many more can recite, years later, the strictures and rules through which Mrs. Gaffney or Mr. Paolucci graded them into silence. (The clearest test of the force of mystique in education is this sort of testimony: a muted human being insisting, after twenty years of silence, that the old rules were *right*, and that he or she did not have the stuff to be an effective writer.)

Of course this school-induced *silencitis* has nothing to do with learning writing at all, however much it may have to do with teaching it. Teachers want to weed out good from bad in their classes, just as professions put forward only those people with certain qualifications—those sanctioned by one particular faction or another within the profession; but none of *that* has to do with learning. So, the teaching of writing has often come to mean, paradoxically, the exact opposite: learning not to write; and because writing is one of the few ways nature has permitted us for getting in touch with each other, the way we view the possibility of learning writing tells a good deal about our vitality as human creatures.

It is clear that something important happens when a diary entry (which no other human being will ever read) is so moving to the writer that it is not only unforgettable, but crystallizes or unravels a problem which has not been definable before. Some people tell us writing *can* do that. And it is clearly important on a public scale when millions of people are moved to a

---

1. I don't remember experiencing *rights*, but I do remember someone whom I respected *listening*. [PC]

new understanding of government by even the "prepared" transcripts of White House conversations. These two examples, from opposite ends of the spectrum of functions of written communication, exemplify our need for and our satisfaction in discovering what has not been known before. (This explains, too, why books like Studs Terkel's *Working* are so appealing. Through Terkel's interviews, we have a glimpse of the *other* side, we can cross over; and the speakers—the used car salesman, the telephone operator—find out who they are by talking about themselves.)

We need these experiences of "crossing over" because no one has yet invented a sentient, conscious mirror. I don't mean that cynically; the mirror is one of our fondest metaphors (think of Gascoigne's "steel glass"; or the glass Fielding wanted to hold up for his readers—and which had so much to do with the early theory of the novel; or the therapeutic mirror Freud hypothesized; and lately, Vonnegut's mirror into a world beyond appearances). This need for knowledge of ourselves exists side-by-side with a kind of self-absorption; but one of the reasons why we read Günter Grass, or Robert Lowell, or Jan Myrdal is because they come back from the hall of mirrors with something tangible, useful.

In listing personal favorites, I am reminded again of the way in which almost everyone has learned either to write, or not to write: Lowell, Myrdal, and Grass, in adding to our storehouse of knowledge, provide the example that communication is possible. The writing teacher who channels students into rules handed down by a profession, or an institution, or a culture works against their capability of learning about themselves. Society always has "good" reasons: write this way or else you'll flunk; write this way or else you won't be able to get a job; write this way or else people will feel you do not speak with any authority; write this way or else people will think that you don't know what you're talking about. But these strictures have to do with learning *not* to write; if everyone heeded them, the knowledge available to us would be monolithic and clichéd, containing no more of the whole truth of experience than any self-sealed system (for example, Euclidean Geometry) can ever attain.[2]

If we can't contribute to each other what we know of each other, and of ourselves, then all we need to do to learn to write is to memorize Mrs. Gaffney's definitions of parts of speech and Mr. Paolucci's spelling rules; we'll all be thinking and saying the same things, anyway. (There may be nothing wrong with *that*, I suppose; the problem would be in deciding *what* it is that we are all to think and say.)

So the question is not: "Can you really teach writing?" but "Can you learn it?" In other words, how much are we willing to find out about ourselves?

People have written to understand themselves and other people, to promote actions, to record, to leave a trail and to obscure a trail, to provide raw material, to untangle and straighten out, to set a record straight—or

---

2. Or, as Dostoevsky called it, "one harmonious antheap." [ND]

crooked, to go where no one has gone before, to set the limits on where it is possible to go, to make a law, organize support for it, map the means to enforce it, or to devise a vocabulary to obscure its defects, to strike against a law, to join in. . . . And at this demarcation writers enter into the same arena with soldiers, politicians, scientists, disciples, vanguards, and lovers. The distinctions among these avenues for expression of the instinct to connect with other human beings cannot be drawn by writing teachers (much less by generals, or bankers, or vice-presidents of marketing); we all have to learn how to make those distinctions together. What writing teachers *can* do is to get out of the way, get off people's necks and let them learn. This does not mean the teacher abdicates his or her role; it does mean that he or she has to join in the learning, in a writing class in which everyone teaches each other.[3]

I am aware that the discipline involved in doing this is nearly unendurable; that the rewards are mild, particularly for this present generation of teachers, and the high school and college students who have been so rudely brainwashed by institutions run for the profit of the few, and the peace of mind of the benighted many. The results will not be of a particularly sensational nature, not in our time. But slowly, surely, more and more people are learning that they have a right to learn; and a step has been taken in the direction of replacing the old phony question, "Can you teach writing?" with a genuine discovery: we can help each other to learn.

---

3. That's the only way to teach: by agreement, cooperation, mutual effort, trust. Write on, Sandy! [KS]

ii

teaching writing

Responding to Writing

PATRICIA CUMMING

If someone tells me s/he has liked something I've written, I get very tense: I am trying to learn to accept a comment like that as a statement of fact, but I still tend to spend a lot of time thinking of reasons why that person should want to be nice to me, or console me, or something.

But if someone tells me that something I've written is terrible, I believe it, instantly.

For a long time if I wanted to keep working on a piece of writing, I couldn't show it to anyone. Now I can, and do, but I'm careful about who sees it. Terse negative criticism can still stop me cold.

"Awkward."

"Poorly organized."

"Unconvincing."

"Sentimental."

Whether or not all this is true, or half true, or possibly true, there's still something I want to say; and learning (irrevocably, at last) that all these adjectives describe it does not help me to say it, or anything else.

"Look, the first part doesn't work for me. It's all those long sentences. Maybe I don't really understand it."

"At the end, aren't you saying the same thing that you said here, in the middle? Or is it different? I can't tell. What did you mean?"

"I think you came down a little hard here. I got your point, but what do you think I am, dumb? Unless you spell it out for me, I won't get it?"

"This word, 'purity,' makes me think of soap, and soda water and virgins. I know what you mean, I guess, but I really can't stand that word."

The difference between the two kinds of comments (aside from the brevity of the first, and the fact that the second points to specific places, phrases, and words) is the personal pronoun "I." It is the difference between judgment and response. In the best of all possible worlds that difference might not matter so much, and everyone would be able to remember at all times that all judgments are relative and (of writing) subjective, depending on the judge's individual values at that moment in his or her life. We could remember that "This is terrible" in fact *means* "This turns me off, I don't like dealing with this kind of writing." Unfortunately, two parents,

---

1. That's not how I remember it; at least, not in elementary or junior high or high school. The correct answer (that given in the teacher's guide) was necessary, but rarely sufficient: if it was not derived in the "right" way, no credit. The hard part of homework, later, in algebra and trigonometry, was finding just the right example in the text so as to be sure of using the correct method. Kronecker, who said, "God invented numbers: all else is the work of man," was wrong. Those workbooks on fractions were Holy Writ, and you were damned if you were the least bit unorthodox. Most people don't meet mathematicians until college, if then. [LR]

eighteen years of school, and various very powerful groups of children and adults make this hard to do: we learn that "terrible" means *bad*, and on some kind of absolute scale upon which survival depends.

This scale has an extra moral dimension when it comes to writing. In arithmetic, if you make a mistake, you are simply wrong, and often your teacher will help you to do the problem over. This is relatively simple to deal with (of course, punitive math teachers do exist, but it's an attitude the discipline as a whole tends to resist).[1] At MIT teachers like the right answers, but what they try to teach is a method of solving the problem, various approaches to it, and even when the answer is wrong they give partial credit for productive ways of thinking about the solution. In English there are large numbers of people, from the most exalted on down, who believe that bad writing is a *sin*. Art and the English language, it seems, are in mortal danger: the barbarian hordes of the vulgar may sweep out of the steppes, at any moment, vengeful, sexual, rapacious, brandishing swords. Even worse, every single child from the moment s/he is born has the capacity—the desire—to become one of these invaders, unless s/he is saved in time.

These self-appointed guardians of Mount Parnassus stand at the furthest foothills, and they stand there with guns.[2]

I think that art and the English language are tough. They have lasted a long time; they have even survived their worst threat, their defenders. Because (of course) sexuality and dialect invigorate and refresh them, keep them alive. Art and English are tougher than students are.

All this is to say: Try not to evaluate other people's writing if you want them to write better (and try not to evaluate your own). This is hard; it involves unlearning habits instilled through most of a lifetime. The best way to begin is to listen to yourself, and try to use "I" or "me" in everything you say about writing. "I like this." "This doesn't work for me." "I get bored reading sentences with too many words in them."

Strict adherents of this method caution you to be careful to observe this even when you are praising something. To say: "This is good" suggests its opposite, and creates the moral and evaluative universe just as strongly as saying, "This is awful." Still when I think "This is a marvellous story!" I tend to say it, though when I remember I add, "I mean, I really like it a lot." My feeling is that praise[3] is okay in any form; saying "This is" makes me feel like an authority, bestowing something good. Dispensing largesse— I had probably better stop.[4]

---

2. I used to think that if I suffered enough they might let me past them. Part of me believes that still. [PC]

3. Once, when we were meeting, someone from a committee examining the arts facilities at MIT came and asked us, "What do you writers want?" Someone said, "Praise," and we all laughed; that *was* what we wanted, after all, more than anything else. [PC]

4. Haim Ginott (among others) discusses this whole concept very persuasively, at length, and with lots of examples, in a somewhat different context (*Between Parent and Child; Between Parent and Teenagers*). He is also help-

One code name for this concept as it applies to teaching is "non-evaluative feedback." Several of us dislike this term intensely (and tend to substitute "non-judgmental responses"), but it has its uses because it sounds authoritative and it does describe the idea quickly for people who do not want to listen to a long explanation of what it really means, and why it is so important.

This idea is absolutely central to everything else we say in this book. It is also the most controversial. You may talk about open classes, workshops and discussion groups with impunity, but if you espouse non-judgmental attitudes in public, it is probably better to have tenure—unless you are teaching in a school where the students' writing problems are so great and the commitment to solving them is so strong that teachers are willing to do what is most effective, no matter what. In those schools some form of this concept usually operates. In others, it seems to be a very inflammatory thing to say, at least around humanists, who will tell you that you are not upholding standards, and are, instead, doing therapy, encouraging mushiness, and other dreadful things. ("What they need is discipline.") Outside of English Departments, people think about their own experience with English teachers, and understand how much pain and frustration they would have been saved if writing had been taught to them as a way of finding solutions, some of which worked for some readers, some of which didn't; had it been taught simply, objectively, without wrath.

---

ful about how to be honest and clear about your reactions, including negative ones, in a non-hurtful way. It would certainly be better for a teacher (to paraphrase one of his dialogues between a mother and her child) to say, "You make me angry. You make me very angry. I would like to pick you up and throw you out the classroom window" than for the teacher to remain polite and give the student an F. [PC]

Exploring My Teaching*

PETER ELBOW

I possess in good measure the impulse to nail down the truth about teaching once and for all, and on that basis to tell everyone else how to teach. Much in this essay hovers on the brink of being plain, pushy, normative advice. Nevertheless, the main thing I've come to believe through the exploration described here—and the main thing I wish to stress—is that better teaching behavior comes primarily from exploring one's own teaching from an experiential and phenomenological point of view: "What did I actually do? What was I actually experiencing when I did it? Can I say what feelings, ideas, or experiences led me to do it?" This approach leads to very different teaching behaviors for different people and even different teaching behaviors for the same person at different times. All these behaviors will indeed be "right,"[1] I would say, so long as they rest upon a symmetrical premise: an equal affirmation of the student's experience, his right to ground his behaviors in his experience, and thus his right, like the teacher's, to embark on his own voyage of change, development, and growth as to what is right for him:

> *I am not in this world to live up to your expectations*
> *And you are not in this world to live up to mine.*
>
> Fritz Perls

After five years of regular college teaching—trying to be Socrates and a good guy at the same time—and after three years of nonteaching while I was finishing my Ph.D. but thinking a lot about teaching (see *College English*, Vol. 30, Nos. 2 and 3), I reentered the classroom to discover an unexpected set of reactions. I found I couldn't stand to tell students things they hadn't asked me to tell them. I knew I knew things that were both true and important, but that only made me feel all the more gagged and mute. I even found I couldn't stand to ask questions—except the question, "What is your question?" Nothing seemed worth saying in a classroom till a student had a question he took seriously. I was no longer willing to listen to the thud of my question lying dead on the classroom floor. I refused to coax interest. I also felt it as a refusal to pedal alone. If they won't pedal, neither will I. No source of energy seemed bearable except their motivation. And not only motivation but experience. If they are not talking from the experience of the text read—even the felt experience of getting no experience from it—then count me out.

---

* From *College English*, vol. 32, April 1971, pp. 743-753.
1. Evaluative. [PC]

These were troublesome feelings. Giving in to them seemed to mean abdicating my role as a teacher. But they wouldn't go away and I was feeling ornery. So with respect to most of the leadership activities of teachers, I'd become by Christmas a kind of drop-out, a conscientious objector, a giver-in to repugnance.

I'm prepared to consider the hypothesis that these feelings are some kind of pathology. Some kind of petulant backlash at having finally submitted to graduate school. Or some kind of atrophy of the deep sexual hunger to tell people things. But on the other hand, perhaps the real pathology is the hunger to tell people things they didn't ask you to tell them.[2] If this turns out to be true, if unsolicited telling turns out to hinder rather than help our goal of producing knowledge and understanding in students, then we will have to be honest enough to set up arenas where teachers can work off this appetite.

Perhaps my metaphor is too unsavory. But not too sexual. The one thing sure is that teaching is sexual. What is uncertain is which practices are natural and which unnatural, which fruitful and which barren, which legal and which illegal. When the sexuality of teaching is more generally felt and admitted, we may finally draw the obvious moral: it is a practice that should only be performed upon[3] the persons of consenting adults.

But since I am not sure which is pathology—unsolicited telling or holding back—and since I don't yet know the grounds for deciding the question, I am merely asserting that it is possible to have these feelings, act on them, and live to tell the tale. Not go blind and insane. It is not a trivial point since so many teachers share these feelings but scarcely entertain them because they feel them unspeakable.

My present introductory literature course is the latest product of these feelings. It is a sophomore course, but comparable to freshman English since it is more or less required and is the first English course taken. Most courses are structured around a class hour, a set of books, and a teacher's perception of the content. If a student's goals, perceptions, and motivation can fit into that structure, fine; if not, too bad. I have tried to stand that model on its head. The core of my course is each student's goals, perceptions, and willingness to do something about it. The other ingredients—the class hour and the teacher's perception of the contents—are invited to fit into that structure if and where they can; and if not, too bad.

The course has three rules.

1. The student must state on paper, for everyone to read: at the beginning, what he wants to get out of the course; at midterm and end of term, what he thinks he is getting and not getting. Each student may pursue his own goals; read anything and go in any direction. The only constraints

---

2. How do people learn to use questions? How can I ask you to explain a function to me if you won't tell me anything until I ask? [ND]
3. I think your preposition has made a mistake. [ND]

are those imposed by reality. For example, I make it clear I am not going to spend any more time on the course than if I taught it in a conventional way.

2. Each student must read something each week, either literature or about literature. I offer my services in helping people find things suitable to their goals.

3. Each student must put words on paper (even if only to say he does not wish to write) once a week and put it in a box in the reserve reading room where everyone can read everyone else's and make comments. (There are about 20 in the class.) The writing need not be on what was read that week, though I ask the student to jot his reading down somewhere on the paper.

Attendance is not required. Anyone who follows the three rules is guaranteed an A. If not, he is not taking the course and I ask him to drop it or flunk. (I try not to be coercively non-directive: If a student's goals are to read what the teacher thinks most suitable for an introductory course and to get out of it what the teacher thinks he ought to get out of it, I try to help him with these goals.)

I wish to describe my experience in this course in terms of five beliefs.

1. *Much teaching behavior really stems from an unwarranted fear of things falling apart.* When I started to act on my new feelings and to refrain from unsolicited telling and asking, I discovered the fear that lay behind much of my previous teaching. I began to realize I'd always been "running" or "structuring" a class with the underlying feeling that if I ever stopped, some unspecifiable chaos or confusion would ensue. In all my teaching, there had been a not-fully-experienced sense of only precariously holding dissolution at bay.

But the unnamed disaster somehow doesn't happen. There is some confusion, desultoriness, and recurring silence, but the new class texture has an organic structure and stability. The class finds a new and stabler center of gravity. And I discover a mental or emotional muscle I've always been clenching to keep the ship from sinking or the plane from crashing. I discover it by feeling all of a sudden how tired it is.

But fears die hard. There are still days when it returns—my security may be low and my refusal flagging. I come in and ask, "Well, what is the question? How can we use our time?" The silence wells up. I can reach for my pipe and throw myself into carefully prying out the old tobacco—which it is important to leave there for these situations—cleaning it, filling it, tamping, and managing never quite to get it well lit so I can have something to keep busy with. All the while trying not to gulp. Not even cool enough to ask myself, "So what is this impending thing that is so scary? What's the disaster if nothing productive gets accomplished? You know perfectly well that they don't carry away much useful from your 'well run' classes."

Some students share this anxiety and some do not. Interestingly, it is usually the ostensibly "good" class—the productive and conscientious one— which persists longest in keeping up some kind of nervous chatter and prevents the class from finding its real center of gravity—usually silence at first and then some question about why in hell they are in this class doing what they are doing: with respect first to the class hour, then to the course, and only then to genuinely assented-to questions about the subject matter. It's so slow. And yet since I won't settle for any but genuinely assented-to questions, it represents a huge improvement and I'm not tempted to go back to the-show-must-go-on. Surely many others must be trapped as I was by unfelt fears in their running of a class.

2. *An actual audience is crucial for writing.* English teachers know it helps for the student to imagine an audience. But this is nothing compared to the benefit of actually having one. The best thing about my course is the fact that each student writes something weekly he knows the rest of the class will read and, for the most part, comment on.

An audience acts as suction. Only a few lucky or diligent souls find an audience because they write well. As often as not, people write well because they find an audience. They may not find a large and discriminating audience until after they get pretty good. But they had to start by being pretty lucky, pushy, or driven enough to find a genuine audience—even if small and informal. Writers like to say that a compulsion to write is the only necessary condition for being a good writer. The formula is elliptical and can be expanded in two directions: 1) the compulsion to write makes you find an audience and then you get better; or 2) the presence of an audience produces the compulsion to write. I sense everywhere a huge potential desire to be heard which the presence of an audience can awaken. A genuine audience can be tiny—even one person. But only exceptional teachers can succeed in being a genuine audience for more than a couple of their students. And a larger audience is better.

I have had the experience more than once of having thought I had finished writing something; sending it around and finally finding someone who would print it; and only then discovering a willingness to revise it again. Lack of character, perhaps, but a common disease which no college course can hope to cure.

The necessity of an audience is supported by the evidence about how children learn to speak: the audience is laid on for free and is eager for all productions; the child doesn't have to deserve it. Whether the infant's audience gives correction doesn't matter much. What matters is ongoing interaction: answering and talking, i.e., nonevaluative feedback. And no audience, no speech. Imagine the sorry results of an infant trying to learn to speak by a process equivalent to our freshman English or writing courses.

The writing of the students in my course improves noticeably. They do not necessarily work on the kind of writing that someone else thinks they ought to. Few work consistently on critical, analytic essays. The majority write explorations of their own experience. More poetry than I expected. But it is clear they are learning the basic elements or atoms for any sort of writing: how to work out thoughts and feeling into words; how to get words on paper such that the meanings get into the reader's head; and how to make the effects of those words on a reader more nearly what the writer intended.

The most solid evidence for the quality of their writing is that I actually enjoy reading the papers in the box each week. And they get more enjoyable each week. The voice and self of each writer continually emerge more forcefully.

3. *Students learn more about literature through writing than through reading.* Many students don't really believe in the reality of words that come in books studied in school. I remember discovering, the first moment I was in France, that I hadn't really believed there were real people who spoke that funny language I studied in school and college. That unexpected, faint surprise revealed that part of me suspected all along that French was an elaborate hoax by schools and teachers to give me something difficult to learn. Paranoia, if you will, but again, a common disease.

And so in the case of literature, I feel students in this class doing with each other's writing the one thing—and a rare thing—that is a precondition for the appreciation and study of literature: taking the words seriously; giving full inner assent to their reality. I phrase the writing assignment as a requirement to "put words on paper such that it's not a waste of time for the reader or the writer." At last students wrestle with the main question—especially in an introductory course: what real value is there in putting words down on paper or in reading them? If a teacher feels the value is self-evident, he should look to some of our cultural and literary critics who have serious doubts. Students share these doubts and it's no good saying they're not allowed to take them seriously till they know as much or write as well as, say, George Steiner. I suspect many English teachers insist so loudly on the importance of reading and writing because of an inner doubt that is too frightening to face. I'm struck by the quiet relief with which many English and writing programs swing into film. Students came to enjoy literature more than they ever have done in a course of mine because this question of whether it's worth putting words on paper at last became the center of the course—and operationally, not intellectually or theoretically.

4. *For learning, empirical feedback is a good thing and normative evaluation is a bad thing.* Empirical feedback, in the case of writing, means learning what the words did to the reader. Normative evaluation means having the words judgmentally ranked according to some abstract standard. I have found that empirical feedback seems to encourage activity; to release energy. Presumably when one gets accurate, honest, human feedback—with all the inevitable contradictions between responders—one learns not to be scared to put forth words. Normative evaluation seems to inhibit words.

The value of having everyone in the class reading everyone else's writing is that it inevitably brings out empirical feedback and diminishes normative evaluation. Students often start out giving normative judgments: they've learned in school that "commenting" on a paper means saying whether it is good or bad. But these judgments are so diverse and conflicting that the writer can see how normative evaluations are usually skewed forms of personal, empirical feedback. When there are many comments on a paper, it is clear that a statement like, "This is disorganized and uninteresting and doesn't really amount to anything," really means, "You bored me and I didn't perceive any organization or meaning here." For other comments show that other readers reacted differently. The effect of this situation—and my urging—is that students get better at giving honest empirical feedback. (They did not, however, usually give enough commentary feedback to satisfy me and some of them.)

I grade as I do because of this distinction between feedback and judgment. When the grade is as meaningless as possible, the student can better believe, assimilate, and benefit from the feedback he gets from me and his classmates. I am frankly trying to channel my responses into personal, honest reactions, and keep them from being channeled into institutional normative judgments. Students write more than they have to, I think, because of a setting with maximum feedback and minimum judgment.

5. *It is good to separate constraints from freedoms with absolute clarity*. I am tempted to think that the amount of freedom in a course makes less difference than how clearly it is distinguished from constraint. Almost any course contains more freedom than is first apparent, but if there is any ambiguity, the freedom ends up inhibiting rather than liberating energy.

I cannot resist speculating on the obscure dynamics here. I find myself and many students reading in constraints that are not there. "If I do such and such I'll get on the bad side of Smith," when in fact Smith couldn't care less. "If I teach in such and such a way, I will lose my job," when the teacher knows deep down that his latitude is immense if he is not needlessly inflammatory. "I wouldn't be reading this crap except that he might put it on the exam," when the student knows deep down he would do better on the exam if he spent a fraction of the time seriously reading a "trot" and discussing it with a couple of friends. "I've got to take this course because they require it in graduate school," when he doesn't take the trouble to find out whether it is really so—and it usually isn't.

There must be good reasons for fooling ourselves in this way. For one thing, it may be a form of reacting to past occasions when we were stung: we were offered free choice but there were covert constraints. Students have had this experience many times. There is hardly a high school course that doesn't begin with the announcement, "Now you people can make what you want to out of this course."

Desires may also make one read in constraints that do not exist: it is hard—especially these days—to accept and experience the universal desire simply to be told what to do—to be held by arms too strong to break out of.

I can think of a third reason for feeling contraints that aren't there: if I feel some task as constrained rather than free, then I don't have to feel how much I care about it and fear failing. In short, I am spared the risk of investment and caring. Whatever the reason for this failure to experience the full degree of freedom or choice that exists, it causes a subtle, pervasive insulation against real learning—a covert non-assent or holding back from genuine participation in the knowledge that is seemingly attained.

As I see it, then, when choice is available, there is usually an initial resistance and tendency to do nothing at all. It is a threatening investment for many students simply to do something school-like when they don't have to. If this can be gotten past, if the choice or freedom can be finally assented to and the investment made, there turns out to be a liberation of energy. But if there is any haziness or ambiguity about the choice, many students get stuck at the stage of feeling subtly constrained. They resent and resist the freedom. The freedom is not assented to, the hump is not gotten over, and there is no liberation of energy.

Such ambiguity can come from a teacher's unspoken doubts and hedges: "You can read whatever you want." ("So long as you don't read trash.") Or, "I am giving you this choice to exercise as you see fit." ("Only I wish I didn't have to give it to those of you who are lazy and don't give a damn about this subject because you won't use the freedom well and don't deserve it.") These unspoken thoughts get through to students—presumably through tone of voice, phrasing, and even physical gestures.

It follows from the idea that freedom and constraints should be clearly distinguished that rules are often a good thing. I used to feel rules were childish. We're in college now. Let's not go around making rules. But there are in fact many constraints at play upon us and our students—from the society, the institution, the teacher's idea of what is proper, or simply from the teacher's character or prejudices. It is liberating to get them into clear rules.

Students only learn to choose and to motivate themselves in spaces cleared by freedom. These spaces can be very small and still work, so long as they are not clouded by ambiguity. A teacher can give meaningful freedom even if he works within a very tightly constrained system. Suppose, for example, that every aspect of a course involves a constraint stemming either from the institution's rules or the teacher's sense of what is non-negotiably necessary. If, in such a situation, the teacher decides nevertheless that the last fifteen minutes of each class period are genuinely free to be used as the class decides—or one full class a week—a new degree of freedom and learning will result.

I use class time for my example because it is usually the area of greatest ambiguity about freedom. So often we are trying for two goals at the same time: to create a free, unconstrained feeling ("free discussion"), and to cover points chosen in advance. (Sometimes, in fact, even to conclude things concluded in advance.) It is crucial in running a so-called free discussion to make up our minds—and make it clear to the class—what the rules really are. Almost any rules are workable so long as they are clear: "We can talk about anything so long as it has something to do with the assignment"; or, "I reserve the right to decide what the questions will be, but we can do anything in treating these questions"; or, "It can go where the class wants it to go, but I reserve the right to decide we are wasting time; but I admit I don't know exactly what my criteria are for the decision; in fact I admit my criteria will vary with my mood."

The only unworkable rule is a common unspoken one: "You must freely make my points." When I finally sensed the presence of this rule and how unworkable it was, I was forced to see that if I feel certain points must be made in class, then I should make them as openly as I can—even through lectures—and not try to coax others to be my mouthpiece.

The problem of class time illustrates the fact that even though it is helpful and liberating to try to get things into a binary system of being either totally free or totally constrained, most of us want some aspects of our course to be somewhere in between. For such grey areas of reality, we have a favorite phrase: "It would be a good idea if you did such and such." I find it hard to break the habit, but I can now see it as one of the most self-defeating ways to ask students to do something. Even though the matter is not fully free or constrained, that is no excuse, it now seems to me, for not making up my mind whether I am saying, "You will get a lower mark if you don't"; or, "You will learn less if you don't"; or, "You will develop less character if you don't"; or, "You will personally disappoint me or make my life harder if you don't." Each of these messages is perfectly valid and causes students little difficulty. But to fudge the issue of which is the true one has the effect of producing needless resistance.

In my efforts to distinguish clearly between areas of freedom and constraint and to make unambiguous, accurate messages about those things that lie somewhere between, I discovered why I hadn't naturally stumbled into these practices before. They are hard. In particular, they put me more personally on the line and make me feel risk. For instance, in the case of sending messages, one of my favorites is, "I think it would be better for you to do X, but it is your choice and it doesn't matter to me." It's unambiguous, all right. But unfortunately it is seldom accurate in my case. I seldom am indifferent about whether they do X. As I began to notice this, I began to realize that in many cases the only thing I was sure of was that I would feel better if they did X; and not that X was necessarily the best possible thing for all of them. But it is threatening to send the new, more accurate message. It makes me feel more vulnerable. And it permits students who probably ought to do X to say the hell with it—sometimes purely out of a spirit of contrariness. But I feel it helps in the long run. It begins to make my word more trustworthy.

Similarly in the case of trying to make unambiguous rules, I found I was more likely than before to be thought of as a dirty rat by the student. I want the area of freedom to be very large, but nevertheless authority is more naked when one is unambiguous. Therefore more students are apt to be very angry about something or other—even about the freedom itself. As this made me very uncomfortable, I began to sense how much of my characteristic teaching behavior is an attempt to avoid being the object of the student's anger.

I suppose this whole exploration of the importance of being unambiguous about freedom and constraint—this renewed attack upon the old problem of freedom and necessity—is merely an extended way of saying that I find an inescapable power relationship in any institutionalized teaching. I feel this power relationship hinders the sort of learning situation I seek—one in which the student comes to act on his own motivation and comes to evaluate ideas and perceptions on their own merits and not in terms of who holds them. I feel I can best minimize this power relationship by getting the weapons out on the table. Trying to pretend that the power and weapons are not there—however swinging I am and however groovy the students are—only gets the power more permanently and insidiously into the air.

It may be, of course, that it is misguided and perverse of me to want to get rid of the power relationship: my own hang-up about authority. Certainly the power relationship can be viewed as a potent audio-visual aid for a mature teacher to welcome and use honestly and constructively. Either verdict, however, points to the importance of recognizing the power relationship.

Because I'm confident the course is working at an important level, I want to share my frustrations. First, inevitably, not enough gets covered in class. It's all very well to make fun of the teacher's itch to "cover" a lot, but the itch is so real. Allowing everyone to choose his own reading makes it harder for the class to come together in a focused discussion. In the future I may ask that we somehow come up with a mechanism for focusing one class a week upon a common text or planned topic of discussion.

There were times when I could honestly have said, "Damn it, this desultory, wandering small talk and local gossip is downright boring to me. Can't we do something more interesting and substantive? Otherwise I'll simply go on sitting here wishing my alarm hadn't gone off." I didn't dare say it, but now I suspect I should have. Reticence about these feelings probably made more oppressive vibrations than expressing them would have done. It's as though I feared I had some super, demolishing power and they were nothing but weak and defenseless. Whereas if I had just said it, maybe it would have helped us all sooner to get past a loaded and awkward way of behaving with each other—strengthened their autonomy and reduced my self-consciousness. To carry this off, however, I'd have to succeed in saying it and meaning it as one person who feels dissatisfied—not as someone who harbors the insistence that the class follow my feeling.

I found, by the way, that longer classes of this sort are more productive than shorter ones. It's worth trying to change three 50-minute classes a week into two longer ones. It's too easy for everyone to wait it out for 50 minutes and avoid the effort and investment of overcoming inertia—holding the breath till the end of the period. It also seems worth informal rescheduling to avoid a situation where you are asking students to break out of their habitual, passive, class role at eight or nine in the morning when their metabolisms aren't even fired up yet.

But I'm sure the problem of low productivity in class won't disappear. Students display strong reactions to past teaching. They do a lot of testing because they have historical reason for suspecting there is a catch. They will inevitably spend considerable time pushing the limits to see whether they are in the presence of that hidden rule underlying so many current educational experiments: "You may do whatever you want—so long as it's not something we feel is a waste of time."

I was also frustrated by what I perceive as a rampant individualism. At the operational level, this took the form of an aversion to working together in subgroups with common reading. Even though many of them had similar goals, this never happened. It discouraged me. The individualism took an epistemological form as well: a tendency to operate on the unspoken premise that "I know what I perceive, feel, and think; if I try to get any of these into words or into someone else's head, there is only distortion and loss, and it's not worth the effort." They were scarcely willing even, to entertain the opposite premise, namely, "I don't know what I perceive, feel, or think until I can get it into language and perhaps even into someone else's head."

So students didn't seem to doubt their own individual perceptions of a text. They seemed uninterested in testing one individual's perceptions against another's. But I persist in thinking I shouldn't force this activity. I feel less worried about their emerging from my course with skewed perceptions of texts than about their persistence in not wanting to say anything about it. I see their wrongheaded, or at least parochial, point of view itself as a kind of proof that required corrective discussions haven't worked in the past. Why should they work better now?

During the term I saw no cure except patience for this student stance of I-don't-need-anybody's-help-to-see-accurately. I had already sensed a quiet refusal in it: they understood perfectly well, as anyone does, that their perceptions were liable to be skewed. The refusal annoyed me. But as I think about it now, I see I can do more. First, I am led to try to guess what experience might produce this epistemological arrogance. And then try to see if I can experience it vicariously myself. This is what I come up with: "Look! For years and years, you English teachers have been saying things and forcing us to do things which all tended to make us feel we have defective sensing mechanisms: our very perceptions are wrong—our own responses invalid. Almost invariably, the poem or character I preferred was shown less worthy of preference than one which left me cold. I was always noticing things that you seemed to show irrelevant, and failing to notice things you seemed to show most relevant. You may be able to convince me I have defective perception in literature; but you can't make me want to rub my nose in it. So now you tell me I can do what I want with a literature class and you want me to go in for more of that? Not on your life!"

So where I once felt indifference and even arrogance about individual perception, I now feel a pervasive defensiveness and doubt. Where I once saw teachers as too unconvincing, I now see they were too convincing. I wish I'd felt this earlier because it dispels my annoyance and that annoyance probably made things worse. For I now see as healthy and positive their refusal to joust publicly with their own responses until they are a bit confident, or at least comfortable and self-accepting, about them. For myself, certainly, I can't really expose my own responses for refinement or correction, as here, until I feel pretty good about them. Only then, paradoxically, can I truly open myself to the possibility that they are seriously skewed, and allow myself ungrudgingly to move on to different, more accurate perceptions.

Another frustration is that I feel much less useful in such a teaching situation. My head is bursting with fascinating things that the dirty rats didn't ask me. (Half way through the term, however, I saw I should join in the activity of putting words on paper once a week for the box. So that gave me a forum that seemed appropriate.) As teachers we tend to assume we are useful to students, and that the more we are used the better we are doing. I think we should take a ride on the opposite premise and see where it leads—the premise that we may not be doing badly if they get very little from us. Einstein put it bluntly in a letter:

> *Incidentally, I am only coming to Princeton to research, not to teach. There is too much education altogether, especially in American schools. The only rational way of educating is to be an example—of what to avoid, if one can't be the other sort.*
>
> *The World as I See It*, pp. 21–22.

Another frustration is that one must put up with great naiveté. But I am convinced, now, that when you allow real choice and self-motivated learning, students revert to the point at which real learning ceased. They revert to what they really feel and think—not to what they normally produce in classes, papers, and tests. John Holt talks shrewdly of how primary school arithmetic teachers often find themselves keeping the class discussion within channels implied by the textbook because the children can thereby produce correct answers; whereas if things wander into novel or unexpected byways, the teacher is forced to confront the overwhelmingly discouraging fact that the children don't really understand the most elementary concept of arithmetic which they have already "mastered." I feel I often see students demonstrate that they don't really understand many things they have a competent academic mastery of. That is, they haven't "really learned" them— they haven't been willing or able to digest, assent to, or participate in the knowledge of these things. For this reason, I feel we should view as progress this reversion to naive stations where real learning stopped.

In the end, I am led back to a new perception of those original pesky feelings: something has been motivating me all along which only now comes to awareness. I sense differently now those refusals to tell things unsolicited, to ask questions, and to pedal alone. I feel them now as more positive. Behind the reticence and sense of being gagged lies a need to be genuinely listened to, to carry some weight, to make a dent. I want a chance for my words to penetrate to a level of serious consciousness. And that need is great enough that I'll pay a large price. I'll settle for a very few words indeed. Behind my ostensible openness lies an intense demandingness. If I didn't really want to be demanding, I could teach the old "well-run" course that students let roll off their backs so easily. It's my desire to be heard that makes me insist that the students figure out what they want to know.

I am like the teacher of the noisy class who says, ever so sweetly, "Now boys and girls, I'm not going to say another thing until you are quiet enough for me to be heard." (Stifled cheers!) But my intuition had enough sense to take things into its own hands and insist that I didn't have a chance of being heard until they made more noise. I think this is true even at the literal level: in my few good classes, I have to fight to be heard, but my words carry more real weight—the weight of a person and not just a teacher. If I want to be heard at all, I've got to set up a situation in which the options of whether to hear me or tune me out—whether to take me seriously or dismiss me—are more genuine than in a normal classroom field of force. I'm refusing, therefore, to be short-circuited by a role which students react to with the stereotyped responses to authority: either automatic, ungenuine acceptance or else automatic, ungenuine refusal.

I don't know whether this underlying need to be truly heard is a good thing or a bad thing: whether the ineffectual parts of my teaching come from not fully inhabiting this basic feeling, or from not having gotten over it. I imagine two different answers from students. I imagine them saying,

> Well, it's about time you had the guts to feel and admit your mere humanity—your desire to get through and your need to make a difference. There's no hope for you as a teacher as long as you come on with this self-delusion about being disinterested, non-directive, and seeking only the student's own goals and motivation. In that stance, you can never succeed in being anything for us but cold, indifferent, and a waste of our time—ultimately enraging.

But I also hear them saying,

> For Christ's sake, get off our back! We've got enough to think about without your personal need to make a dent on us. What do you think we are? Objects laid to gratify your need to feel your life makes a difference?

My teaching has benefited in the past from experiencing more fully the feelings which generate what I try to do. So I trust that this new clarification of feeling must be progress even if I don't yet know what to think of it.

I Won't Write

PATRICIA CUMMING

Many of the essays in this book have been concerned with the act of writing itself; and with situations where the essential meaning of that act can be restored. But sometimes writing has to be done under conditions where that kind of freedom is not (usually) allowed.

I

I had lunch last spring with a friend, a professor of history at a nearby college; he told me what a number of professors tell me when they find out I teach writing: "I wish you could do something about *my* students. They can't write." He also said that, in his large lecture course, they were planning to cut down on the time allotted to section meetings and to replace it with additional lecturing. "The sections don't seem to serve any useful purpose," he said. "The students don't seem very interested in them, they don't talk. . . "

I suggested that he keep the section time, and that in it he should ask the students to read their papers aloud to one another and to him. "If you just do that—and nothing else," I said, "the writing will improve."

He told me that he believed me, that it would work. "But, then," he said, "no one would take the course! The students would hate reading their papers aloud—they don't care about them, really. And the class would be bored stiff. They don't want to sit through twenty sophomore papers on the Industrial Revolution, et al."

Perhaps my friend was right. At first the students might have felt this to be an intolerable imposition—not only to write papers, but to read them aloud, to be responsible for them as well. But I wish he had followed my suggestion. He is a kind person and would have been patient with them and their papers, and would have helped them to be helpful to each other. He is also open enough at least to consider alternatives to straight expository prose.

In any case, the underlying problem of most college writing would have been out in the open, for both students and teacher: is it in fact possible to write such a paper and make it interesting, accurate and informative? If so, how? If not, is it really necessary? How much is it really an educational experience for the student, and how much is it simply a tool for evaluation, for the convenience of the professor? And if it is simply an evaluative tool, what does it evaluate?

The answers to these questions probably differ for each student and each instructor, and they may vary for each at different times. It must be borne in mind that an essential ingredient for good writing is *time*: the time to make two or three drafts, to think, to revise, to edit. And that the more remote and uninvolving the piece of writing is, the harder it is to do.

There are of course interesting and involving topics concerning the Industrial Revolution, and it is possible to present standard material and ideas in other forms—dialogues, journals, parodies. The problem is (and in the kind of class I suggested it might be possible to discuss it) whether a student should take the risk of exploring these forms in order to write something of interest to others, or whether s/he should bore everyone, including him or herself and the professor, and turn in what s/he thinks the professor thinks is an "acceptable piece of historical writing."

My friend realizes that it is hard to be interesting, and especially to students (he tries to do this in his lectures); his remark implies that he believes a student audience probably won't sit still for the kinds of rhetoric and emptiness which replace thought and concern in many papers, and which professors doom themselves endlessly to read. Unlike students, professors feel they must accept being bored: they are paid for their time (instead of paying for it), they have a Goal (to improve the student, impart knowledge, values, research tools, respect for accuracy and/or the English language, and so on); hence they are prepared to endure some suffering. But that suffering is involved is evident in any college faculty at term paper time. And, of course, in writing those papers, students have suffered too.

It is often asserted that suffering promotes learning; in some situations it may; I'm not sure it does in this one.[1] It is certain that it creates feelings of anger and rebellion and hence, in conscientious people, guilt.[2] The angry professor gives sarcastic comments and low grades; one, at one of those recurrent meetings where the "problem of student writing" was being discussed, was very clear about this. At the suggestion that professors should write long comments on each paper he said, "I refuse to spend hours of *my* time on papers they have taken only 20 minutes to write," and walked out.

Others of us are afflicted with an uneasy sense that boring papers reflect bored students, and blame ourselves for somehow being responsible for it all. How can we read reams of nonsense every term, read and *not* retaliate; try to continue to understand, trust, remain open (those papers are hostile, after all)?[3]

To write well, even fairly well, is hard. Even aside from inner difficulties, which may afflict one no matter how simple the assignment is, a certain amount of effort is involved in revision, editing, recopying. Faced with an assignment they do not care very much about, many students, not unreasonably, put off doing all that work as long as they can, until they have only a few hours before the deadline. Then, guilty and angry, they do what they

---

1. In fact, since Aeschylus at least it has been asserted that suffering promotes wisdom. But experience with term papers (both the reading and the writing of them) might well throw doubt on this truism. [ND]

2. I object! I consider myself extremely conscientious, but also angry and rebellious and not the least bit guilty about either. [ND]

3. I have one friend who solves this problem quite simply—by returning papers late. [PC]

4. I take exception to that "we"—because those same qualities looked at

can. As my friend saw, clearly enough, they hate the result, and would not want to read it aloud. They end up hating writing even more than they did, and will probably put off writing the next paper even longer. And this has done nothing more for them than to destroy their self-respect and self-confidence: they would agree with their teachers that they "can't write."

This is true to the point where many professors who *do* spend hours commenting on their students' papers, in the most constructive and helpful ways they can, find that the authors never pick them up. These students find the whole thing so distasteful that they never want to see what they have written again. This is discouraging to the professor, who finds him- or herself in the position of having worked hard on something, only to discover that no one bothers to read it (the same position students have found themselves in, time after time. How were they to know this course would be different?).

In any case, what finally happens is that a grade is given—which translates or expresses some of the above in one way or another, depending. The grade *is* real; it follows students all their lives. It may also have a further measure of reality, because the ability to figure out what people in authority want, and produce what they consider interesting, useful or true on paper, is an important one, and does predict success. Grades are, in other words, a good measure of a person's shrewdness, adaptability and willingness to perform (at no matter what the personal cost) upon demand. These are all qualities (among others) we want our doctors, lawyers, engineers, corporation executives and public servants to have.[4]

Nevertheless, we and our students are still in a university and we are not supposed, really, to be measuring and grading our students' shrewdness, adaptability and docility.[5] We are supposed to be educating them, and in some cases also encouraging or releasing creativity, which, as a number of studies show, does not always flourish under structured circumstances.

No matter what our motives are in giving grades (and, like deadlines, they can be useful), they do represent power (and power corrupts), authority, force. And, as Gary Woods points out in "Confessions of a Disloyal Student," force does not teach, except about itself. I am not sure you can *make* anyone write better though I suppose you can frighten them into it temporarily,[6] especially the cynical or the docile; but perhaps they too would be better served in another kind of situation. Real writing skills come from having something to say, and someone you want to say it to, from taking real responsibility for it, from the self-confidence and sense of crafts-

---

with a slightly different bias suggest a lack of self-respect and a willingness to toady to any authority that presents itself. [ND]

5. Being "original" on demand is still evidence of a kind of docility; a harder kind; for A students only. See Peter Elbow's excellent article, "Shall We Teach or Give Credit?: A Model for Higher Education," in *Soundings*, Summer 1973. [PC]

6. I don't believe that. In fact it has been my experience that anxiety and stupidity are usually indistinguishable in a classroom. [ND]

manship gained from working carefully until something comes out right; and from showing it to other people and knowing how to use their responses constructively. Threatening a student with a C makes none of these things happen.

This is why English Composition courses often fall short of what they set out to do, and even though both students and faculty agree on their importance. Students have a built-in resistance to assigned papers, one that often goes back to grade school when an enthusiastic but misspelled account of a summer met with "C- Sp!!" in red on the top. In our freshman writing course at MIT it sometimes takes one full term to deal with that resistance. The students have to test us and the course over and over again until they are *sure* they have full autonomy; then they begin to use the course to pursue their own interests in writing in their own ways. It can be a painful process. There seems to be no way to circumvent it or cut it short; nothing seems to be happening for weeks. But it is worth it in the end. To give people back a sense of owning their own writing, the feeling that it is theirs, instead of something squeezed out of them by teachers, is an important thing to have done.

I think, finally, this is what I have against written comments on papers, though I used them for a long time, and some students want them. But if you write on someone's paper, it is no longer *theirs*; it is a good feeling to give a paper back to someone exactly as he or she wrote it.[7] Then talk to him or her, but let the student take h/h own notes. I did this in a literature class I taught last spring, and it felt better. I also said more, and, ultimately, it took less time, than written comments.

Then *say* when you have been bored, angry, disbelieving, turned off, and, if you can, why (it can be a simple matter of spelling or punctuation, as well as phrasing or lack of organization). The student will tell you what s/he really meant to say; you can suggest how it could have been said, and find out something about how s/he goes about writing. Some people write one draft slowly; others (like me) have to make many, many drafts; and while if you wait for inspiration you may have to wait forever, there are definitely good writing moods and terrible ones, and there are good editing moods and terrible ones. In both cases you can learn, with practice, to recognize them in yourself.

The ability to know oneself and to write precedes the form the writing may take, and I believe that a poem, a short story, a literary or historical essay or a lab report are equally useful in teaching these skills. They are hard in any case, and you might as well learn them on something you are interested in doing. Unfortunately, most writing courses are taught by English departments, where there is a good deal of unconscious pressure on the instructors (particularly if they are non-tenured) to turn out students who will do well in upper-level English courses. The academic essay, in all its

---

7. This does meet with a lot of resistance since students tend to equate no comment with no interest. The conference is essential. [ND]

forms, which is taught so hard and intensively in college, is in fact an extremely specialized kind of writing—useful to future graduate students and professors, whose jobs and careers do hang on the ability to manipulate it well, but quite divorced from the other kinds of writing one may find oneself doing after school. Publicity violates all its rules entirely; fund-raising proposals have a form and language peculiar unto themselves; and journalism has its own extremely specialized format. The one exception to this is probably some forms of technical writing: the way you learn to write up your research in college is probably the way you will write it up in your job. At any rate, the rules of any given form are intricate; they can be endlessly fascinating for anyone who wants to master them; and they are confusing and irrevelant for others.

I don't think I ever really believed that the "discipline" I acquired from "learning how to think clearly on paper" was ever sufficient reason for putting myself through and over the hurdles writing a term paper involved, and I was a docile Radcliffe girl of the fifties, and out of desperation got to be pretty good at it. Sometimes I did think things through that I might not otherwise have thought about, but they tended to be small things; my real discoveries in my courses were too large and disorganized for term papers, which I early learned were easier and more successful in proportion to the minuteness of the topic. It would have been different if I had been asked to tell other students about what was really important to me about the books I read, but that was not the point.

As a result, I did not write prose for years after I left college, and only started again because I had to do publicity for an organization I cared deeply about and felt responsible for. In any case, nothing I had learned about writing from those term papers was particularly useful to me. I *had* been writing plays and poems, and feeling that I could do those made the difference. Even now, the knowledge that I have succeeded in writing publishable poems is what is carrying me through this article. With a little help.

Three conclusions about writers:

1. The single most important fact in getting people to write better is their own feeling that the writing is in some way important to them and to others.

2. A friendly, honest audience is probably the best way to make this happen, to provide the advice that all writers, even professionals, need at times.

3. Writing should be taught when the writer has some real reason or need to work hard on it, and to learn whatever specific forms that that kind of writing demands.

One about teaching:

Teachers—and not only writing teachers—can be very useful in setting up a situation where the audience can be helpful to and not destructive of the writer.

II

The fact is that, whatever their ultimate value for nonprofessionals in the field, term papers are here to stay, particularly in the Humanities, to the point that many professors, when talking about their students' "writing," mean, quite specifically, term papers in the professors' own fields. I have, therefore, two suggestions for dealing with the problems of learning to write them. Both are simple, and are radical only in the sense that they emphasize the educational process rather than the grade curve.

The first involves only a rearrangement of the teacher's time. It's a simple idea, but every time I mention it, especially to teachers of English (who do much of the assigning and grading of term papers, and who often do want to teach writing), they look at me as if I had suggested something way beyond the bounds of possibility. One professor, who had thirty-nine papers to read that weekend, put her head down on the table and covered her ears with her hands. She didn't want to think about it. And yet, she does want to teach her students, and comments on all the papers at length.

Let us assume a teacher who believes that the ability to write acceptable term papers is essential to survival in college. (It is.) Let us further assume that this person believes that this skill ought to be made available to every student in his or her course, regardless of race, sex, creed, or ethnic origin. Let us further assume that this is important enough to the professor to divorce the teaching process from the evaluating procedure (grading) at least in part. And let us assume that the teacher cannot devote any more time on the process of teaching term-paper writing than s/he is now spending.

This professor could assign several short papers rather than one or two long ones. Students who received A's on the first paper would be excused from writing subsequent ones. They would be given other projects (preparing a class report, extra reading in some area of a student's interest, field trips or research, etc.). Students who received lower grades would either be asked to rewrite their original papers, or write another, using the experience gained from the failures in their first attempt—preferably discussed in conference. At the time the second paper was due, another group of students would (presumably) have written A papers. They also could then be excused. The teacher would be left with a much smaller group, the students who most needed help, and could work intensively with them, reading over successive drafts, for example, until they had brought their work up to acceptable standards.[8]

"But we can't give all A's!" Why not, if your students meet your standards? If the institution wants you to hand in a balanced grade curve, and you feel you must comply, you could use other criteria: attendance, class projects, class discussion, tests, finals, etc. Writing term papers and

---

8. One student, an unwilling writer of history papers, believes you would have to write one more paper, on your own, to feel sure you would be able to do it subsequently. [PC]

grading have become so deeply intertwined as to appear almost inseparable, but it will only be by separating the two that Johnny will indeed be allowed to learn to write. It is as simple as that. If every teacher could be measured by the quality of his or her students' papers, if teachers, high school and college, could be seen to have failed in their function if a significant portion of their students were handing in substandard work, the quality of college writing and the College Board written scores would rise dramatically within a year.

Like a garden that produces beautiful tomatoes all summer long, this process could be far more satisfying than the discouraging spectacle of stunted, misshapen produce that now occurs at the end of every term. Students would have a reason to work harder on their papers the first time, because doing so would free them to pursue their own course-connected interests in ways that were interesting and useful to them (this might include writing other papers). Teachers would be rewarded by being able to *teach*: this is, after all, their profession, and most people do want to practice it; they are frustrated by lack of time. Students would have real hope that they could learn how to write papers well (more students lose this than gain it under the present system), and teachers might actually enjoy reading the papers they received—imagine all the clear, interesting, well-organized and neat papers that could result. Both would have accomplished something they could regard with satisfaction.

"But," my friends who teach English ask, "what if the teachers cheat? What if they give A's to students who don't deserve them so that they could get out of grading all those papers?" The fact that this possibility has instantly occurred to a number of teachers is an indication of the depths of the basic, and often largely unconscious, distaste the present process evokes. The answer is (of course) that, if teachers are not to be trusted, a second reader should be provided. Any student knows that this could be difficult because no two teachers are alike in what they consider "good," but the ensuing dialogue between readers would be to everyone's benefit. It would be especially useful if the writer could be present.

Two readers, talking about the paper with the writer there, are better than one; and a group is better than two—for any kind of writing, not simply the poems and short stories we often receive in "Writing and Experience." One of the premises behind this book and the basis of my second suggestion is that if you give people an audience for their writing, one that will discuss it constructively, the writer will take the time to make it interesting and clear to that audience. In order to test this premise in another context I chose an environment that was as far removed from our elective writing courses as possible: a laboratory course called "Measurement and Instrumentation," given by the Department of Mechanical Engineering at MIT. The substance of this course was to teach students experimental procedures ("A Comparison of Strain and Stress Ratios in Steel and Copper Bars") and how to write them up in lab reports.

Lab report writing is a kind of anti-writing; the purpose of a good lab report is to make readers read as little of it as possible. The abstract should make it unnecessary for most readers to read the report at all, though a few may also want to scan the results section as well; virtually no one will read the entire report. Serious debate exists about whether or not personal pronouns are permissible; subjective impressions and feelings are, of course, unacceptable.[9] Writing lab reports is about as far away from the kind of writing most students do in our elective writing courses as is possible. This course was, therefore, a good environment in which to test the premise that, if you give people an audience for their writing, one that will discuss it constructively, the writer will take the time to make it clear to that audience.

When I started teaching the course, I read several books on technical writing and I attended the first lecture of the course, which dealt with guidelines for writing the reports. Nevertheless, I had had no personal experience with the form, and I was fairly certain I was not going to be able to understand much of the material that was presented. I knew that the other students would understand the content of the papers and that the regular graders would evaluate them (for both form and content). What I wanted to bring to the class was my knowledge of how to set up a group which could discuss the papers of its members in a fruitful way, and I hoped that the students might learn how to set up similar groups, formally or informally, later, when they needed them.

As a result of teaching this class I too learned to write lab reports, and to respect the form as an extremely useful and concise way of organizing and presenting information. I used the form to report on the class to the Department of Mechanical Engineering; that report follows this article.

The student evaluations of the course were all favorable; except for one dissenter, all believed that the discussion seminar had helped them to write better lab reports and should be continued. My recommendation was that I could use my teaching time most effectively if I held a similar seminar for the instructors grading the course, using pieces of their own writing (research reports, theses, etc.); in it we would not only discuss their papers but talk explicitly about which comments were most useful to them, and why; and which comments were not. They would then be able to set up similar course-related discussion sections for their own students, and these would probably not take much more teaching time than is presently required to read, comment upon, and grade the reports they now receive. And would be much more effective.

This model could completely change the teaching of writing in colleges and universities (and in high schools too). Students would work on writing not only in English courses, but where and when it was most important to them, and the faculty of their departments could learn how to run discussion seminars. The skills necessary to run these seminars are not difficult—they rest on the same principles on which any discussion section

---

9. In one of my classes we had a somewhat intense discussion about whether you could use jokes. We finally asked the Professor; he said *he* enjoyed them, but not everyone would find them appropriate. [PC]

10. Some community colleges and schools with open admissions, where students may need to work on writing at a more basic level, are in a somewhat

is run—but it would be important for faculty members to read and talk about some of their own writing in their introductory seminar. The principles are not as important as the experience of being a writer in this sort of situation. Besides, teachers often have as much trouble writing as students do; and if the only result of these seminars were to free teachers to write, it would be worth the time spent.

Ultimately, a university-wide program of course-related writing seminars would be much less expensive and far more efficient than numerous courses in English composition.[10] It also has the advantage of placing the responsibility for clear writing where it belongs: in the hands of every department graduating students qualified in its discipline.

Everyone wants students, scientists, engineers, and professors to write better, and everyone wants someone else to make this happen (generally young instructors in English, who are having or have just had problems enough with their own dissertations). Therefore, some sort of college- or university-wide requirement is probably necessary to put this plan into effect: a requirement that each student, before graduation, must participate in a writing seminar in connection with some course or paper in his or her major field. Otherwise, many departments and their faculties will not want to take the time to implement it, however much they may feel (abstractly) that good writing is a good thing.

In most colleges writing teachers could set up and lead the faculty seminars.[11] They would also be available to visit the subject-related writing classes given by department faculty when it seemed appropriate, and to lead seminars for new teachers of these courses so that problems could be discussed.

One further point needs to be made about the question of whether the very specialized writing skills learned in these subject-related seminars are transferable to the students' writing in general. I believe, as I have said, that the techniques acquired in learning how to do one form of writing well, and the self-confidence that accrues from it, can make all kinds of writing easier. I can imagine that a writer of lab reports, schooled in the avoidance of personal pronouns, might have trouble writing a love letter or a poem; but I have known many people who were able to do both, and the problems in their poetry came not from their expertise in lab reports but from their high school English teachers who disavowed every word written after 1850 (exception made for Tennyson, of course). Once people have really started writing and acquired a sense of freedom, fluency, and discipline—and, in spite of the work, have felt the joy that comes from being able to speak meaningfully to others—then they will go on writing.

---

different situation. See: *Uses of Literature*, Harvard English Studies, edited by Monroe Engel (Harvard University Press, Cambridge, 1971), especially the articles by Clara Claiborne Park, Robert Cumming, and Adrienne Rich. [PC]

11. The authors of this book also give a summer writing program for faculty interested in exploring this method of teaching. [PC]

An Interdisciplinary Experiment in Teaching Lab Report Writing*

PATRICIA CUMMING

ABSTRACT

In the fall of 1973, two experimental writing sections of 2.671, Measurement and Instrumentation, were given by a member of the Humanities Department in conjunction with the Department of Mechanical Engineering. In these sections students read their lab reports to one another and to the instructor, and discussed the problems they had in writing them; the class commented on them and made suggestions. Most of the students and the instructor felt that this method helped them write better lab reports. Certain modifications could be made, however, so that the course reaches a wider number of students and uses teaching time more effectively.

INTRODUCTION

Lab report writing is a highly formal exercise, and the organization of the information it contains demands a high degree of abstraction. Students who are faced with a mass of information, much of it of great interest to them (the construction of apparatus, the use of pertinent equations, a successful set of calculations) often find it difficult to realize that much of this material is not really relevant to the report and must be consigned to an appendix.[1,2]

The ability to manipulate this form successfully is an important one for engineers, and this fall two subject-related writing seminars were set up as a joint undertaking between the Department of Mechanical Engineering and the Department of Humanities, in order to explore one method by which these skills might be obtained.

METHOD

Two sections were offered, meeting one hour a week, composed of volunteers from 2.671, limited somewhat by scheduling conflicts. In the end

---

*A report presented to the Department of Mechanical Engineering, MIT, January 1974.

1. The writing in the apparatus section was often fresh, clear, and accurate. [PC]
2. They have trouble deciding what information is relevant and primary because they have not been taught to decide on the thesis of their report *before* they begin to write. [RR]

70

there were six in one section, eight in the other. Students were told they would be graded pass/fail on attendance (although, at the end of the term, this turned out not to be possible). Six units of credit in Mechanical Engineering were given.

In class, each student read his lab report to the group; copies were provided for the instructor and the other students. The class and the instructor commented on the structure, language, and technical problems. Each student read every report he had written; when there were no new reports to be read, we talked about other students' reports or did various writing exercises (response to this was mixed).[3]

RESULTS

With one exception, all the students who took the course and who were present at the final meeting felt that their lab report writing had benefited from it and that it should be continued. The students had a number of suggestions for varying the format; many of these are useful but would require more class time. The instructor feels that the basic method of teaching the course proved effective, but that the sections should be taught by the regular staff of 2.671, with some initial assistance on the problems of teaching writing *per se*.[4] In this way the class could be more integrated with the subject; some of the problems of monotony would be avoided; and fewer meetings on the writing alone would be necessary.

DISCUSSION

MOTIVATION

I offered to teach these sections because I wanted to test a method of teaching writing which had proved successful in elective and general writing courses (having students read their papers to others, followed by discussion); and I was interested in testing it in a situation where the students did not want to become "writers" but had some other reason to want to write well. In these classes, however, the students' professional commitment was not always clear:[5] one finally told me he took the course for the extra credit; from the laughter that followed I gathered that others might agree. Nevertheless, by the end of the term, the students in the class were working hard on their writing, and their reports reflected this.

---

3. i.e., Smarterbook (see Appendix I) and free writing. I also asked them to abstract other students' reports. I tried to gear these exercises to technical interests, but one section of students resented this and opted to write about people and places rather than about apparatus and experiments. The other section resented Smarterbook. [PC]

4. The students need to feel that instruction in technical writing is an integral part of their training as engineers. Participation by the engineering staff is vital to the success of a writing project. [RR]

It was my initial understanding (from the proposals for the class submitted by Prof. Griffith and me) that members of the staff of 2.671 would be present at all meetings. This proved not to be the case; and though some students would have welcomed more technical expertise on the part of the instructor, it is also true that in a writing class, as in a laboratory, the most lasting learning occurs when students must really search for the answers to their questions.[6] The best discussion occurred when I was not sure of the answers to the students' questions about format and they had to ask other students, read books, and question the course graders in order to bring this information back to the class. This is, of course, precisely the situation they will be faced with when they are out of school, and learning how to find the answers is more important than any information they might receive from me.[7] By the end of the term the students certainly had a clear sense of the structure of the lab report.

Good writing comes from taking time to revise. At the beginning of the term, the papers were clearly written in great haste; by the end it was equally clear that the students had worked hard on them. Students were willing to do this, I believe, because they knew their reports would receive careful attention from the class, and that they would be present to answer for ambiguities and imcomprehensible sentences.[8] Several students said that written comments they received from graders, while often useful, did not answer all the questions and uncertainties they had experienced while writing the reports; the class made a real attempt to do so, and the writers felt grateful for this. Subsequently, they felt it was worth making an extra effort. This is not to imply that graders, faced with hundreds of reports, can or should take more time on written comments. It does suggest that their time might be better used in sections with groups of students; and that verbal comments, expressed in a helpful way, are often much more effective than written ones.

LANGUAGE

Somewhat to my surprise, problems of language did not often occur after the first group of reports, where the writing tended to be hasty and ill-considered. The students themselves objected strongly to long sentences, sentences beginning with conjunctions, misspelling, and lack of organiza-

---

5. This often changes for the better by the time they take 2.672 second semester because the engineering projects are much more challenging. [RR]

6. Agreed. But many questions concern conventions demanded by the engineering professions (e.g. the specifications for chemical abstracts). The engineering staff should provide the answers to these questions. [RR]

7. Students can always tell whether you know the answers to the questions you ask. If you don't, they are often willing to put real energy into finding them out. If you do, the polite ones will often give a semblance of talking about the subject; others will be bored. If I teach this course again I will know more; students will learn less; though they will feel more secure about it all. [PC]

tion; by the second reports all these had improved dramatically. It was clear that (with a partial exception of the one foreign student) they all had a basic knowledge of how English sentences should be written, even if the writers did not at first always take the time to work them out carefully. In fact I found that the writing was often crisp, expressive and accurate. The most serious discussions we had about language concerned the use of the personal pronoun and the advantages and disadvantages of passive versus active constuctions.[9,10]

TIME

Given the small number of students in the sections, one meeting every two weeks (after the first weeks when every student had written a report) would have been sufficient. Even with larger sections, fewer meetings would, I believe, cover most of the students' papers (it takes about 15–20 minutes to discuss a report). Reading a number of lab reports, one after another, can become somewhat monotonous. This can be varied, but while other projects, such as reading and abstracting other reports and doing various writing exercises, were useful, they were not, perhaps, strictly necessary.

Since I ended up teaching only 14 students, the use of my time was somewhat inefficient; and even with larger sections I do not think it would be possible to do this on the wider scale that I believe the Department would prefer.

RECOMMENDATION

I suggest that these sections should be continued, meeting one hour every other week, and that they should be taught by the regular staff of the course. Students had many questions about the factual and experimental material in their reports and would have liked very much to have talked with an instructor about them. Further, the instructors' grading time might best be spent in these sections, where their comments could help a number of students at once. Running a writing class is not as difficult or as abstruse as it may seem: it draws on the same kind of teaching skills as running any discussion section; and it was clear to me from students' comments on the

---

8. Students also will prepare their reports carefully if they know their laboratory instructor thinks that writing is important and will spend time evaluating the expression and organization of the text as well as the technical content. [RR]

9. The personal pronoun, especially "I" (and hence a freer use of active verbs) is now being used more and more widely in the professional journals. However, usage does vary and personal pronouns are usually kept out of the abstract. Avoiding them takes some skill. [PC]

10. I am still crusading to outlaw the use of the indefinite "it" as a substitute for "I." [RR]

help they had received in the laboratory that the 2.671 instructors do possess these fundamental skills. No one outside of the Department of Mechanical Engineering can possess as intimate a knowledge of exactly what is required in a lab report as a Mechanical Engineer; what expertise the writing instructors possess is in knowing something about how to help MIT students to express themselves. This knowledge could best be transmitted by a seminar led by a member of the writing program where the staff of 2.671 discussed some of their own reports and learned from their own experience what kind of discussion and comments were most helpful to them. Alternatively, we could meet with the staff members and talk about writing, and how they can use their own teaching abilities to encourage it. Atmosphere is decisive in a writing class; it is far more important than a careful knowledge of English grammar.[11] A teacher with a large red pencil and strong opinions about the use of the colon may impress students but so intimidate them that they never want to write again; while a group with no special ax to grind but a concern for accuracy and comprehension can really help people to take the time to say what they mean and mean what they say.

---

11. Amen. [RR]

Twenty Questions

KEN SKIER

The teacher who says "Write!" before discussing the why, what and how—with each student, individually if necessary—is asking and imposing far more than he or she realistically should. The teacher wants the student to write. That's reasonable. But first the student needs to know what that means.

"WHY SHOULD I WRITE?"

This question comes up—rather often at MIT—and I answer it differently each time it is asked.

"Because it's required."—I say that to the student who responds to nothing else, who doesn't want to be here and can't convince himself it's real—and I gag each time I do it. If I have to say it to three students in the same class something's wrong.

"Because it's good for you."—They've heard that before and, like medicine, it can be ignored.

"You write and you get better at it; the class and I can help you."—I believe that to be true, but it sounds like a hype, and self-improvement doesn't sell very big.

"Try it—you'll like it."—This should always work once, but after that I risk credibility.

There are other ways, but they work best one to one.
"Why should I write?"
"Because you've got something to say."
"Me?"
"You."
"Me?"
"Everyone does. You live and you learn. You've got a lot to say."
"How do you know?"
That can be the killer. How do I know? I don't. Not if I give a writing assignment before I've talked it over with the students. Not if I fail to carry on an "Opening dialogue"[1] to let them know what I expect, what I will and will not do. They may find it hard to believe that I want something written by *them*, by those particular individuals, with their unique outlooks and experiences and expectations for the future. I want something from each of them that no one else can write: *not* "a piece of Freshman writing", but a personal statement from each student.

---

1. See the chapter of the same name. [KS]

That can be tough. They've never had a writing assignment before where they couldn't substitute papers, never been expected to write something that actually went with their names. What have they got to say? How do I know there's anything there?

The only way to know is to show them.

It's an odd occupation, but I see the teacher's role here as showing the students themselves. Not *in toto*, full relief, head-to-toe, every angle accounted for—just a glimpse; a shadow of a reflection of something that is theirs. If I can do that, my job is almost done: the rest is really follow-up.

I can't ask them to write in a vacuum. They're people, and there's more to them than I see in my class. If I'm going to ask them to open up and share something—with a piece of paper, a collection of contemporaries, and a teacher—then I've got to do the same thing, myself. I try to let them see me as a person, *not* "an instructor." I want them to write: I write, too. I want access to their words, their thoughts; they deserve the same from me. I want something to happen in the class, and I want it to be real, on a very human level: they have a right to expect the same from me. If I play a role —and only a role—they're going to play roles, too. I can't claim "professorial privilege" and expect anything but disparities.

"Write what you care about. Care about what you write."

I make two rules for the class when I give an assignment—*no*, not so much rules as requests, since they're obviously unenforceable. "Don't hand in a piece of writing if it doesn't mean something to you. You expect me to read it, you expect the class to read it, you have the common courtesy to care a little about it before you ask us that." I don't expect it to be great writing; I don't even expect it to be particularly good writing, but I want it to be honest writing.

Write what you care about.

When they ask me why they should write, I tell them, "because writing means something."

"What does it mean?"

"Whatever you intend it to mean—although it might come across as something else entirely."

"That's an answer?"

"It means what you want it to mean—to you. To someone else it might be something else."

"Then it doesn't mean anything."

"Maybe not—to some of your readers. I can't guarantee I'll understand what you write—though I can tell you I'll try. I'm pretty sure some of the people in the class will get what you put into it, but even that's not certain. We'll try to understand, to interpret, to feel. No matter what happens, though, you'll learn something."

"From a meaningless piece of prose?"

"If you write about something you care about, it can't be empty. And if you care about what you're writing, it won't be meaningless."

"Why?"

"Because it'll mean something to you."

That's when I've got them. They can't argue with that.

But it doesn't mean they'll write. A guy won't write about his social life if he thinks he risks his ego; a girl won't write about herself if she fears for her reputation. For that matter, a girl won't write about her social life if she thinks she risks her ego; and a guy won't write about himself if he fears for his reputation. They know they have something to say, and they know there are things they care about, but they won't bring them out in the open in a class or a writing assignment. School is for students, they figure; not people. They leave part of themselves outside when they step into that scheduled room.

My job is to bring them in. All of them. All the way. Or, at least, as much of them, as much of the way, as possible. I try to make it safe enough for them to come in. It's a matter of trust. But I want them whole: the fears, the hopes, the frustrations and expectations; the little things they look forward to and the words and phrases they use to say what they mean. They've got feelings, and they can express them, but they start out afraid to do so in front of this audience.

That's where writing comes in. "Fiction is a way of undressing in public—without exposing yourself."[2] I'm asking them to reveal themselves, to write about things that are important to them. I don't want interchangeable math solutions, physics answers, or assigned essays on literature: I want something they can say is true—as personal as a palmprint or a name. I want them to look inside. That can be frightening. They might be afraid of what they'll find. They might be afraid nothing's there. That's one of the reasons why I bring wine to the class.[3] It breaks the ice. It breaks the image. It helps us all to open up.

If I'm going to ask them to risk parts of themselves by writing, I've got to convince them they're not going to lose. They've got to trust me. They've got to trust each other. They've got to know their feelings won't be greeted with laughter; they've got to know they'll be listened to, read.

I must take the time to let them get comfortable with each other, with their own and with each other's words. Some people will be able to talk or write more easily than others. It will be jerky, stop-and-go, very uncertain for a while. Then, suddenly, with an almost audible click, something will come up that connects. "Someone is talking about himself — about something that matters." It's recognizable, the act of revelation; the undercurrent of understanding that it's finally come. "That person cares about what he's saying. It means something to him. And I can feel it. I understand it. I've felt the same way." It connects. It can happen when someone is reading aloud, during a discussion of someone's writing, or in a rap session on random events. Something is shared with the others. "It's different in this class. That wouldn't happen anywhere else."

Then I've answered their question.

---

2. Joe Brown, 1971. [KS]

3. If it meets in the evening, for 2 or 3 hours. Wine just won't work in a one hour class, which meets two or three mornings a week. [KS]

Why should I write?
Write because it connects.

WHAT SHALL I WRITE?

But they won't necessarily know what to write yet; a lot of them will be lost.

"I'm not the storytelling type."

"You don't have to tell stories."

"But what shall I write?"

"What do you care about?"

"Nothing much. I'm too busy with all the work I have to do."

"Do you care about that?"

"No. Most of it is required."

"Do you care about this?"

"The assignment?"

"Your piece of writing."

"I'm not sure. It depends on what it involves—and what else I have to do."

"That makes sense. Well, do you mostly want to get it out of the way, or is there something you really want to say?"

"I don't see what you mean. . .?"

"That's all right. What are the other courses you're taking?"

Anyone who can't talk has no business being a teacher. By talk I mean carry on a conversation, a give and take constructive dialogue that builds a connection and brings the conversers closer together.

"Where are you from?"

There are dozens of stories in their lives, and they know them, they remember them, they'll tell you if you let them.

"Were you in the hospital long, then?"

They've got families, and roommates, and professors who give them problems. There's all kinds of things they care about, and can talk about, and write about.

"That's a great story! Why didn't you tell that in class, to the others?"

They don't tell their stories because they're afraid, or because they're shy. There's nothing special about *them*—why should they take up a listener's time? They're not interesting people. They'd rather listen to the others. They've got an elaborate defense mechanism, a labyrinth of excuses. They don't know any more why they don't talk. Some people are just like that, they say.

But they can write. They can write and not be interrupted; they can write and not be ignored. They know they'll be read; they know they'll get a response; they see they've got something to say and the only step remaining is to say it—on paper.

I can convince them very easily: I convince them by being interested. I may be their first supportive audience. I try to reinforce their attempts to talk, to tell stories. My attention to what they have to say exceeds anything else I have to offer. And after a while, the other students will make this service of mine superfluous. That's when I know I've succeeded.

But what about the ones who don't talk? What can the teacher do then? I keep trying. *Nobody* has nothing to say.

"What do you care about?"

"I don't see what you mean. . . ."

"What are you interested in?"

"Huh? Oh . . . math, I guess, and physics, and I used to like history."

"Would you care to write about any of those things?"

"Are you kidding? I have enough work to do in those areas already."

"Well, what are you interested in?"

"I already told you—"

"No, I mean what are you *really* interested in? Where does your mind wander to when you don't pay attention in class?"

"But I *do* pay attention. It may sound strange, but I'm a serious student."

"I know. I've seen you in class. But nobody follows a discussion sixty minutes out of every hour. And in a lecture, thirty minutes out of an hour is attentive. There must be times when you look at a problem set or reading assignment without seeing it. Where do you go when you're not there?"

"Oh. . . I see. Nowhere."

"Do you have a car?"

"I used to. My father made me sell it before I came to college. He says I can get one next year . . . if my grades are good enough."

"Do you ever think of going places?"

"Sure. Especially during math lectures!"

"Anywhere specific?"

"Sometimes."

"Why not write about that?"

"Write about daydreaming?"

"If you want. Or write about where you'd like to be when you're some place you'd rather leave. Just try describing the place, as an experiment."

"I'm not sure."

"OK. You can think about it. Do you ever write to anyone?"

"My parents. But that's not interesting. And my girlfriend. But I can't bring that to class."

"I understand. You miss her a lot?"

"I miss her too much. She's four hundred miles away and I won't get to see her until Thanksgiving."

"I know the feeling."

"And I write her a lot, but like I said I can't bring it to class."

"I know what you mean. But—do you think you can fictionalize her?"

"What do you mean?"

"Write a character description. Call it a piece of fiction, but base it as much as you want on your girlfriend."

"I don't know if I could do that. It wouldn't be interesting."

"Is it interesting to you?"
"Sure."
"Then try it."
"OK. I'll think about it."

The key is to help them find something they're willing—no; *want*—to write about. Little things. Big things. Something that happened on the subway. A snatch of conversation they overheard in a hall. The way they reacted when a cousin's fiancé cracked up on the Turnpike. Their favorite place for fishing. The time they were forcibly showered in the fraternity. Being lost. Being found. *Anything* that made an impression on them, anything they care about. People tell stories to people all the time. "You know what happened to me yesterday afternoon?" I just want them to write it.[4]

"HOW DO I WRITE?"

So we've come this far. They're willing to write something, and they've got something to write about. A person, a place, a relationship. We can find a hundred and eleven things if we spend half an hour; they'll care. It's *them* we're talking about now; *their* writing. They just want to know how.

"One step at a time," I usually say. "Sit down with a paper. Have a pencil, a pen or a typewriter. Make the words fall out on the page, make them follow each other on down until they fill up that page, and then another. Keep going until you've said what you started out to say—or maybe something else entirely—but see to it that it's *said*. We're talking about words, just words. Nothing to be scared of right there."

"But I sit down and nothing happens. What can I do then?"

Too many things to count.

"Why can't you write?"

"I can't think of anything."

"No ideas?"

If the student says s/he's got nothing to write about, we talk. Sooner or later s/he'll have told me—or given some darn good hints about—what s/he wants to write about. With enough time and care on my part, this problem shouldn't remain.

"I know what I want to say, but I don't know how to say it."

Typical problem. Everybody has it. No writer escapes it, and *I* certainly don't have "the answer." But we talk it out. I let the student tell me what s/he wants to say and sooner or later s/he says it, one way or another. Then, I say, "Write it! The way you said it. Or as close to that as possible. Just so the story gets *told,* on paper. It can be revised, told from

---

4. This seems crucial (so this note is by way of adding an exclamation point). Students—in their role of students—seem to feel they *ought* to be interested in Big Questions, the result being often Big Boredom for all. [ND]

different perspectives, completely reworked later. But first get it *down*. That's simple enough. It doesn't have to be perfect. It doesn't have to be complete.

"At the very worst it won't work. Write it again a little differently. At the worst you've done some bad writing. Nothing wrong with that—every good writer has written badly. (Just ask one!) This is only the beginning. You're learning. Clean it up a little if you can and bring it in. This isn't your thesis—it's a little piece of writing and maybe it's your first. If anything about it works, you're ahead of the game.

"Read it to the group. Listen to their reactions. Watch their faces. See what they liked, what they missed. See how it affected them, what they think it was about, what you were trying to say. *That's* how you learn about writing, by learning about *your* writing. Don't explain your work. Don't defend it. Just watch. Listen. Pick up on what they picked up on. You'll see different things, from different angles. You may learn to like some parts of your piece that you didn't like before . . . or you may decide that the whole thing fizzled. You can't help but get new ideas.

"At this point there are two things you can do. You can take what you've learned and re-do what you've done, trying to tell the same story but with a little more storytelling ability. This is called revising. If it's something you care about, you'll want to say it, and once won't be enough—especially if that once didn't satisfy you. You can rewrite what you've written, or write it in a different way, a way that maybe you couldn't have written the first time, because you didn't know what you know now. One step at a time. It gets you there.

"Or you can write something else. Keep in mind that your first piece of writing had some better parts and some weaker parts, and pick out one of the parts that didn't work quite so well. Your dialogue might've been strained, or your narrative confusing. Choose one, just *one* problem. Don't try a shotgun cure. One step at a time.

"Now write something else. Keep in mind what you liked about your first piece, and what you didn't. Work at getting this piece to have one less problem. Bring it in. Read it. Watch their faces as you read it. Catch the reaction. Listen to their words."

Writing Exercises for Non-Writing Classes

NANCY DWORSKY

Many classes in which students are expected to learn to write, or in which they might well learn to write, center on other subject matter: literature, history, sociology, psychology, anthropology, *et al.* But term papers in these courses don't teach writing. Numerous shorter papers may do better, but not very much. The basic problem seems to be one of getting students to integrate writing into their everyday intellectual activity; because only when it is a common tool for thinking and for understanding experience does writing improve and remain improved. I have found a number of exercises useful in non-writing classes that I think are generally adoptable.

First, there is free writing. Its virtues as a separate activity have been discussed elsewhere. Its value in other classes appears in two situations: (1) when a class seems totally dull, listless and unresponsive, and (2) when a class seems lively, alert and engaged in discussion. In the first case the instructor saves him or herself a lot of anger or self-doubt by giving up on trying to elicit interest from a roomful of turnips by interrupting the class and demanding ten minutes of free writing. At the very least it brings the students' minds back into the classroom. If, when they are done writing, they are willing to read what came out (and after the first one, almost all become eager. Sometimes the instructor has to volunteer to be first[1]), they establish some lively communication among themselves that can sometimes be used when returning to the material at hand. The teacher learns what the class was really thinking about and can judge whether it is at all possible that day to draw attention to the grain production in Soviet Central Asia in 1932. And everyone has spent some time writing that was otherwise being frittered away in classroom boredom. Free writing is not boring.

---

1. Unfortunately not all classes (mine, for instance) are so obliging as to jump eagerly to read their free writings after the first exposure, even if the instructor jumps first. I think a caveat may be in order for people trying out this idea and others mentioned in this book: If something doesn't work, go ahead, feel a little disappointed, a bit frustrated, but also try to avoid anger, anxiety, and depression; it probably wasn't anyone's fault. As all schools, all instructors, all classes, all students are different, so is the success of any particular technique at any given time. These ideas have worked for us, sometimes very well, so they stand a good chance of helping you. But nothing's a certainty. [SWR]

2. Here is the full assignment: Think about one of the following "sins": insatiable sexual passion (that's what "excessive love" is); theft; suicide; sodomy; fraud; wrath; sullenness. (If none of these seems worthy of your attention, pick another that does.)

Imagine yourself doing it. Close your eyes and conjure the scene as clearly as possible, with all the details—smells, colors, weather, etc. Then write the following exercise:

How has your mood been affected by imagining it?

The advantage of free writing *after* a lively discussion is a bit more complex and varied. It has been my experience that a lively discussion engages no more than about five people. In a class of twenty, this is a large proportion of the class. (I think this is why humanities teachers always want small classes. If five people engage in a lively discussion in a classroom with forty-five people in it, it doesn't feel anywhere near as lively.) If you stop the discussion ten minutes before the end of the class, you engage different attention from three groups of people. Those who have been doing the talking have a chance to sum up their thoughts on the subject and their responses to others. Anything they've learned in the course of the class will become solid thereby. Those who were listening with interest, but could not take an active part, have a chance to express their opinions and comment on others. This can change disgruntlement into satisfaction. And if the teacher is reading the free writing (and he or she should be) it can bring attention to sharp and interested students who, for one reason or another, are not speaking up in class. The third group are those who have not been paying attention, have been bored and unhappy, wish everyone would shut up, etc. This group is usually larger than the teacher, happy with an alert class, has had any inkling of. It's a good, if humbling, thing to discover that in the best of classes a large number of the students aren't there.

Another kind of exercise adaptable to many courses is the Smarterbook. You can make up an exercise directed toward specific material. This can be helpful in clarifying a student's attitude toward a subject before he or she considers someone else's attitude toward the same subject. The example I'll give feels a little like cheating, because the subject matter was so appropriate for the method that the assignment could scarcely fail. But I'll give it anyway because it worked so well. When teaching the *Inferno* I make up a Smarterbook exercise directed toward a sin of the student's choosing.[2] He is supposed first to do the Smarterbook (ending, whatever the questions, with ten minutes' free writing), then to find the same sin in Dante and write an essay comparing his own attitude with Dante's. One reason

---

What does it taste like?

If it were an animal, what animal would it be? What piece of music?

Say something about this act from the point of view of someone who loathes it.

Say something about this act from the point of view of someone who enjoys it immensely.

Describe someone you love doing it.

Take a blank piece of paper and write for ten minutes without stopping—anything that comes into your mind. If there's nothing in your mind, write "blank blank blank" until something else comes to mind. Don't worry about sentences, spelling, punctuation—just keep writing, and don't look back.

Now read in the *Inferno* the Canto appropriate to your sin. Read it carefully and thoughtfully. Then write an essay comparing your attitude toward this action, as you have discovered it in the exercise, with Dante's attitude as it is exposed in the Canto (consider his landscape, similes, etc., as well as description). Speculate, if it seems interesting, on what might account for similarities or differences that you find. [ND]

that this particular assignment works so beautifully is that often students find, by doing the metaphoric questions, that they come up with imagery similar to Dante's, and this tends to get them thinking seriously and positively, instead of adopting a stock tone of twentieth century superiority to thirteenth century narrow-mindedness. The first time I gave this assignment, I left it optional whether the students handed in the exercise along with the essay. This caused many of them to skip the exercise as obviously unimportant. The result was just what I would have liked to predict: it was perfectly clear who had done the exercise and who had not because the quality of the essays was much higher among those who had done the Smarterbook. What that exercise did was to engage their interest in the topic, focus their attention on their own thoughts and feelings, and hence give them a firm ground from which to look at the other material.

I use Smarterbook exercises whenever a topic is apt to excite prejudices that the student isn't aware of. This includes many more topics than one might expect. For example, I've found when teaching the *Iliad* that many students have strong anti-Achilles prejudices that go back to fifth grade where they learned he was childish and irresponsible. Until and unless they confront this judgment for what it is, they are unable to read Homer above a fifth-grade level. A Smarterbook exercise on Achilles brings their attitudes into focus so that they can see them on the one hand and the actual text on the other hand. Not only do these exercises clarify thinking; they provide more experience in using writing as a tool of thinking.

The last method I have discovered for getting a class to write involved the whole structure of the class hour. It reflects my belief that discussions are only useful to those who are actively taking part in them, and hence a discussion class of fifteen to fifty people, since only some of them are speaking, is largely a waste of people's time. What I have found effective is this: I assign for a specific day a piece of writing on a particular topic. The writing is to be a student's response, impressions, feelings, or an anecdote from personal experience, or a fantasy—anything, so long as it is obviously personal and informal. (How, you may ask, do you make such an assignment when the topic is the Dred Scott Decision? In that case, you could have a monologue from the defendant's point of view. Or over-population? Have them write up an experience with birth, or death. Anything goes as long as it provides a handle for the students to grasp a situation personally, not abstractly and ideologically.)

Each of these assignments is due in class on a specific day. A certain number of them must be done in the course of the term. None are accepted late. None are refused for any reason if they are ready on time.

When class meets, the students break up into groups of about five, read their papers to each other and talk about them. The teacher stays out of it. (At least I've always had to stay out of it. If I join a group, I kill it. They all sit and wait for me to say something definitive about each piece of writing.) At the end of the hour each group must hand in a written statement on what they've been talking about, or have found themselves interested in—again, a wide open assignment that allows just about anything, as long as it's written. Before the class is over, you read off the reports of the groups to the whole class, interpolating comments if you feel so inclined (provided they aren't the kind of comments that make students inhibited and afraid to be honest in the future). This isn't to hold the groups up to one another, but because they really are interested in what's been happening in other groups.

When students are first told to do this kind of writing they tend to react as though it's an invitation to get away with something. They also complain that it's a waste of time because everyone will just horse around and do nothing serious. But the same thing happens here as in a writing workshop, though the topics of discussion are different. Soon the students become embarrassed in front of their peers for writing vacuous nonsense— their fellow students make a demand for quality more effectively than teachers can. And they find that they often have interesting discussions, hear points of view that they never would have thought of themselves, find they share things that they thought were uniquely private. They learn a lot, and are willing to tell you so, when it's all over. And they've been writing. All the time.

If you have a coherent set of assignments worked out, you can keep them in separate folders for each student and return them at the end of the term. This way each student has them all together and can look over them as a whole. You don't need to pass judgment on his performance; he'll be quite capable of doing that himself.

When you're running a class this way there is one great drawback: you, the teacher, rarely get an opportunity to say anything. For many of us, this is obviously unacceptable. One thing you can do is give lectures. I have found students more willing to listen to me when, at other times, they have opportunities to talk with each other.

One other question inevitably comes up sooner or later: how, given that I teach the way I do and assign the way I do, do I grade my classes? Well, I like to grade on solid grounds and I like to use the power I have to my advantage. So I generally grade on attendance.

Writing Exercises, Writer's Block

DAVID WRAY

When I can't write, I sound something like this:

"I can't write. Oh, I want to write so bad, but I can't think of anything to put down on paper."

My friends who are sympathetic and helpful might hear me complain this way and say, "Gee Dave, I hear you had a great time up in Maine last month. Why don't you write about that?"

"I don't want to write about Maine. I was thinking that maybe I want to write about a desert."

"Great! What desert do you want to write about? Gobi? Sahara?"

"Well, I've got this place in my head, and it's not anyplace I know, but that's not what's getting me down. I just can't think of any stories there."

"Write a mystery story about a boy, a girl, a donkey, and a silver chalice."

"No, no, no, no. It's got to have only one character, and it has to be some kind of personal exploration, maybe a survival thing."

"So write it."

"I can't. I can't think of anything to write."

I don't think that I'm the only person who gets writing blocks in this way and the great thing about such blocks is that they can be gotten over.

When I feel blocked, I know only the fact that I don't want to write. Even if in some sense I do want to write, or if I feel that I ought to write, what really seems to be happening is that there's something about how I'm feeling that I'm doing my best to ignore. I find the helpful questions that my friends ask irritating because they prove to me that I do know what I want to write. More accurately, I know that I don't want to write and I'm willing to be very creative to avoid it.

This is the point where writing comes very close to therapy, because often a person who has trouble writing is having it because of some psychic self-abuse.[1] Writing appears threatening to such a person because it's a way of confronting himself directly, but the problem is that the person doesn't want to confront the problem.

When a student is in a funk, when that student is feeling slothful, vague, and angry, that's when a teacher can fulfill all his midwife-type teaching fantasies by asking more and more questions until the student has virtually written a short story, complete with plot, characters, and dialogue. Factors that tend to cut such dialectic short, however, are how much irritation a student is willing to put up with, and how irritating a teacher is willing to be. While it's not a capital offense anymore to force people to think, aspiring Socratics should note the rate of axe-murders in their area before embarking on their careers whole-heartedly.

---

1. At MIT, students are big on this. [DW]

Helping friends to write is hard for at least two reasons: There's the ethical problem (should one intrude oneself in ways likely to be very personal?), and then there's the possibility that the intruder might be one of the central problems of the intrudee. In the case of the teacher-pupil relationship both questions must be considered, and it's my belief that good teachers agonize over them, never reaching final answers.

But for some teachers, there's an important institutional re-definition of this relationship that tries to hide these questions. It becomes the object of teaching to *make* students learn; it can be said that teachers have society's mandate for doing so, and thanks to the insanity of our times, they are supposed to do this in as impersonal (objective [objectionable]) a way as possible. They cannot help becoming one of their students' main problems because a mandate is nothing else than a license to ignore things that are important.

Be that as it may, writing exercises can be extremely valuable for teaching people how to write, or they can be goddamn wastes of time.

Many writing exercises are wastes of time for both teachers and students. They're usually things like: "Write a minimum of 2000 words from the third-person, semi-omniscient point of view," or "Write 600-800 words of exposition on steel production in post-war Germany." Excuse me for being judgmental, but exercises like these are terrible! Students hate them! If they happen to learn anything while doing them, they forget it as soon as possible because they can't see how such knowledge affects them other than by making their teachers happy.

There is no good way to justify using these exercises in teaching situations. They are solely devices for judgment. Using them, teachers can see who knows how to write already and who doesn't, and the only constructive advice usually offered to students who are "not verbal" is, "You can do better than this. Write better, students." Deep in the hearts of these teachers is the belief that writers are born, not made, but this is contrary to the experience of every writer who has worked hard developing his craft.

Now it becomes necessary to ask what kinds of writing exercises can help to teach writing. What is needed are kinds of exercises that work to prove to the down-trodden student that his creativity works, the kind of exercises that (when coupled with the teacher's dictum to do them) force the student to fix concrete ideas in his mind and to play with them. They must be his ideas, and he must come to know them inside and out, backwards and forwards, even to the extent of knowing what they will never be. They have to be the kinds of exercises that will build islands in the mind on which to stand and view imaginary objects as real, if only for the short time it takes to describe those real impressions with pen and paper. This is exactly what Smarterbook exercises do.

Smarterbook exercises consist of many unlikely questions that all require explicit answers, and they terminate in ten minutes of free writing. If a student likes Smarterbook exercises, he can use the questions to stretch out his creative muscles. The process of answering the questions can focus his energies until he's finally allowed to take-off in the free writing on some story line or experiment he has found himself exploring. If a student doesn't like the exercises, if he finds the questions tedious and aggravating, the exercise still works. The student actively resents the authority that can make him do such trash. When he finally reaches the free writing, he can utilize his anger at having been forced to acknowledge his imagination by writing some brilliant polemic against the stupidity he's had to confront. He will explore to great depth the idiocy of the teacher who gave him this writing exercise, and he'd almost rather write a story than be stuck with doing another of these exercises. The beauty of this experience is that the student still has the place in his mind built during the exercise, and he has broken through his writing block for a while by expressing some of that anger that he's been keeping bottled up.

Anyone can write a Smarterbook exercise, but there's an art to designing them so that they work best in the context of specific writing classes. The exercises that appear in this book have been found to work well in writing courses at MIT, and it's my belief that they show a good many of the styles of questions that can work anywhere.

Smarterbook exercises begin by making the student choose something concrete: a person, a place, a thing, a number—almost any class of nouns will do. The important things to note is that choosing an entity from a general class of objects is basically a creative act. Questions that follow should involve synaesthesia, shifting perspectives, the choosing of more entities.

Types of questions are: metaphors (Your object is an animal. What kind of animal is it?), allegories (Say a prayer about your object), shifts of perspective (Your object has been made very tiny, and it lives in your armpit. Tell how it views the world), fate and freewill points of view of the entity, relations (Pick another object. Imagine your two objects making love. What kind of children will they have?), and so on to all kinds of questions that have yet to be discovered. One way of making up questions is to flip through a thesaurus and try them out in your mind as they occur to you. For example, I just noticed the word "fear" in a book. The question that first occurs to me is, "Imagine that your object is afraid of something. What is it afraid of, and how does it show its fear?" This might be a useless question for some purposes, but a fearful person might find it liberating to think of things, creatures, or other people as being afraid, too. Good exercises come from a lot of thought, a lot of experience, and specific tailoring to the needs of a class.

Smarterbook-type exercises have applications beyond being warm-up exercises in creative writing courses. There was once a course at MIT whose whole substance consisted of doing these exercises; I'm told that the quality of writing from the students in the course improved noticeably.

Poetry workshops sometimes use a Smarterbook-like exercise. Students may be asked to pick an object living or dead, and to identify with it. Their task is to write a first-person poem about that thing. This is always a good way for people to get to know one another because they often say more about themselves than their object. I've had good results by doing something similar to this, asking people to do crayon pictures and then to identify with something they've drawn. The poetry that I've gotten from this has been interesting and sometimes beautiful.

Joe Brown often uses biography exercises to begin courses, and sometimes to keep a dynamic air of expectancy in them. He may ask students to pair off on the first day of class and talk to one another, and then to write short biographies as introductions to the rest of the class of the persons they've met. Another exercise he uses which intrigues me is to ask students early in the term to write character sketches, stories, or whatever of one other person in the room. The person can be chosen by any means, but it's important that only the author know which person he is to write about. For the rest of the term people will be looking to decide whether pieces of writing are biographies or not, and if it's decided that a particular piece is a biography, then to figure out whose biography it is. This helps make members of a class interested in one another, as characters and as people, and it adds an element of what might be called reality appreciation that students direct towards one another's writing.

Exercises similar to these can be used in other kinds of courses (see Nancy Dworsky's "Writing Exercises for Non-writing Courses") often with great success. When the fare of a course is ideas, exercises like these can be much better in revealing the ideas to the students than traditional papers "about" them. In making the exercises, teachers should emphasize direct confrontation of the ideas by the students. If ideas of philosophy are to be communicated, students should experience the problems actively from the same points of view as the philosophers who discovered them.[2] If appreciation of literature is to be promoted, students should gain that appreciation by attempting to deal with the same issues that exist in that literature. Exercises can be made that would make philosophical distinctions clear. They can be made to enable students to experience the sharpness of perceptions in the classics. Bonds of humanity can be felt by students who have never consciously missed them. It's all part of a new type of education that demands the primacy of experience.

Meanwhile, the task in creative writing courses is to change people from being writing-blocked to being self-unblocking and motivated, to move them from complaining about not being able to write, to:

"I'm having trouble writing."

"What's the problem?"

"Well, I wrote fifteen pages in the past couple of days, but I just don't know where the story's going."

"Are you going to stop writing it?"

"Hell no. I'm caught up in it too much. I can't stop, but it's sheer agony to go through with it. I have no idea when it's going to be finished."

---

2. An example is an exercise often used to illustrate Berkeley's ideas on the relation between perception and thought: Imagine you have a glass of milk in your hand, and that you're standing before a refrigerator. Open the door. Place the glass inside, and close the door. Now, how do you know the glass is still inside the refrigerator? [DW]

The Judge in the Classroom

NANCY DWORSKY

The most pernicious and unjustified attitude I have run into in ten years of teaching is the belief that I, the teacher, know how *good* a student is. When I teach a subject, I feel I know that subject and know it well. And I'm willing to claim authority on that basis. As a teacher of writing, I believe I am particularly knowledgeable in pointing to language that works and does not work for me, and articulating how it works and to what end. If students acknowledged just that authority in me, I would have no trouble teaching and they would have no trouble listening to criticism.

But teachers aren't seen that way. They're seen as judges, and their opinion has the power to make students think well or ill of themselves. They are authorities on what is *good*, and students want to be judged *good* or taught how to be *good*. So when a teacher responds directly and precisely to a piece of writing the student is apt to hear himself either praised or condemned rather than instructed.

So we try to be nonjudgmental and we talk about things like non-evaluative feedback and how to be supportive rather than critical. But to be really nonjudgmental, both the student and the teacher must give up the premise that the teacher's job is judging and the student's role is being judged. This is monumentally hard to do. But until it happens, there's no constructive criticism possible—no, not even if it's called something else.

At a risk of emphasizing the self-evident, I want to stress how insidious and omnipresent the judge in the classroom is. Also, to admit that it isn't there by accident or mistake. There really is, through the whole educational system, a function of judging who shall do what in later life. The teachers make these judgments. I object to this role for teachers, because I think it works against their primary function of educating; but just because I object, it doesn't go away—not even from my own classroom. The simple fact is that I am in a position of power as a teacher. To refuse to exercise this power is difficult. It often even necessitates withdrawal of support and encouragement from students who are seeking it.

This is something that tends to be overlooked because we generally like our students and we do sincerely want to encourage them. But as long as they trust our authority, our encouragement supports dependency, and dependency is detrimental to education. An example that made this very clear to me: I was teaching a class in which I told students to keep journals on their reading that I would check but not read through (the check being there to show that I did indeed consider them important). Some wanted me to read them. They said they just wanted my response to their thoughts. I refused. Even if it was true, they didn't want to hear that I found their reading puerile, superficial and dull. They wanted to hear that it was interesting, sensitive and profound. I didn't want to be cornered into giving a predetermined response that would finally support an authority that I don't have. I prefer to let the students feel angry and abused. When they have learned not to trust me, I will be open and honest with them.

But even when this great day comes, when we have classes full of students whom we respect and take seriously, and who respect us without either trusting or fearing us overmuch, we still have problems of *constructive* criticism. "Be non-judgmental" does not say anything about what we should positively be doing. What kind of response is useful? Peter Elbow has invoked the image of the owl swallowing a mouse whole and spitting out the bones to suggest that all students should learn to take in all responses and only retain those they can use. That seems to me a fine idea for what students should do, if they can learn how. I clearly can't teach them how to do that, since what's useful is going to be a very personal thing. My question is, precisely how can teachers respond more usefully?

There seem to be two general rules that can be followed. One is to take into consideration what a student is trying to do and to distinguish it from what you wish a student was trying to do. The other is to be honest. An example: a student is trying to write exciting science fiction. I am not excited by science fiction. I am tempted to tell him or her that the story is boring, but if I do that the chances are I will be judging it by the wrong criteria. I will be rejecting it individually because of my feelings about the whole genre. The truth is that I'm the wrong audience to read the piece. There's probably little I can say that's helpful. The student needs someone else for useful criticism.

Of course it implies evaluation when I tell a student that I can't work with a genre and don't particularly want to. It also implies an evaluation when I find a student's work interesting and strong. I don't know of any serious and honest response to writing that doesn't imply evaluation. As long as the student isn't trusting me as the authority over what he or she should be writing, it doesn't matter.

Why shouldn't the student trust me in this matter? Why shouldn't I want my students to write fine literature instead of pulp? It seems to me improper and arrogant to have such standards. After all, there wouldn't be any fine literature if there weren't also pulp, so why should I discourage the pulp writers? It is enough that I be what help I can for writers to learn to do well what they want to do. Teaching writing is no more, nor less, than that.

Bad Students—Three Exemplary Anecdotes

NANCY DWORSKY

I

Good students are all alike; bad students are bad in their own ways. Bad students produce many different responses in teachers from anger to despair, sometimes even causing self-doubt, until the teacher remembers that the fault is with the student. But a good student—in any field with any pedagogical criteria—is one who makes the teacher believe he or she is a good teacher. This I learned, not surprisingly, from a bad student. A very bad student indeed.

He was a dolt in a freshman class on the Western Tradition. He seemed literate enough and competent enough (had he not been, I would have judged him worthy of help or at least sympathy rather than condemnation; after all, I wouldn't want to be unkind). But he didn't want to think and he didn't want to learn. Well, that's all right too. The student who rebels against being stuck in a class of no interest to him also has my sympathy. No, what was really offensive in this student was that he had a great deal of energy and enthusiasm that he was willing to expend on trying to figure out what I wanted so that he could answer questions correctly in class and discuss problems correctly in essays. I loathed him.

Furthermore, he loathed me.

Finally, it all came out in a conference over a paper that I had graded C (we were still grading in those days) and he was angry about it. He had done his best to do it right; he had written a beautifully organized essay, typed, in clear and proper diction; he was not accustomed to getting C's. I told him that in reading an essay I looked first for what it said, then for how it had said it, and finally for whether it had been worth saying. His essay was vacuous, so I was unable to go even to my second criterion.

After conferring for about a half hour, he became angry enough to overcome his years of training in mannerly behavior before authority. And he told me, clearly and succinctly, that he had spent eighteen years learning to play the system, that I was part of the system, and it was my duty to reward him for playing properly. (An outrageously *bad* student!)

Of course I replied: Tough luck, ducky; it's an absurd universe, I'm an absurd god, and I've changed the system on you. The only behavior I'll reward is your thinking for yourself.

We did not part friends.

I've thought of this student a lot. At first, I was sure that in some fundamental way I was right and he was wrong. And I guess I still believe that, though I wouldn't be so hard on him today. Also, today I wouldn't be grading him—and that would make it easier for us to talk with each other instead of against each other.

But there is also a place where he was right. His expectations of the classroom had been painfully learned through time. He was not responsible for the school system that had nurtured him, had taught him about authority and obedience—and about trying to preserve your own soul without being squashed by the institutions of the world. I really was another authority for him to cope with; that's the role I was playing. My judgment of him said that I objected to his family, his schooling, his relationship with the body politic. That's true. I do object to all these things. But what rights over him do I gain by my objections? I had no right. Just power. And so, finally, I was ashamed.

II

Early in the term one year a freshman brought into the writing class a piece about his kid brother. At that time we had all things xeroxed, so it was unnecessary for him to read it to the class; we each did our own reading. Silence followed as the class waited for me to say something.

(A new class always waits for the teacher. In my more bitter moments, I assume they wait to see what they're supposed to think. Actually, they're being mannerly by standards they've been taught. But also, the one who speaks first is most embarrassed, and that onus might rightly fall on the teacher—except it works against a writing class.)

I could not speak to the piece I had just read. Conviction backed by self-control forbade my saying anything vicious; honesty prevented my saying anything supportive. From where I read, the piece was pure sentimental twaddle, written in a soap opera vocabulary inappropriate and unnatural to a budding computer hack, extraneous to his interest or experience.

Being in the position of power, I could remain silent as long as I chose, but I was afraid the other students would tear the author apart—from embarrassment, if not from meanness. Still, there seemed few alternatives, so I asked how people responded to it.

The tone was set by an Iranian student who was homesick. He had left at home a twelve-year-old brother whom he would not see for four years, who would be so different when they met again. He responded to the writing by bringing his own feelings and memories to bear. And he spoke simply and directly, in his own diction. Others in the class followed him, very simply, talking about leaving home, and what they feared to lose.

I listened, both touched and appalled. That these students, new to MIT, with all their thoroughly documented, much vaunted competitiveness and mistrust of one another, could meet so personally and straightforwardly, was touching and warming. That this response could come from such an execrable piece of writing was appalling to my well-trained sensibility.

But as I listened, I came to understand some things that I had not seen so clearly before. First, there was the matter of audience: I was simply the wrong audience for that piece of writing—wrong time, wrong age, wrong experience. Second, there was a clear distinction to be made between what was in the written text that could be explicated from it, and what could be inferred into it from the reader. When the class was through talking about it, I found that I could speak to it both kindly and cogently—which I certainly was incapable of before. I could say something about audience that was meaningful because it had just been demonstrated: I was the wrong audience. And I could say something about diction: being the wrong audience, I picked up on words that sounded empty and fake. And I could, and did, say these things without hurting the student's feelings. Partly, the support he had gotten from the class protected him. But partly it was because I had stopped feeling judgmental toward him. My thought that he was a bad student had been replaced by my interest in what was happening between words and people.

This student, by the way, was a black man from New York City. He had a hard time writing—trusting his own language and his own tone. I got angry, during the term, with his slap-dash way of doing assignments, and with what seemed like disdain for anything resembling work, though I was confused when I learned he was in an experimental program and so was not required to take this course. The last thing he wrote for the class was a defense of required freshman humanities. He said he had never enjoyed or seen any point in humanities courses in school, and so would have avoided them in college. He said he had learned something in this course he would have missed, and he was looking forward to studying some literature. I wished him luck.

III

Thinking about Bad Students always makes me think about plagiarists, because without a doubt they are the worst, most offensive, least defensible students to be found. Any teacher knows that. At some colleges it's one of the few grounds for not simply expelling, but expunging!

I tried for a long time to work from the assumption that what could be plagiarized shouldn't have been assigned. But that's foolish. Anything could be plagiarized from one year to the next if there's a student file system. And to try always to think of papers that no one would want to plagiarize is arrogant and manipulative: there are no possible assignments that could or should please everyone. Furthermore, what about the student who simply prefers to plagiarize? That's the one who interests me, and from whom I learned things that I'd like to pass on.

The first student of this kind I knew was plagiarizing for a class other than mine. I tried to convince him that he could write his own bad paper just as easily as copy someone else's, with none of the fears of discovery that were paining him. But something else was going on in his mind. There was a fear of inadequacy, but there was also a great depth of hostility toward school, toward the teacher, toward the whole class structure. It was as though getting away with handing in someone else's paper was a way of preserving a sense of himself, his self-respect. (Resonances of Aristotle's discussion of moral action for a slave!)

I thought of this student when I got a paper on *Endgame* from a bright and capable person that was clearly not his own work. At least it was clear to me. Colleagues teaching sections in the same course, to whom I showed the paper to see if they would recognize the source, were timid about judging it. And they advised me to be cautious: it was a very tricky situation. I would have to locate the original before I spoke to the student about it. Somehow, I knew I was too lazy to do that particular piece of research. And I couldn't imagine why I should have to. If I did all that work I didn't want to do, I'd become really angry and punitive. As it was, I just wanted to talk to him about what school was about from my point of view, and what papers might be about if he were interested in learning.

So I called him in to talk about these things. And while we were talking (in truth, I was doing most of the talking, because he seemed rather nervous at that point) my phone rang. It was a colleague who thought he had found in his stack of papers an identical one to mine. And while checking with the student on whether this was indeed a friend of his, another colleague appeared at my door making faces and signs. He had one too. Now this was, if nothing else, an absurd situation, worthy of the play assigned, and worthy of the staff that had assigned it.

It was my student who had done the work of going down to the Boston Public Library to find a rather esoteric piece of criticism—it was, in fact, a production review for a Catholic periodical, and it was the reference to St. Veronica that gave the student away. The other two, fraternity brothers of the first, attached to the humanities only by a steel chain of requirements, had copied his discovery.

My student and I could chat amicably enough about how I had used criticism in class without footnoting my sources (he was a gutsy kid when he got over feeling nervous) and whether this was in fact a model for his performance. But what could the other instructors discuss with the fraternity brothers?

It turned out that the other instructors were thinking dire thoughts about department chairmen, deans, or at the very least, F's. I wondered, "why?" And, if that was too sticky a way to look at it, "why not?" Dealing with these questions seemed a more fruitful use of energy than simply acting on rules and impulses. So we got together a conference, as I remember it, of all the students involved, the faculty involved, and the president of the fraternity—thrown in maybe as referee, maybe to add solemnity—I'm not sure at all what he was doing there, except he seemed a paternal but non-official figure.

A few things came clear from this conference. First, it was obvious that the students had absolutely no sense of guilt about plagiarizing. Fear, yes; guilt, no.[1] We were on that infantile level where parents give commands that are in no way comprehensible, but the consequences of disobe-

---

1. I am advised that this lack of guilt is not common to all students in this situation. Students from liberal backgrounds suffer greatly from guilt. The more authoritarian the background, the less the guilt. [ND]

dience are dire. To some degree, the students saw it as a simple contest: if they were caught, they lost. It was unfortunate, but it had nothing at all to do with right or wrong, and the consequences had nothing at all to do with justice. Further, the students seemed surprised at evidence that the teachers saw it any other way. They just couldn't deal with the possibility of serious moral involvement in actions that were, from their point of view, matters of expediency and survival, if not part of an effort to maintain self-respect in conditions of slavery.

As we talked, another thing emerged that was even more surprising. The teachers were suffering from hurt feelings, and were demanding punishment as retribution more than from any deep sense of moral outrage. Here we had been trying so hard to teach these students—whatever that meant to each of us. At the very least, we all shared a love for our material and a sense of its value. We wanted our students to feel these same things. Yes, and we wanted them to recognize us as mentors who had introduced them to this great and beautiful world that so enriched their lives and understandings. And what had these swine done? They had treated pearls worse than swill, not deigning even to wallow, and had treated us as enemies, jailors, hostile powers, instead of the kindly nurturers we really were!

Now we had a classic Sartrian situation set up: by treating us as enemies they were making us into enemies: we were calling for punishment, for retribution, against the helpless, guilty only of striving for survival! It becomes impossible to punish the plagiarist. That would mean giving up the identity we cultivate and acquire, to live out the role that they have cast us in. I absolutely refuse to let my students have that power over me.[2,3]

---

2. Well, you fooled me, Nancy. I'm not so sure that I agree with your definitions of good and bad students, but I'm with you all the way when you say that grading gets in the way of communication, of understanding, of closeness of any kind between "student" and "teacher." I won't go so far as to say that grading gives the instructor-as-grader the godlike stature you suggest, but it certainly puts the two people—grader and gradee—on different levels. As Gary would say, it forces them to fit into certain roles, and that hinders, rather than helps, understanding and communication. [KS]

3. So what did you do, Nancy? What did the other teachers do? What did the students think? And what did they go on to do? Write a short essay on each of these questions and hand in your answer sheet at the end of the hour. [KS]

Confessions of a Disloyal Student

GARY WOODS

POWER

Almost everyone is crammed into a hierarchy of roles somewhere, like it or not. The teachers on the senior faculty simply can't understand what the role of power is, why the juniors are upset, and simply can't see the problems and responsibilities they have in exercising it—promoting, firing, giving tenure—to the incredulity of the juniors; but those juniors too are completely unable to see how much power they have and what's wrong with it—the rules for students, requirements, punishments for plagiarism, grades, etc.—to the incredulity of this student. True power always seems to lie just ahead and what is behind is just, well, direction or discipline or one of another thousand euphemisms. Roles do that to us. When I am teaching I too cannot understand why someone would object to the infinitely reasonable and certainly "easy" requirements of the course. "But we all agreed on the reasonableness of these criteria," I cry, and the students say, "But it's wrong, don't you see?"

Even if the person on top in any hierarchical situation is himself/herself concurrently also living in a subordinate role, it is impossible for him/her to understand completely why his or her own particular rules, with their criteria, their reasonable expectations, are the stuff of oppression for those below. Oppression, because no method except reason can ever legitimately be used to change or affect the behavior of any human being. There is no education-by-violence.

The senior faculty cry out, "But our rules *are* reasonable, we have to decide *somehow*." And the junior teachers say the same things to their students all the while gazing incredulously at the seniors, saying, "But these are our *lives*, our *jobs*, you're talking about." We *are* an ascending order of niggers and the next nigger up is oppressing us no matter how benevolently, compassionately, or even sympathetically—the role becomes destiny. And if I get in that role I will do the same thing, I know. This is not a judgment of teachers as people, not a judgment of their integrity, not a moralistic assertion that they themselves represent the forces of evil—what I am saying is that once the role is accepted, either in whole or in part, it overpowers *any* lone human being, even the strongest willed and most revolutionary.

There are always some junior teachers who claim to, or *do* see the "reasonableness" of the senior faculty, who do think that there is a heart-rending dilemma in the plea, "But we must decide somehow"; always some juniors who feel like seniors feel, feel part of them and are on their side—and they are perceived as hypocrites and traitors to their peers. And there are students who feel the reasonableness of the teacher, who feel themselves to be in that teacher role (or even adopt it): they are Toms and I have been one of them.

PLAGIARISM

I *do* think it is important to examine whether one's reaction to plagiarism is a knee-jerk from high class grad schools or not. How serious an offense is it?

A teacher has the right to feel angry, insulted, hurt and certainly betrayed if plagiarism is an important breach of faith to him/her. You have the right and responsibility to openly vent all those feelings to the student. You can get pissed off, blow your stack, call him names—anything that you would do to anyone else who betrayed you or insulted you. And, telling the student what you feel personally is going to be by far the most effective way of "reforming" the student: almost all of us have no compunctions about screwing the system—the system, establishment, MIT, institutions in general, are accurately perceived as being oppressive—if a plagiarized paper feels like a way of screwing the system it doesn't seem such a bad idea; but if a plagiarized paper instead means screwing a person, insulting or betraying a fellow human being, I think almost no one would be willing to do it; people just aren't often that insensitive if the decision is presented in that light. It is difficult for me to believe that the student in question wasn't feeling that he was screwing the system somehow, "getting away with something" at MIT, and that he probably never even considered the other possibility.

Once this "crime" is committed the teacher must respond with essentially one of two alternatives: (1) in the name of the system, of law and order, or of egalitarian justice (depending on perspective) exercise power to punish the student, show him s/he can't "get away with it"; or (2) maintain that coercion/power has no place in education; that a personalistic/humanistic form of educational intercourse is possible; and tell him or her why s/he has done something wrong to the teacher; show him/her that this act is not only screwing the system but also screwing a person. In that case the student may learn something, may even suggest doing another paper.

From this experience the student can learn two things. If the response is punitive s/he will learn that you have to be very careful when you screw the system, that pushing the system inevitably results in being squashed by that system or its agent, and that fear of retribution is the strongest argument against whatever offense was committed. But I have a craving for a kind of society where people don't refrain from harming one another solely out of fear of the law, of punishment. The second response may teach you that before you blindly try to get away with something you should look to see if you are hurting someone, doing an injustice; it may teach you that education can be a humane experience.

GRADES

The system of channeling, grading, evaluating, credentialing and demanding performance serves only the smooth functioning of a hierarchically (i.e. authoritarian) organized society. No one else benefits from formal, public grades. The plea that "we must evaluate somehow, grades have to be assigned in some fashion" is simply specious. There are many creative ways to subvert the grading, channeling system. One is the use of pass-fail (pass-incomplete) grading whenever possible. Another that Lillian Robinson used to use was to give everyone the same grade and let them decide on what it should be (it always came out A). Giving all A's is a common route. Allowing the class to propose and vote on a system is another. There are a few other, more exotic ways of grading in an unlimited A situation, which is the rule at MIT. In the situation where grades are a limited commodity there is always the Marxist system (to each according to their needs), i.e. an A average student would get a C, someone with a B+ would get a B and someone with a B— would get an A. Clearly giving all A's is not a complete denial of the system, but in the context of the grade system it does give the individual teacher a chance to make grades a little more meaningless. And then there's Nancy Dworsky's system of grading by class attendance.

iii

classes

How I Survived My Education

JOSEPH BROWN

Epiphanies occur all the time but we're always missing them. Perhaps our rhythm's faulty or we blinked our eyes a second too soon or we're a little hard of hearing, or simply slow to comprehend. I'd been getting signals for two years, but it took a certain amount of repetition and a rather special conjunction of circumstances to explode the illumination that led to other, newly sprung perceptions about myself and writing and the teaching of it.

I was "doing" *King Lear* at MIT; that is, I was leading a discussion of *King Lear* in a section of a staff-taught freshman course called The Western Tradition. It was spring and we were well into a reading list that began the fall before with Homer and would end soon with Freud and his *Civilization and Its Discontents*. The first semester had gone rather well: the reading was interesting,[1] the discussions (or dialogues) sufficiently lively to keep me from being bored, and I remember thinking at the end that for my first run through of a required course no one in the classroom need feel empty from the experience.

The second term, however, was something else altogether, and when *it* was done, looking back at the whole year, I began to suspect a touch of self-deception, to doubt the grounds of my confidence beyond acceptable paranoid limits. But that was later, when the bad moments were transforming themselves into a new perception. The time I'm speaking of now was irritating, unpleasantly so, but not yet the stuff of revolutions.

The week before we began *Lear*, one student, Mike, in what I took to be a fit of despair over the agony of a requirement he could no longer bear, had taken after Dante, in particular the *Inferno*, with a protestant zeal. I saw myself in those days as the great classroom debater taking on those less able than I to see subtlety though eager to follow, making them learn by model to see more sharply, to discriminate fine scratches beneath the skin, and—if I failed—to discern the darker truth of a freshman's irrevocable inadequacy, as then, with Mike. I had been trained, after all, at Harvard by one of the greatest living Dante scholars (to say nothing of T. S. Eliot) to believe that no single human creation could quite match perfections with *La Commedia*, so when my eyes focused on Mike's angry, outraged face, I wasn't prepared for the spasm of doubt that lightly blocked all my earnest arguments, only a wink, casually ignored but oh how real: Maybe he's right! Could it be that Dante's not indisputably worthwhile? Why shouldn't a poet be asked to justify our attention regularly? It passed, of course, this absurd hesitation, but my subsequent inability to win the debate addressed

---

1. Or should I say: I liked it and assumed I'd done a job of imparting my passion to the students? [JB]

2. Even now, reliving the experience, making it come out better, still

silently another question: I was having such trouble speaking to Mike's doubts because they were my own, undermining a life spent preparing for just such a moment of intellectual persuasion, only to lose it. For a while I chose not to hear the question, although the attack on Dante had not been an isolated episode. A little earlier in the term we had been doing the *Confessions of St. Augustine,* a most trying book, and when one of my colleagues suggested we reproduce the lyrics of Dylan's "I Dreamed I Saw St. Augustine," I snatched at the device as an inspired assault on the class's resistance to the soul of the book; but one student, Phil—I see him now so clearly, sitting in the right corner of the room, having only to look at the backs of heads, I hear so precisely his anguish and frustration at having to deal with my ignorance—resisted aloud, quietly, my attempt to be cleverly pointed, contemporary, in tune with what was very important to him in a context that up till then had quite ignored his real interests. In response to my question about the meaning of the phrase "a coat of solid gold," he said: "Either you know it or you don't, there's no way of explaining it." He did not speak angrily. In spite of what was on his mind just then, he indulged me with sweet patience, and so I felt impelled to announce certain great principles, as, for example: the anti-intellectualism of such a position, having been loosed on the world, would also destroy the liberator. I was not then of course as articulate or as aesthetically in control of my irony as I choose now to remember. I concluded with a definitive judgment: he ought not to be in college if he found activities of the mind so offensive.

"As a matter of fact," he said, "I'm dropping out."

A silence.

The words, confirming my judgment, died away, throwing me into despair: we ought to be talking about his determination to leave—he was, as I think back to it, quite ready to do so (he came no more to class, he had come to this one to tell us), and there were others in that room (as I later discovered) who would have welcomed the discussion, who were close to some special edge of their own[2]—but at that point in my life I was not prepared to desert for any period of time the lesson plan, to drop out. I could not strip myself of the protection books had come to mean for me, a necessary separation between me and those empty, hostile people stretching out before me in neat rows, waiting for the word, my judgment approving their lives: it was the way I had been taught, and it worked! There I was, doing it for the next generation of students, working the magic, believing they cared, without question, and so the class ran down, towards its appointed end, and I began to comfort myself with "facts": they were scientists and engineers, after all, it was *their* fault, not mine, the silences, the sullenness, the emptiness of the discussions, it's what happens when you cast pearls, etc. I was secure in my judgment and my despair grew, as it will in the face

---

trying desperately to redeem the failure, I can see myself establishing connections between Phil's choice and Augustine's career, which hardly progressed evenly: it is not inappropriate to doubt the value of what one is doing, we sometimes stand mute in the face of great pain, etc. [JB]

of one's security, against the more radical instincts and emotions one filters out of any experience in the name of reason or order.

And then the crucial day: we were speaking of the end of *Lear* and I was proposing the ambiguity of those final lines when Shakespeare attempts to reaffirm a moral world, and I asked them to compare it to the final lines of *Oedipus Rex*, a play they had read last September, and there was this awful silence, and I saw in their faces surprise that I should expect them to remember such a detail as the ending of *Oedipus,* amusement even, until, irritated, I began pushing them into anger: how dare I assume they ought to remember, that they might make the effort required to remember, and finally, most hurtful of all, that they would care enough to consider remembering what was apparently (but stupidly) important in a world that was not, from their objective hillock, of any substance or effect, and then I had my epiphany: most of them hadn't even read *King Lear*. We'd been talking about it for a week, they'd been coming to class for those discussions, and except for two or three of them, the play did not touch them because they had not read it and probably did not intend to. Perhaps it was penance that drove them to class or fear that I'd flunk them if they didn't come, and they hadn't even read the book. It was more than I could bearably understand. So in the way of a paranoid spasm I began to brood on all the other discussions that term, Mike's invasion of Dante, for example, and immediately concluded they'd read nothing. Mike's exegesis was a real *tour de force*, and it was all a farce anyway, twenty people captive in a small room, one of whom was working from assumptions so radically different from anyone else's in that space as to make intellectual (let alone human) engagement out of the question—I remember so powerfully, even now my teeth ache with the perception of it, the sense of futility and, of course, betrayal: how comforting it is to be a martyr, how pleasant to insure the enactment of that role, and ultimately how unsatisfying always to be "right" in all the slippery rationalizing we use to disguise a failure to be honest, and true to the situation making such immediate demands on our sense of what is appropriate and substantial and resonant—so I drew myself up (I'd been sitting on the edge of my desk, which was placed on a raised podium at the head of the room) and affirmed my moral superiority: "I cannot carry on a discussion with you if you haven't read the play," and walked out.

At the time it seemed such a good thing to do: it felt positively cathartic. I stood at the elevator at the end of the corridor and they still sat in the classroom, obviously stunned by my act, absorbing the lesson of my chastisement, preparing to reform. I could hardly wait for the next meeting, by which time they would all have read the play—nay, studied it carefully—and be ready to give me precisely the answers I wanted to the brilliant questions I'd spent hours creating. The vision was utopian as I descended.

I'm being somewhat heavily ironic, of course, in part, I think, to conceal a pain whose source is my very real love for the play, tangible, sensuous, and my corresponding sense, even now, when I know better, of their worthlessness in not sharing that love. They did not transform themselves in time for our next meeting. No one ever referred to my aberration. We all behaved well, waiting for the term to end. But from that pain came an elementary conclusion: they will never, unless they are willing to be recreated in my image (like Joyce's ideal reader of *Finnegans Wake*), be capable of experiencing the play as I did, and do; it is presumptuous and stupid to make them try, let them come to it out of their own experience—I now know all these things and believe them and still struggle with myself to affirm them in action. But the bias dies hard: that sense of superiority my teachers fed me lingers, muted, in my present determination, on the whole a sound one, not to force students, in their required courses, to discuss writing that does not matter to them. But I am getting ahead of myself.

The new course was called *Identity and Autobiography* and it was my first attempt to put into practice what I thought I'd learned from the epiphany of the preceding spring. Like *The Western Tradition* it was a staff-taught course, one of four or five an incoming MIT freshman has to choose from, and during the summer, Myra Brenner, Nancy Dworsky, and I met to plan a curriculum. The setting was a tiny study, really only a little larger than a typical New England privy, five hundred yards or so from the main house on Martha's Vineyard, just within call of the "murmuring surge," and everything we outlined that weekend seemed indisputably right. We were inheriting a course which had been organized on sound historical and literary principles, a study of concepts of the self in nineteenth-century England and twentiety-century America, with an impressive reading list that began with Rousseau and ended with Mailer. We turned the course around to focus on the selves which inhabited an MIT classroom in the late Sixties, reborn of high schools of every size and assumption, of varied institutional freedoms, and to establish a context of school, family, work, and God (or nature) for those selves. The reading list, limited but also impressive, included, among others, Kafka and St. Augustine (ever my nemesis), there for exemplification and, occasionally, relief from the painful exigency of having to be present in a new way in the classroom; but always, we decided, we would end with the selves we bring here and now, to Cambridge, at this very moment in time. We were uncertain about the amount and nature of the writing we would expect, but we were not afraid of making demands as to the degree of their commitment: they were all to do their considerable part to "make things work," although we were not sure exactly what that meant.

We started that year with a "gestalt" exercise: you pair off in class with someone you don't know, stare into his eyes for five minutes without uttering a word, then each asks the other a question which will elicit comments that begin to tell you who he is. For the second half of the hour you pair off with someone else, except this time you offer yourself up cold, not in response to any particular question. There was an agreeable buzz in the room during what most of them took to be "nonsense," a little uneasiness about the menacing eye contact, and they were pleasantly disturbed by the assignment for next time: write a brief biography of the two people you met and introduce them to the rest of us. They said later they expected to be asked to write an autobiography.

The next time, however, we had troubles: I called for volunteers to read what they had written. After the jovial, sociable intercourse of the first class I was not prepared for the devastating silence, eyes avoiding eyes, twitching. I had also done the assignment but had determined not to be the first to read. When one student did at last step into the arena, the relief everyone else seemed to be feeling swallowed up their residual energy, and response—what little there was of it—crept out like snails. Obviously I had certain expectations but except for the out and out fantasies, I can't begin to imagine, as I sit here writing this, what I wanted from them. They, of course, were waiting for me to set the direction of the discussion and I refused, having decided they must learn not to depend on me (without telling them what I decided), and so confusion resulted and anxiety and in the end indifference.[3]

Then we settled into two weeks of hell.

I had decided, after that second meeting, well, this is, after all, an experimental course, why not go all the way with the experiment, so I threw out the lesson plan, all of it, saying, "OK, we're in this room three times a week, 10 A.M. to 11, for three months. How are we going to spend the time?"

---

3. Another memory introduces itself: halfway through the hour, unable to bear the silence, I read my two biographies, and one student said: "What a great piece, it's the best one, that's the way it should be done!" I got angry, saying, "You killed it," thinking, Apple-polisher, and the class died. Remembering it now, I believe he was only trying to cheer me up. [JB]

4. Here is the description of our course (with a new title) on the basis of which incoming freshmen were supposed to make an enlightened choice, followed by the description of another course, one of the oldest and at that time more popular offerings. I think the differences which emerge between the audiences spoken to are clear:

A. Our course: The sequence of 21.013-21.014, Modes of Self-definition, will focus its attention on the students themselves. Through discussion, writing, individual and group projects, and reading where pertinent, students will approach such fundamental questions as: what do we mean when we speak of a "self"? and how is this concept shaped by experience in familial, cultural, and societal circumstances?

To the greatest possible extent each class will provide its own questions for exploration as they relate to individual concerns. This implies an informal class structure in which conventional assumptions about the nature of learning will be challenged and traditional expectations about a formal course will be questioned. Of primary importance will be the student's writing (including the keeping of a journal), parts of which will be used in class as a focus of discussion. In addition, students will be encouraged to use means of expression other than languages, if they so desire.

B. The sequence of 21.011 and 21.012, the Western Tradition, treats the nature and evolution of the modern sense of the human condition, as it has found expression in masterpieces of imaginative literature and philosophy. Works are studied largely in chronological order, as they inform or alter decisively the central tradition of experience and expression to which all significant

No one quite knew.

Some of them didn't want to be there, of course: they were mathematicians, physicists, engineers, and humanities was required, so why didn't I make things as simple as possible by assigning books they didn't want to read and papers they didn't want to write and we would all be unhappy together? Some of them didn't want to be in college at all: later in the term, after we'd discovered, less resentfully, a less boring routine, Jack, one of the noisier, unhappier of the group (he would drop out at the start of the second term), said: "Question time, everyone: how many in this room are going to drop out?" Three raised their hands. "How many are seriously thinking of it?" Three more. "How many have entertained the thought?" Four. Half the class.

So it was at that moment I discovered empirically what others already knew: programs which suggest that forced learning is ultimately negligible attract students on their way out of the system but willing to give it another try.[4] We did (and perhaps still do) attract the alienated, sometimes neurotically independent students, and the pain they cause to themselves and each other is sometimes unbearable.[5] I have seen this process occur at elite schools like MIT, at community colleges for lower class whites, and at

---

works of modern literature must be referred in order to be fully intelligible. The first term, the Classical Heritage, takes Nietzsche's *Birth of Tragedy* as its defining text; it begins by opposing Homer's *Iliad* and the *Book of Genesis* as representatives of two outlooks, the heroic and the moralistic, between which, as Nietzsche believes, Western culture must forever seek a compromise as it articulates its sense of values. The subject proceeds to works of Aeschylus, Sophocles, Plato, Aristotle, and Virgil, in order to study the evolution of pre-Christian conceptions of honor, justice, heroism, and destiny. The second term, the European Heritage, examines the modifications worked upon the classical tradition by the Judeo-Christian experience, through study of the Bible, selected readings from St. Augustine's works, and Dante's *Divine Comedy*. It follows the later history of the Western ideal as reflected in works by Shakespeare, Swift, and Rousseau, touching upon the rise of Christian humanism, the challenges offered Christianity by the rationalism of the Enlightenment, and the romantic rediscovery of the mythopoetic and the irrational. The sequence concludes with Dostoyevsky's *Crime and Punishment* and Freud's *Civilization and Its Discontents*, both of which respond to the sense that the Western tradition has reached the point of crisis while bearing testimony to its continued relevance to the existential and psychic predicaments of modern man. [JB]

5. It's true that some students and some of the wildest and most creative ones do stay at school or come back because of our classes, individualistic and rebellious, hating the rest of it because they distrust all institutions, all structures (until they make their own), but willing to endure because of the measure of freedom we give them, and because we and our classes will listen carefully to whatever they come up with as they pursue their relentless quest for a more perfect life, in a more perfect world. And this sometimes makes me uneasy. At first I thought because we were fudging the issue for these students: if the Institution is so *wrong*, wouldn't they be better off facing that fact squarely without any ameliorating circumstances, like sympathetic teachers and writing courses, and

urban ghetto schools, and in all of them the students, less satisfied than their peers, occasionally more disruptive, more sullen, are the ones who make incredible demands on themselves and others, work hard, play hard, and are the most serious, once they survive their various crises—if they survive.[6]

So it was, the first year of *Identity and Autobiography*.

After two weeks in a regular classroom we moved to the commodious lounge of one of the dormitories, where the seating arrangements were more varied, and it was here the revolution took place. The change in location was no small part of it. Ten minutes into the first meeting in our new environment, Bernie, who had been rather talkative the first weeks, willing to give more to the group than the rest, stood up (he'd been lying on a rug in the middle of the room) during a rambling discussion of a student paper that attacked everyone in the room for being stupid, and said:

"I can't take any more of this. I'm leaving."

He paused.

"Who wants to come with me?"

Bernie hadn't been able to carry it off alone: he was looking behind him to see if he was leading anybody. There was a long silence. I started counting to myself. If no one joined him by ten, I would. At five someone stood, breaking the ice, and in a few minutes there were four others willing to leave with Bernie, and they did, and the fifteen who stayed behind sat or lay there giggling nervously, doodling, and then I said, "Now what?" and for the next thirty minutes we talked about what we were going to do. We made plans for the rest of the term: we organized, I remember, into reading groups, writing groups, movie groups. The class never again reached that point of tense, energetic interaction Bernie had succeeded in bringing us to, but he had dramatically affected the life of the course.

I see now that Bernie wouldn't have been able to act if it weren't for the paper—a scornful, rather unpleasant put-down—we had just been reading, but the class would have slowly died if it weren't for Bernie and the four who came after him. The dissidents, by the way, met regularly, every week, in the evening, did more work than anyone else in the regular class,

---

using their energy to change things, either in college or outside? Then I realized I felt uncomfortable, not because of what might or might not be in the best interests of these students (they *are*, after all, the best judges of whether or not a college degree is useful to them, or worth it, and under what circumstances), but because I felt *we* were being used as a kind of whitewash. For a long time we felt peripheral and under attack because of the way we taught ("lack of intellectual rigor and respect for *authority*" are some of the kinds of phrases used); it was made fairly clear to us that we were only there on sufferance somehow, and that we were out of line with the true purposes of this institution of higher learning. Our jobs have never been secure, and we have never been allowed to forget that.

But now I see that this uneasiness comes from accepting an overly monolithic view of the institution (and the world)—the view held both by these students, and some of our colleagues, however their reactions to it differ—the Insti-

continued to meet the rest of the year, and four of them became very good friends. Only Bernie was never really a member of it: apparently they had to get rid of their leader.

The fifteen of us left behind, feeling chastized by their departure, never mentioned the unholy five during that class hour, but I remember we discovered them afterwards in the small foyer leading to the front door of the dormitory and when I stopped to talk to them, they told me they had just sat there, paralyzed by what they had done, only able to discuss what might be going on in the room they'd deserted, afraid to guess what we were saying about them. It took them a while to accept their daring. Bernie said they thought I might flunk them.

"You blew it," Bernie said.

After a month he had come back to us for a while, first asking my permission, a bit diffidently, neither a member of the cell he had created nor part of the larger conglomerate he had precipitated into a functioning class. But he was getting more and more difficult, never satisfied with what we were doing, always griping about his peers, the Institute, the world at large. The class itself walked unsteadily toward its destination, pleased to have survived a crisis that in another place, under similar circumstances, might have destroyed it—or so we chose to believe. What happened each time we met was so chancy—we were never sure of it, even when we planned something—that we all became giddy from the implication of our plunge into what Conrad calls the destructive element. It was all around us, every day, and it became easier to suffer because we had made a natural commitment to the whimsical lottery of learning how to get along, to survive without a plan. We were drunk with the absurdity of it; it would take the smallest breath to raze our belief in the value of what we were doing, and yet we persisted. So when Bernie said you blew it he was using a hammer on a very delicate needle indeed. I had defenses, of course. Once, Bernie told us that he had been to Woodstock the summer before and it was a bad scene all around—drugs, despair, paranoia—so we mustn't heed the then official judgment of it as a New Utopia, and when he moaned on, complaining

―――――――――――――――

tution is (and should/must//should not/must not: be) *this* one thing, and this alone. In fact, MIT, like most social structures, is incredibly complicated and diverse: we *are* teaching there (and not only us, but people like us in every department); and we are as much a part of the full reality of the world we and our students must face and understand as is beginning calculus, a traditional, authoritarian structure, or those vast, immutable, marble corridors. I do not believe I should keep my sentences short. But what a feeling of release, prompted by Joe Brown's example, to let them go on, complex and various! [PC]

6. Four of the ten who raised their hands that day didn't, at MIT: Jack disappeared into the wilds of upper New York state; another transferred to Amherst; another to Boston University; the fourth went home to California. A fifth left for a term and came back and finally finished. It was, I'm sure, their only way to survive, leaving MIT. [JB]

about it and the inadequacies of the people he was forced to be with all the time, I heard the bitter monologue as yet another example of his unleashed inability to thrive in a genuinely free atmosphere—oh how self-righteous I was. So when he said I blew it, I nodded comfortably and asked how and he merely repeated it, in the familiar accent implying, "If you don't know I can't explain," and was silent. I can still see that accusing finger stretched out toward me across the room (he had waited until the end of the class), the smile on his face, the anger in his voice, his chin clean-shaven for the first time since the memorable day he had walked out on us. Life with Bernie was an endless encounter.

Well, I did blow it. But not in the way Bernie believed.

In his unhappy frame of mind that year, disturbed, destructive, frustrated, Bernie was looking for a guru, someone to lead him out of the hell he was living in and feeling, someone to save him, and everyone he met he cast in that role, to see how far he could go along the road, any road, to some triumph of the spirit, no matter how small or incomplete, and I seemed to be a good candidate since obviously I had something up my sleeve or in my head or on my soul when I threw away the course syllabus; but then I blew it, I didn't lead him anywhere, I let it all die. Naturally I told him he misunderstood what I was trying to do: I was no longer leading anybody; power, even if it saves you, corrupts irredeemably. I was only trying to show him a little light from a small acre maybe halfway up the mountain, inviting him to share the view for a while (a short while, since, after all, it's my acre and my climb and you have to work to get there and keep it—I hadn't, of course, changed as much as I thought), so although I did blow it, as we all must (I was enjoying my lecture now), since nothing ever really works, I blew it in a totally different way, on grounds more critical than mere salvation.

Nevertheless, Bernie dropped out at the beginning of the second term.

Now I know he was right partly in the way he meant: by abrogating all authority, by refusing to enter into the class with my personality showing, by concealing that part of me which is the lover of words and books simply because I associated it with the old way, by denying what, at certain times, more often than not, I indubitably am, someone, for example, with a

---

7. (A) But did any one believe this, including the authors of the course descriptions? *College. Learning.* You can't shake off that mystique, not at least in the first term. [PC]

(B) Now, of course, we are much more pragmatic. We are pretty sure that if people do some writing they will take something away from the course that has some value for them, or will have, later—a record, however sporadic, of who they were (or at that point thought they were) at that year in their lives. Something they made and can keep, if they want to make it. In addition, as Macrorie points out in *A Vulnerable Teacher,* many students often write something that merits their own self-respect and wins the real respect of the group; and in gaining that they have received something in return for their struggles to get into college and their tuition money. And if they don't write—or write superficially—we've finally, reluctantly, come not only to see, but also to

trained wish to read books, talk about them, and even sometimes write (about) them, I blew it.

I hung back too often in that commodious dormitory lounge, unwilling to intrude on them with my authority, trying to encourage them to be more insistently there by absenting myself, to talk more, even take over if necessary, rendering me superfluous. And what it looked like to some of them was that I wasn't interested, that I was bored with what they were trying to say and do: they would get into a subject they were enjoying, would look at me for confirmation of its value and see me not listening, and slowly the conversation died. I assumed, of course, the talk died because they were at a loss to sustain it, or too new to the experience of taking so much responsibility for the life of the class on their own heads, or simply uneasy about it, or bored themselves.

I blew it, Bernie, because I refused, in my determination to make them free, to take any responsibility on my own head for what was happening even as I dictated the terms of *their* commitment: how obvious it sounds, how stupid of me not to see it while I was doing it, and how I made them suffer for it![7]

Very little in the world, however, is permanently horrible: the next year of *Identity and Autobiography*, now called *Modes of Self-definition*, went much better. We were less fearful of the risk of failure; we knew, in other words, what *not* to be anxious about. We became freer to improvise, to listen for changes and wishes and demands. The freedom to fail nourished our self-confidence about what we were doing, so we could begin to shape our ends more naturally by structuring chance. If something was said or done casually in class that radically shifted our attention, we simply followed the shift and made it part of the class. We were giving assignments again. It was Nancy Dworsky, I think, who proposed a final project at the end of the first term which would require everyone to make something out of words or wood or plastic or sounds, an assignment that released all sorts of latent energy and imagination in incipient engineers and scientists. We received poems, stories, allegorical chess sets, we heard jazz concerts and autobiographical tapes, we were invited to observe the assembling of incred-

---

believe, that's *their* decision, based on their lives, and the way they want to or must use their time and selves in this situation. Too many of them in the same room can ruin a class, of course, though we're more able to keep that from ruining it completely, because, however haltingly, we're able to talk with the class about how we feel about what seems to us like lack of commitment, and ask (genuinely) what we should do about it, if anything, and accept, seriously, whatever answers we get. We have stopped—usually—feeling so terribly *responsible* for everything that happens, though we care. And I suddenly see, now, that one of the things that went wrong at first was exactly that position of responsibility—which we, as teachers, dramatically and defiantly abdicated; but we did not abolish the post. We turned it over to the students, who did not of course want it or accept it: it's too heavy a load to bear, whether or not you are being paid to carry it. [PC]

ibly complex objects whose symbology was sometimes obscure, but in all cases what was done was done with the whole group in mind. The projects were not for me alone; everyone shared in their wit and mystery. It was the first tentative step toward the idea Peter Elbow introduced more formally into the course: all work, which meant, in effect, all writing, becomes the common responsibility of the whole group. There is no teacher who singles out the best, the most interesting, or the worst papers or passages, to make a point to the class—a point, usually, that the class is already quite aware of. Rather, the group itself determines the nature and extent of the "discussion" of the papers; and, by fiat, they are *all* read; the author learns, in collaboration with his audience, whether what he has done "works," whether it is, in the old language, "good." Judgments are not suspended; they are merely established in a new context, under freer conditions, at the point where the bearer and the receiver of them can meet in a mutual commitment to the truth of what is being said, within boundaries drawn by everyone, with just that degree of honesty which is acceptable to each member of the group. No one gets more than he needs or demands in the way of critical response.

It is a most delicate negotiation, this coming together of a collection of people with disparate motives and anxieties and the consequent forming of a group which begins both to learn and to teach what it means to write about honestly and well those things most important to each member of the group. Such a congruence does not come easily, or all the time, but when it does happen—when everything works, that is, when we want to write and want to hear what others feel and think about our writing—such an experience makes real all our wildest imaginings about the essential community of education.

And then there were Bill and Steven.

Bill came into the class by chance. He had been a student in one of my courses three years before, dropped out for a while during the great radicalizing upheavals of the late Sixties, came back to the Institute to finish his degree in preparation for a teaching career. He was married now, eager beyond a teacher's most unreasonable fantasies to learn what he could that final year about teaching, and so when he discovered he had an hour to kill between classes and that one of my sections of *Modes of Self-definition* was meeting then, he asked me if he could drop in for a while, to see and hear what the freshmen were about that year—and stayed and stayed, through the whole semester, absent only once. And because we knew each other fairly well and discovered quickly that there was really no need to compete for the attention of the students, we began to share the teaching of that class in a way I had not thought possible. With his flair for dramatic gestures and his insider's knowledge of what it meant to be a freshman at MIT, he was able to do and say things quite alien to my will, experience, and personality. I think we came on like Laurel and Hardy; but comedy or tragedy, it worked to bring the group more easily, quickly together in preparation for a new beginning. More writing was done in that class that year than in any of the others, more attention paid to the writing, more discussion of the character of the selves that made that writing.

Bill was, I believe now, the first of our TAs, unsung and unpaid, doing in an off-hand, crotchety manner what has become a regular and important part of our program.

Steven was another sort of catalyst altogether.

At this time, again by chance, I had the opportunity to work in an experimental program at MIT called USSP or the Unified Science Study Program, begun by Jerrold Zacharias as an alternative mode of education for freshmen. USSP tried to give students more freedom to plan their curricula, to learn at a self-regulated pace; it encouraged them to discover and work on projects which might be only peripherally related to the regular program. For me the value of USSP lay in the chance it gave me to learn whether the sort of teaching we were doing might also be useful to students whose backgrounds and aptitudes were quite different from those of MIT freshmen: there were men and women in the program from the University of Massachusetts at Boston, North Shore Community College, Keane State, Tufts, a great many of whom did not come to college with a passionate commitment to science or engineering.

Two things happened that year, one of which didn't surprise me.

It took just about as long for the group to get going as in the more homogeneous workshop of all MIT students: in a room full of 20 students, about evenly divided among high science achievers, somewhat more casual middle achievers from the urban branch of the state university, and the low achievers of a two-year community college, we had just as much trouble finding our way into the heart of the enterprise.

What I didn't expect was the lingering resentment some of the MIT students felt toward the outlanders, a resentment springing in part from the fact that the people from the community college, for example, were getting an MIT education at community college rates. But there was the less frivolous resentment they felt when they discovered themselves with students who could write poems or stories or personal essays so much more easily and effectively than they—that there were skills that being skilled in science didn't automatically entitle them to. Perhaps they already knew their limitations from high school and had forgotten about them, or thought college would be different. Perhaps they never knew them. For some it was a liberating experience as they began to take pleasure in the skills of others, even in learning them. Some chose not to expend the energy they saw necessary to catch up with their "dumber" peers. But the experience illuminated even those who professed to learn nothing.

Steven, for example.

He was an Objectivist dueller.

That is, he was a disciple of Ayn Rand; and that meant his greatest pleasure came from instigating debates in the classroom in order to win them. As a matter of fact, Steven was quite adept at the strategy. One of my sharpest memories of that term is of the time I covered my ears with my hands and shouted: I won't debate you, Steven!

He was also a dueller.

That is, he kept fencing equipment in his room and was rather famous in the dorm for the passion and skill with which he pursued, as an amateur, whatever human target he could hold still long enough to foil for him, no matter how sloppy.

Steven didn't stay the whole year in the workshop. He decided early on that since it required little effort to pass, the course was obviously not worth his attention. He liked to work hard, he told me, under famous men who knew exactly what they were doing at all times and could tell him what he was doing wrong and how to correct his mistakes, whether in computers, fencing, or writing.

Yet I watched him discover one day (and then, I'm afraid, forget) the possibilities of language, and the great distance he had to travel to reach the point where he could begin to write better than his beloved Ayn Rand. The epiphany occurred as he sat listening to a slight, witty poem about kids in a supermarket, done by a woman whose intellect he did not particiuarly value but who clearly could do naturally with words things it would take him months to learn; and even then he could not be assured of success. He sat there listening to her and I imagined him saying: I like that, what a marvellous poem, and isn't it wonderful to be able to write things like that. Then: I wish I could do that, it looks easy, I wish someone would show me how, why doesn't Brown tell me how to do it? He prides himself on not teaching me how to write good poems, no rules, he probably doesn't know any! And anyway, it's not worth the effort.

A caricature no doubt, but I had been learning all sorts of things during the growth of the course: to listen, for example, to the students I was teaching, to learn to trust what they were teaching me, to recognize Steven for what he was and could become without judging him, to meet him and his writing on the terms he set and let his peers show him other selves and other kinds of writing that have to be met on *their* terms. And if he chose to forget what he learned as soon as he discovered it, no one was to blame, least of all Steven, who, in spite of what he believed, could not be *made* to remember.

By this time the authors of *Free Writing* were helping me to learn to *believe* in what I was learning, supporting my sometimes feeble sense of its "rightness," its value to me at that moment as a teacher bringing his whole self into the new life of the classroom—no, not the whole self. One holds back: there is no life, no writing, which does not affirm mystery at the imperceptible still point. The trick is not to feel guilty about it, or at least, not to be paralyzed by guilt.

We learn to cultivate realism—which means not to be excessive in one's claim about the truth. All that has happened—the good and the bad —ensures the continuity of our experience, and the possibility of failure; but we have learned not to be destroyed by that possibility. Some people have given up teaching altogether. A writer I know announced the principle to me before dropping out: "I have nothing to say." It's not true, of course:

he speaks elegantly, movingly, of what passes before his eyes; his students will miss him, I think; but silence, he says, is better.

And some of us stay.

Like the man I know who writes stories, writes them magnificently, making beautifully wrought fragments he shores against his ruins; until, unable to survive that way, he breaks down (almost, I would swear, to see if the pieces *can* have a better shape), goes off to the hospital, is silent for a while; and then begins speaking again and we begin reading the words in our fiction workshop, we listen as he has taught us by his own listening, we learn to cultivate that lovely mode of behavior by which we discover others —and the silence has enriched the melody.

I remember interviewing a student who had just spent the summer wondering whether he would return to college for another year. The college was DIT[8]; the student was quiet, nervous. I was supposed to be gathering data for an evaluation of the experimental program he had been a member of for two years. Here are my notes on the conversation:

Edward acknowledges pressures from his family and friends not to drop out, asserts that the decision to stay was finally his, an "internal one" whose source could not be traced to any one place or person. Nevertheless, as he looks back on that difficult time, he concludes that the program made a difference—how crucial, he cannot or would not determine—and in his quiet, skeptical way suggests its importance to his life. He thinks of other friends, as bright as he, already dropped out, in the army or "working days and running nights," their lives fixed forever, and sees himself partly attracted to such a life, free of hard choices, real achievement, and the risk of failure—yet he is powerfully relieved to be saved from it.

These are what matter: risk, freedom, and the pleasure of being responsible for one's acts. We all wish our lives to be full of them, they give the edge without which there is no value. They are the only things worth learning about; the stuff of our dreams, and our words.

---

8. See Jean Colburn's "Free Writing in the Motor City." [JB]

Writing Class

LEE RUDOLPH

He comes back to us with a story
and won't tell us. He says,
Tell it to me. He passes his hand
over my mouth, and draws out a bird,
a starling. Look, he says, it has a grub
in its beak. And it flies off.—
But he said nothing of the kind,
you tell me; *he said nothing; and he had*
his hands over my eyes the whole time: he was holding
my head up from behind.

At night, he serves each one of us
tea, and a tennis ball. He puts one word
into each ear (a fortune in a cookie),
he says To pay our passage.—*That's not so,*
you say: *it was admission to a play;*
he sat between us, he was holding
(one each) a hand.

When the night was windiest, and the moon full,
he took us to the beach: to overhear
the dialogue. But—*No, that's not clear:*
he was moving his mouth in speech,
but it was the voice of the ocean
inviting us, and I think he knew better
than even whisper: I think he was holding his breath.

Waiting for the Professor (or Someone Like Him)

KEN SKIER

Patsy: "I want you all to free write now about a first class you had either as a student or as a teacher, and what made it a good experience or a bad one, and how you felt about it. I'll do it, too."

Cami: "Are you gonna collect these?"

Peter: "Anything you write you will have power over. You don't have to give it to anybody. But if they ask nicely, you might want to . . . ."

Joe: "This is a hard assignment."

Seth: "Especially since it's not free writing."

Seth (again): "See if you can get Sandy to do this one."

Enter Sandy.

Seth: "SHhhhhhhhhhhhhhhhhhhhhhhhhhh."

This semester I know what I'm doing. I know—there's no doubt about it. Fifth semester of Freshman Humanities, third semester of student teaching, fifth semester with Joe—what could be easier? I'm experienced. I work well with Joe. And this time the class will click—they all picked *Writing and Experience* as their first choice, they want to be here, they want to write—what can go wrong?

I have no time to wonder.

My lease expires and I move from my crummy apartment, de-roaching all my books and papers and hauling them on my back through the sickly sticky end of August Boston sauna blues—while my parents move, and I have to pack and unpack stuff for their place, and prepare for my senior year, putting up half a dozen friends and friends of friends in my new-found roach-free, air-conditioned digs for the duration.

The chaos of the summer—split up by a month-long mysterious headache that they say was a migraine—promises to fade into the free and easy-going friendly days of the fall.

September. The semester starts, and on the day of our first class Joe and I talk in the afternoon coolness of his office. Half-empty coffee cups hover on shelves, books and student papers spread in splendid disarray, my feet on Joe's desk and both of us acting calm. Cool. Collected. Confident. Prepared.

After all, we know what we're about. We wait, and we talk.

At two o'clock I check my watch and say, "Well, I guess I'll go stroll into the class." Joe says, "Sure"—he's on the phone with someone—"I'll be along in a minute." So I pick up my bookbag and walk into the class.

Modern, carpeted room, more a lounge than a lecture hall; a living room really: conversation core of sofas surrounded by comfortable chairs against the walls. Cork tile on the ceiling, hidden fluorescents for indirect light, and large windows, offering unobstructed views of the other inside faces of the Humanities building.

I walk in quietly, sit down silently at the end of a sofa. The room is almost empty. Several students sit and open bookbags, waiting. I open my bookbag and wait.

A student, red-haired, curly, brisk, efficient, looks my way. He doesn't look twice. I am only another student, more than likely a freshman. He is waiting for the prof.

I clear my throat.

"Is this 21.023?"

"Unless my schedule card is wrong."

He is confident. Another student looks up.

"I hope so."

He laughs. A third student smiles. They are waiting for the prof.

"Oh. Well—"

I raise my voice. They raise their eyes. Wondering. Looking. What is going on?

"—I'm glad this is 21.023, because that's the class I'm supposed to TA."

Someone laughs. Curly makes a joke.

"*You're* the TA?"

I nod. I smile. I am trying to be engaging. Two women students walk into the room. They sit down, open bookbags. They are waiting for the prof.

"My name is Ken. I'm a senior. Joe Brown is the teacher, he's got an office across the hall, and he'll be here any minute."

I nod out the door, in the direction of Joe's office. Some people look. They don't see Joe. They don't even see his office. You can't see it. There are doors between here and there. I shrug and I smile, disarming, engaging. I am trying to set the right tone. The mood, the mindset. Just as the first page, the first paragraph, the first goddamn sentence of a story establishes the mood, sets the scene, prepares the reader, so does the first class unavoidably establish the foundation, the footing, the direction for what will— must—follow in suit. Step off on the wrong foot and you'll be limping for the rest of the term. Confirm certain operating assumptions of the students and you'll be fighting an image, a set of expectations, an authority which is implied—thought not necessarily imposed—by the teacher, and accepted by the students. You—teacher, student, or TA—are responsible for reinforcing this relationship, if you don't reject it at the start, and move to establish a more reasonable one.

So I sit there. They expect a *Humanities Professor,* and they're going to get a goddamn *Humanities Professor,* unless we—that is, Joe and I— straighten things out at the start. So I say,

"This is a writing course, but it's not only a writing course. It's called *Writing and Experience,* and that means it's about you. Each of you. This is your course. We won't give you any assignment based on 'the material.' *You're* the material. If you want, Joe and I will be equal participants in that process. We'll write and try to share parts of our lives with you. We'd like that. But it's up to you. You tell us what you want. What we want is to get to know you, at least a little. I'm Ken. I like to write and I like to read people's writing. Who are you?"

They mostly look at me. One woman looks wide-eyed, without blinking, watching me like a hypnotized woman watches a gleaming swinging watch. I know, because I move somewhat as I speak, and her eyes and head move from side to side with me. It makes me stop. I wonder what they are hearing. (A hypnotized woman watches the watch, but what does she see? Can she read the time? Is she even listening to me?) Some of them look out the door, waiting for the prof. Waiting for Joe.

We talk for a while—mostly me, asking what kind of class they think this will be, what kind of classes they've had in high school, what they think of MIT, where they're living, where they're from, what they want to do in this class, this semester, this institution, this city, this life. Small talk. Small jokes. Still an overriding sense of anticipation: When Will We Get Going, When Will the Professor Appear, What's Going On Here? They are talking—and not just to me: talking to each other, as well—but not much. Killing time. Trying to put something on the first bare pages of their virgin spiral notebooks. Some questions about phone numbers and office hours and my suggestion that they think about what they'd like from the class, followed by silence, blank stares, followed almost immediately by my own suggestions of possibilities, opportunities, alternative ways to work the course.

After a while I pass around my legal pad and look about the room. Ten, twelve people. We have no idea what size class to expect. I decide to go for Joe.

I stand up, smile, say something no one notices, and step toward the door. There is a chair between me and the door. I can step over it or go around. I am feeling energetic, charged—able to leap tall buildings in a single bound—.

I lean forward, lower my shoulders, pump my legs up and down in the manner of a sprinter. Idle looks, casual interest. Then I take off—one, two, three—up in the air, land on the chair, and spring up and out higher and further . . . *Beautiful,* a meteoric ascent, almost straight up and slightly forward, through the doorway and into the *SMASH*!!!!!!

Not through the doorway.

Not into the hall.

The doorframe dents inward, upward, under the impact of my skull. I bounce back, down, rebounding like a ballbearing on an oil drum. The small talk stops. They all look at me. Concern. Fear? Apprehension, my way. Someone, a big basketball-looking fellow, stands up and strides toward me. Absolute, cemetery silence. I know I have succeeded, at least a little. I notice the silence. That means they were talking. My head rings and sings and my scalp is on fire. My skull is a bell. My migraine will bury itself in my brain and fester. My world will be red, purple, orange, streaked with the changing raging colors of pain.

Ten or a dozen open mouths, twenty or more open eyes. One open head. I touch it. My hair is dry. No blood. A good sign. I stand up.

"Low doorframe," I say, and smile. Weakly. Wanly. Winningly. I hope. What a way to show I'm human—that ought to destroy the authority, the image of power. I stagger out to Joe's office, my head swimming.

Behind me, a babble of voices rises in the room.

"Did you *see* that?"

"What a *sound*!"

"Holy Fuck I thought he'd never stand up . . . "

Well, at least I gave them something to talk about. Maybe I even got them excited. That's my role.

We spend the rest of the class talking, explaining to them that this is *their* class. I refrain from rubbing my head. Joe tells them to call him Joe. When I wince, I try to contort it into a smile.

For part of the period we divide into pairs—dyads, Dr. Schultz, psychologist-author of *Joy*, would call them—where one person tries to get to know one other person. We return to this theme later in the term. In maybe a month, we write our names on paper and drop them in a hat, then draw out another name. The names we draw are our "subjects"—the starting points for pieces—prose, poems, possibly even plays inspired by our subjects. Author and subject anonymity are allowed. There is no due date.

[In December, a student submits a long story about a likable clutz. I like the story. I identify with the character. I ask her who the subject might have been. She grins and points to me. Then she looks embarrassed and leaves. She and her friend walk out, giggling. They don't hit their heads on the doorframe. I am unaccountably pleased.]

At the end of the hour and a half, in that first class, Joe gives them an assignment. Smarterbook—think of a place you know. But we don't want to limit them. So I add, "That's only a suggestion, you know. We want you to write something, but you decide what that will be. If there's something you really want to say, then write about that, regardless of what it is. It doesn't have to be about a place—though most things happen in places. If you have nothing specific that you want to say, or write, try writing about a place you know. You can use the Smarterbook—all or part of it—but you don't have to. Use it as a guide, a set of suggestions, directions—but don't do anything if you don't want to. We don't want forced writing. Far better to work on your calculus, your physics or chemistry. I can't believe you'll get through three problem sets a week without daydreaming at least once. Wait until that happens. When you notice you're daydreaming—when you've been staring at a problem set or the wall for a while, but your mind hasn't been there—try writing about where you've been. Anywhere at all—real or imagined. Your subconscious is telling you something. Listen. There's obviously some other place where you'd rather be. Write about that."

They stand there, books in arms, bottled up against the doorway. They want to leave, but they're waiting for me to finish. I wonder if I'm speaking English. When I got my migraine in July, it caused aphasia. I knew what I was saying, but no one else could understand. Am I spewing forth gibberish? I stop and smile. Joe says *ciao,* and they flow out.

We watch the procession—recession?—and begin to relax. This is going to be a long semester. Joe stretches and groans and looks at the ceiling. I've never seen him so satisfied so early in the semester.

"You know, Ken, that wasn't nearly as painful as I expected."

First Class

DAVID WRAY

I didn't know how to be a TA. I thought I did when I asked to be one. I studied for a month all the things I thought would help me. I talked with Joe Brown, the professor, I thought up exercises, I reviewed in my mind the virtues of good teachers and the faults of bad ones. I did everything I could think of to change me from being me, to being an authority able to teach freshmen how to write, all the while hiding from myself what I was doing. I was terrified of going into my first class and being judged.

Thinking back on that first class I realized that I just didn't have the courage to face it without crutches. I wanted power, authority, and skill, and I didn't know where to get any of them. So I did the next best thing as far as I was concerned. I tried to counterfeit them.

The first thing I do in any scary situation is collect advice. The more scared I am, the more advice I collect. And the more advice I collect, the more sure I become that I won't be able to succeed, so I waste my time massaging that advice, memorizing all my frightened brain will hold. With my first class I wasn't taking any chances so I copied advice down verbatim. I figured that whether I thought I understood the advice or not, there was a chance that knowing the exact words at the right time in class might make their complete meaning clear and useful to me. Of course advice is rarely this useful, but useless activity is a comfort, and I have yet to ask anyone and be refused advice.

I plan, too. When I'm scared I do enough planning for ten people, doing my best to figure out all the possibilities.

I was over at Joe's house one day, asking him for advice, when he made a motion with his head as if to say, "These questions are fun but let's get to work." And then he asked, "Dave, what are YOU going to do with *your* first class?"

I was speechless . . . for five seconds, then I almost asked his advice. Then I thought, "This will never do. When he asks me a question like that I have to give an answer." So I started to think out loud in the following way[1]: "Now let's see, the goals of the first class should be to start people

---

1. Planning for a course in this way is another useless activity. Any course that attempts to use individual experience as a base must be open in ways not allowed by behavior designed to control what happens. For success, everyone in class has to take a share of the responsibility for the course by being honest, by being themselves—and that's hard for everyone, too. [DW]

2. This is the first time I've seen anyone own up to hating an unknown class. I've never experienced my pre-class feelings that way, but once I came upon some notes I had written myself long before about what I wanted to tell a first class about the course. They were written with incredible venom. I had no idea that I approached *anyone* that hostilely, let alone a class. Fear and hatred often masquerade as each other. [ND]

toward knowing one another and to generate feelings X and Y. If the class is A, then we'll hit 'em with exercises G and F, and then we'll close with a discussion of H. But if the class is B instead, then we really ought to do J the whole time. Oh, and we ought to tell them right away that no matter what, we expect them to do L,M,N,O, and P by the end of the term." We had many planning sessions like this, and even if they didn't prove exceptionally useful, for the most part we enjoyed them.

The only preparation that really did help me was doing writing with friends and experimenting along with them in things like Joe Brown's writing clinics and Ken Skier's taped story-telling sessions. We were doing things that were important to us, and we learned a lot about the learning of writing. I knew that if I ever got hard up for something to do in class, if none of the advice or plans were working, then all I'd have to do would be to introduce something that I did with my friends. I counted on this heavily for the class because I assumed out of hand that the students would be interested in the same things I was.

The only good thing about the preparation that I did for the course was that not all of it was useless. It usually turned out that things I considered exciting were useful while the tedious work that I did—well, I guess the only person it ever hurt was me.

Anyway, I'm human. I try hard doing whatever I'm doing, and I was worried about going into something new. I was scared. I thought, "It's my responsibility to see that these people learn something, and it's my responsibility to have something to give them. Maybe I'm really qualified. More likely I'm good at some things and bad at others, but maybe I'm so ill prepared that it's going to be a joke and I'll spend the whole term coming to class and trying to hide my ignorance."

The first day dawns and I hate my class-to-be so much that my face tends to color with rage. I say I'm embarrassed. Joe calls it stage fright.[2]

We meet an hour before the class for reasons which lose themselves in the rising tide of fear that I am coming to feel. Instead of pacing, I had turned to writing poetry, this being the only thing I could do that would calm me enough to keep sitting.[3]

"Maybe you ought to read them your poem, Dave, to show them how you're feeling."

---

3. Dear Elizabeth,

I'm sitting before my professor's door, the one for whom I'll TA. It's an hour till the time (I'll fill it with rhyme) when I'll sample the didactic trade. "Am I nervous?" you ask with a grin, as you view my body a-quiver. "I'm not nervous!" comes a voice through the din of teeth all pounding and chattered.

So I'm sitting here waiting for the prof to get back—and lo through the door come he, and what do you know right down to his toe, why he's just as nervous as me. "What good will it do to sit here and stew, afraid of just a few freshmen?" he asks from experience though he acts just as tense, his fingers make "snap" goes his inkpen. [DW]

"I don't want to do that, Joe."

"OK. Well. It's time for us to head down to the room."

"Do you think they'll be early?"

"I don't know. Sometimes they are."

I grab my shoulder pack like it's a security blanket. Inside there's a notebook with an outline on the first page. Each entry of the outline is a key word or phrase for a body of information in my head. Everything I have come to believe about being a teacher falls somewhere on the outline. When I'm nervous when it's my turn to speak, that piece of paper will tell me what to do. I feel as prepared as I'm ever going to be.

There were three people in the class at 1:30, which startled me. I was reminded that I had no idea how many people were coming. The chairs were arranged in a circle, and no one was sitting next to anyone else. There were seats for maybe thirty people. Joe said, "Hi," and sat on one side of the room. I was silent and chose to sit next to the door. Class was supposed to start at 1:30. Damn it, where is everybody?

"My name is Joe Brown, and this is 21.024, Writing and Experience. This is David Wray, my teaching assistant."

The silence fell sharply as I rummaged through my pack for my notebook. "I think we're missing some people, Joe. How many are registered, anyway?"

"I don't know. The computer broke down so they couldn't send around those enrollment sheets like they usually do. Do you suppose they sent everyone to the wrong room?"

"I don't know. What should we do?"

"Well, we ought to see who comes here, at least. Start a sheet of paper around so people can sign it. Here, pass this around and give it to people as they come in."

"Should we talk about the course now?"

"We might as well. Why don't you talk to get things going?"

Four pairs of eyes looked at me expectantly, and advice seemed to flit through my mind. [*Advice:* Establish your presence immediately. Say something even if it's as insignificant as making a joke while erasing the board.] I had to fumble with my notebook. "Put your class, address, and phone number on the sheet, and indicate whether or not you're on Pass/Fail." That seemed innocuous enough, but already two people started to glance out the window, and one of them was Joe. In the air I felt a tension as if power were balancing between Joe and myself. Suddenly I knew that if I'm going to get people to listen to me at all this term, I'd better get them to listen to me now. I noticed that I had the beginning of a headache. Then I found the outline that I was looking for.

"This is going to be a continuation of the class last term except for some minor changes. We've increased the page requirement"—three groans went as one—"and we're going to try to make available some new techniques in fiction writing such as role-playing and storytelling." There were no groans, but no one was interested, either. I regretted that I hadn't made a good news-bad news joke.

"How many pages do we have to write?" asked the student with the bushy beard.

"And what's your office number?" asked the woman.

"Do we have to type our papers?" queried someone else.

Before I could answer these dubious signs of interest, the beard refocused his eyes from looking outside and suggested that we write our names, room number, and other information pertinent to the course on the blackboard so they could fill out their roll cards. That way we wouldn't have to repeat ourselves as more people came in. Two students walked in as if to punctuate his remarks.

Good suggestion. Joe looked at me to see if I would get up because I was closer to the board, . . . but I wouldn't do it. I was too hung up on trying to swing the situation round to initiate the rigid plans I'd designed with such care. So while Joe got up to perform the necessary task, I studied my outline trying to figure how to get us to a writing exercise. [*Advice:* Get the students working right away.]

I ignored Joe writing on the board, and said, "We didn't think that the page requirement last term would be enough for you now that you've had a little experience, so we thought we'd increase it to thirty-five pages." Five students wrote this fact in their notebooks. Three sighed and two groaned. One of the new boys passed the sign-up sheet to two girls just coming through the door. Joe smiled a welcome, and I went on, "We're going to count the pages according to the MIT standard page"—more groans and a "What's that?"—"We'll set the number of words you can put on a page with double-spaced pica type as equaling one page. Then you can turn your pages in to us in any form you want as long as we can count the words. But the best form . . ." Bush-beard was waving his hand agitatedly, "Yes?"

"Can we make that MIT standard page with really wide margins?" He looked proud of himself for that question.

I wanted to be reasonable. I said, "Look, all we're doing is saying that you can hand the stuff in to us any way you want, and that we want you to do some fair amount of writing."

"But I don't think that thirty-five pages is fair. It might be OK for some people, but I'm taking some heavy lab courses this term. All you wanted last term was twenty-five pages. I don't think it's fair increasing the requirement like that in a course that freshmen have to take."

And someone else said, "Yeah!"

I didn't know what to do. So I got a little angry and said, "This is your class. How do you want to run it?" And nobody said anything to that.

I think one reason those first few classes were so bad was because I always thought in terms of an us and a them, and Joe and I were *us*. It had to be either my way or theirs. I'd try to sell them on my thing only to fail, because we didn't have common goals in the course. And when it came to choosing which goals to respect, mine or theirs, I always chose mine because of their obviously superior merits.

Much that should have been discussed the first day was not spoken, and much that was said was not heard. I don't think that this is something inherent in the teacher-pupil relationship, but I do believe that it is a part of any master-slave relationship. Non-communication will always result whenever one human being tries to control another.

People kept dribbling in after that for the entire class. We found out later that there were many scheduling difficulties in the process of being resolved. Students were sometimes trying to decide between our class and someone else's, or they came to talk to Joe to find out if they could take the course by doing the writing without coming to class. They didn't want to talk about the great new things that we could offer them. They'd been able to survive last term, and new things could only complicate their lives and be dangerous. They might not like them. But when I saw what a disaster the class was becoming—their fault, of course—I let fly with my ace-in-the-hole. I told them of the wonderful new experiments we were going to do this term.

I told them about storytelling sessions, where a person could tell a ten-page story before he could finish one glass of wine, and how this made page requirements something not even to consider. I told them of writing exercises that were fun to do and never failing in their ability to loosen bound creativity. Even Joe told them that he'd discovered some new things that he was looking forward to trying this term. But the class remained cold with mostly everyone looking bored or hostile.

They didn't like anything we told them. Besides that, Joe had to constantly introduce me as people came in. Otherwise they tended to ignore me, and that bothered me. I was bothered so much that I was ready to consider myself a failure and shut up if I hadn't gotten help in a most unlooked for way.

It was just about the end of class which had swelled to the size of fifteen people, thirteen men and two women, and a third woman walked into the room. A beautiful woman with dark hair and light green laughing eyes who came into the room like a gay forest breeze on a somber meadow.

Talking had stopped. I guess we were all pretty discouraged. So when she asked, "Is this 21.024?" it was bush-beard who welcomed her to the class and motioned her to a nearby chair.

Someone who had gotten the hang of things by then got up and said, "This is Joe Brown, and that's Dave Wray over there, his TA." Then the guy looked around the room, took a deep breath, and said, "My name's Bob. I've been trying to write a book for a month." He sat down.

A girl across the room stood up and said, "My name's Susan and I've never been able to write at all, but I want to learn," then she sat down.

And so introductions moved around the room tapering slowly into talk about writing and about what people were doing. I was very surprised to discover how interested some people were in what I was doing. I started to feel good about the class.

Joe asked if anyone had brought anything to the class that they wouldn't mind reading out loud. There was a ripple of heads turning to see if anyone would volunteer, and I thought, "Damn, I hope Joe doesn't want me to read my poem." But I was saved by the girl with the green eyes.

She said, "I have something, maybe," and then looking over to me, "but I hope you're not like the TA we had last term."

Shocked, I asked her, "Why?"

"Well, he was a real sex maniac. He saw sex in practically everything I did."

"Well, was there?" I asked.

She smiled an exquisite look of haughty contempt in reply, then she made as though to read one of several pages in her hands. A few people sat up in interest.

When she read she seemed to be talking to me, and the images that flowed out were: "Waves lapping, licking" at her body, sending "pulsing, panting pleasure, pouring" through her mind. She said it was all about a sailing trip she had taken the week before, and I said I thought it was all about sex.

She laughed, but a lot of people wanted to talk about this. I told them just exactly where I saw sexual allusions and just exactly what I thought they alluded to, and people got very excited. They raised their voices and several tried to talk at once. And some of them appealed to Joe for help against my opinions, but Joe saw sex in the story that even I couldn't see, and before I knew it a lively, interesting debate was going on.

More people came in. We talked some more, and we barely had time left to do some free writing before the class ended. (You should have heard the bitching when we stopped the discussion to do free writing.) Anyhow, the class ended and I had to extricate myself from all the people asking questions, so I could rush off to a class in which I was a student. Joe congratulated me on the day's success.

The point of all this is not that "sexy coeds" are necessary to give writing classes their proper starts, but rather, it's just plain unpredictable how a class is going to turn out until it's over. It happened that this class really got going because of Green-eyes, but maybe that's because the beginning was so uncomfortable for everyone that we were ready to exploit the slightest excuse for relief. The virtues of the class that made such escape possible were commitment and flexibility. We were committed to explore only things people cared about, and we were flexible enough to follow through with our commitment no matter where it might lead us.

First Class

PETER ELBOW

I can't remember the actual class very clearly. Though as a matter of fact I remember one girl in it. The class was two years ago. I keep running into her on campus in the interim. Saying hello very smilingly. At one point in the class—in the middle—I suggested that we all go off with one person and talk. Get to know them a bit. I got her. Or she got me. We strolled around outside for 15 minutes. She was very pretty. Seemed very self-assured. We made conversation. The next day I learned from the person in charge of the program that she had strongly requested a change of seminars and that he'd given it to her.

But I shouldn't make a joke of it.

It was my first class at Evergreen. What we did wasn't very important, and what they were like—on that day—is all an unremembered blur. (Though I do remember them from later in the term when they emerged to me as people and I got to know them.) I tried to do sort of "loosening up" or "getting to know people" activities. I was very nervous. The only thing I remember—and with some pleasure—was when I suggested that we all lie on the floor and close our eyes and just rest and breathe and listen. That was a relief. Not to have to deal with each other. That brought the panic down to the level of being able to be felt.

But what I do remember strongly—if not clearly—was the feeling. Because later on that day I stopped to write about it. The panic. The feeling that they all knew what they wanted, they all knew what they were doing. They were sitting there waiting for some teacher to do something to them. They seemed so assured.

As I close my eyes I remember the utter dread. It's not that I mistook them for being *literally* more powerful or smart than I. But in terms of guts or vibrations it seemed that they could utterly scorn me. In my dreams they would turn up as people who would hold me up, beat me, blackmail me, get me into a dark alley, rape me, rob my house when I'm gone, rape my wife. *They* are the people with the power, the leverage.

As the term goes on, reality would creep in and gradually they would become real people and I wouldn't any longer be putty in their hands—and they tyrannical. Not again till some new class with new unknown people— or till I had certain dreams—would that tyrannical panic return.

A Vigorous Educational Experience

STEWART SILLING

My first class at MIT began with Joe Brown introducing himself, pacing up and down in front of the blackboard, looking seedy in a scholarly way. With a tiny fragment of chalk he wrote his name on the blackboard. I wrote "21.023" on the cover of my MIT spiral notebook and opened it to the first page. I wrote down his name. Brown said something about a teaching assistant, a junior, sitting in the back of the room. Brown wrote "Ken Skier" on the board, and I copied it down.

Brown handed out a stack of nicely xeroxed papers and made us move our desks into small clusters in order to discuss Building 7, one of MIT's domes. I thought that idea was crap, but I went along with it. I felt that this kind of awkwardness served no pedagogic purpose, and the teacher was trying some cute teacher trick to get us to talk to each other.

I certainly had no interest in talking to any of them. I wanted to sit in the class and learn, to be taught something. The groups began to aggregate, and I stood around and gawked like the leftover kid when we had to choose up sides for dodgeball back at PS 114. I finally squeezed into Ken's group.

And did we introduce ourselves? Did we tell a little bit about ourselves? We did. We then proceeded to a pointless and uncomfortable discussion of Building 7. Brown cut the discussion short with an announcement that he "would like us to try some free writing." Oh boy, a composition. I was good at those.

The rules for free writing turned out to be that we had to write continuously, without even lifting up our pens, until told to stop. This kind of writing was not exactly my idea of freedom. My God, I thought, what these people won't do to make us spontaneous.

Writing it was misery, and boring. It felt like signing some kind of irreversible contract. I felt doomed to embarrassment. I pictured this hot-shot literary smarty-pants professor smirking at the papers, sneering at our clumsiness, our inability to think or express. I figured I had nothing to say, so at least I would make mine formally correct, and I took long pauses to organize and sharpen up my sentences. Brown had jocularly told a few people not to stop, but he left me alone. (This was encouraging. Teachers who appear to sense that you think they're acting stupid often turn out to be good.) He vacillated on the matter of handing in the papers, so I snuck out at the end of the class and tore mine up.

Linda was the only girl in the class. She chain-smoked, which annoyed me from the beginning. I hate smoke. I hated it when my father smoked. But I especially hated it when people smoked as glibly and brazenly as Linda did, every class, sitting on the floor in a half-lotus with her legs around an ashtray, constantly pecking at the cigarette with her finger.

Our first homework assignment was to write about "a place you know." That was by far the best writing assignment I had ever been given.

In fact, the way the assignment was worded was so kind as to be inspiring. I thought that anyone who would give assignments as cool as that couldn't be all bad, and I began to think that Brown had done those dumb tricks in class in the knowledge that they were only tricks. You see, my experience had been that teachers took those things seriously. They thought they were there to perform and to make the students perform. Thus, physics teachers showed filmstrips of roller skates with bricks on top of them racing down the street. My old English teacher's attempts at turning the class into an encounter group of sorts made her a laughingstock.

I wrote about the apartment building in the Bronx where I lived until I was 8. I was surprised to find that there was a subtle, good feeling in writing it. It was the first nonanalytical writing I had done since junior high. I wrote about the sound of the lights, the rows of hexagon tiles flickering and swirling, the coldness of the stone steps. I wrote about the same things that always flash through my mind when I think of my childhood. That's the satisfaction: getting it all down, being able to force it out of your memory and get it into English. Most of the time there's nothing to say, but when there is, it's delightful. I had a hint of that delight then.

Next class, we were in a new room, seated around one large table. Brown called for a volunteer to read his assignment. Nothing doing. Another call for a volunteer, another worried silence. This went on for several minutes, and at one point Brown said, "Are you waiting for me to call on someone?" Was he just trying to make us feel stupid and ashamed? It was obvious that we were all afraid that we would each be the worst in the class. It looked like Brown was trying to make us get used to reading by plunging right in, but his tactics seemed excessive.

I finally suggested that all the papers be put in a pile and that Brown pick one at random and read it. This was agreed to, and, much to our relief, the first paper truly stank. Then we were supposed to give our reaction to the piece. What reactions? It failed to affect anyone. There was nothing to say. We all sat silently.

We read about five papers that day, and none of them drew much response. Nobody had anything to say. The papers read at our next class were reacted to a bit more strongly, but most of the reactions consisted of trading anecdotes about things the writing reminded them of. There were pieces about the woods back home, the old high school football field, fantasy places, that sort of thing. I think I was one of the first people in the class to bring up a matter relating to writing itself. I said I didn't know what Linda meant when she said a New Hampshire mountain retreat was "a good place to get away from *The New York Times*." I really didn't know what she meant, although I think I do now. When I told her I didn't understand it, her reaction was typical of hers and some other people's throughout the term. She insisted that the open-minded and perceptive reader *should* know what she meant. But she didn't even say that directly. She said, "Oh, come one, everybody knows what that means." I found this irritating.

By the time the class got around to my piece, I had already begun to hate my writing. I thought my piece was better than anyone else's, but I still hated it. This was a problem that was to continue: a few days after I wrote anything, I always despised it. I wished it would go away, although I never actually tore up a finished piece of writing. I felt my writing was unfair to me. It took so much out of me, but no one could understand what I was writing about, and I knew it. Even if it was better written than anyone else's, it made me vulnerable, subject to all kinds of embarrassments. It could give the class the wrong impression about me. They might think I was out to impress the teacher, or I was artsy-fartsy, or I thought I was better than they because I wrote in a sad, personal tone instead of the usual buddy-buddy straight talk. I was not writing for them.

I was very nervous, but I think I did a decent job of reading it. When I was finished, no one said anything. They sat around looking bored.

Eventually, Brown said to the class, "Do you get any feelings about the place? Does it seem menacing? I think I sensed that menacing aspect of it." That made me feel somewhat better; I had elicited a reaction.

"Does anyone sense that?" Brown said. No, they did not. They just sat there.

Finally, one young man in a cowboy hat said, "It's too bad it had to come near the end, if you want a response. I think you came out on the short end on that. I mean we've been listening to so many of these things." Fuck you, I thought, then don't waste my time.

The class moved again, this time to cozy old Building 20, a cheap wooden structure put up in World War II as a temporary barracks. We had no assignments after that, just a 26-page requirement for the term. The next piece I wrote was a description of a man walking through the snow in the country.

With that piece of writing, I inadvertently forced the issue of style on the class. The piece seemed quite sensible to me when I wrote it, but some members of the class were unwilling to accept several of my phrases. For example, a few people, including Linda, said that they did not know what I was talking about when I said the man's footsteps in the snow sounded "electronic" and that my comparison of the taillights of a passing car to sunglasses was without redeeming social value. It so happened that the idea of stoplights on a car looking like sunglasses had occurred to me when I was about seven and had remained dormant in my mind until I wrote the piece. Thus, I felt comfortable with the idea. And I wanted it there on the piece of paper. I told the class that I didn't think those particular comparisons were unreasonable. Ken said they sounded like things that I might think, but they didn't really fit the character who thinks them in the story. But the character was myself, a fact which I denied to myself but really knew all along.

I was acutely aware that what Linda was criticizing me for was the same thing as what I had criticized her for. Thus, the discussion introduced another problem for me: If two different people criticize different pieces of writing for the same fault, does it mean that both comments are valid and that the pieces of writing are equally bad? I wanted to believe that my writing was better than Linda's even though both of us drew similar reactions in class. Linda's "strained metaphors" seemed oily and presumptuous in their conception, but I was trying very hard to make my metaphors, which some people called strained, likable. I looked at other people's writing and thought it was shallow and dishonest, and I wondered if that was what my writing looked like to them. And, if so, were they right?

My writing was not that important to me, although it contained some important thoughts. I just disliked having to put myself in a humiliating situation in front of a particular group of MIT freshmen of whom I was becoming less and less fond.

One day Ken told me that he sensed that I wasn't getting the kind of response I wanted and suggested that the class might not be a good audience for me. He said that not everyone can write for just any group of people and that I should try to find someone I wanted to be read by. He said he knew from experience that having to write for a class which you feel doesn't know what you're doing can be unpleasant. I said that writers can't pick their audiences, so mine might as well be them. I thought writing was a means of communication solely for the benefit of the reader. Thus, I temporarily became convinced that it was all my fault that the class was a bad audience for me.

I was particularly annoyed at Linda. More than anyone else in the class she demanded more from me than she gave. She seemed hurt or resentful whenever I said that something in her writing was unclear or implied that I didn't like it, but she herself was not a sincere reader. She wanted every feeling in my writing laid out in a way that would always get her involved immediately. She always compared my feelings to her experiences. ("What do you mean? I never felt that.") She would not let my writing across her well-guarded boundaries (or, alternatively, my writing was not strong enough to get across), while I usually tried to take her writing into me and let it mingle with my own feelings.

Actually, I liked Linda. There were some things about her that I couldn't stand, but she was all right. I liked Joe (that's what I found out I was supposed to call him). I liked Ken. Joe didn't use any classroom tricks anymore, except for some anonymous Kafka that he slipped in once.

Around the middle of October, Joe asked me what I thought of the way the course was going. I said I wished I could get the class to react to writing more strongly. I said that although some of Linda's comments were objectively valid, I felt she had no right to say them. Joe frowned at that statement, and I felt pretty stupid after I said it. It seemed like a childishly inconsistent remark, although on thinking it over I can't seem to find the inconsistency. It appeared to contradict the assumed premise that everyone is supposed to say what they think. It's a free country, right? And I said what I thought about her writing, right? Not really, I later decided. When I made comments about someone's writing I was always very careful not to make my remarks appear dogmatic, sarcastic, egotistical, bitchy when technical, or personal. I felt that Linda's comments about my writing were not good-natured, they often made me feel bad, and they were usually wrong anyway, so why doesn't she just shut up.

Joe said, "If you could tell the class something about them, what would it be? That they're stupid?" I thought he was being sarcastic. I was afraid that Joe was suggesting that I had misinterpreted the bored silence of the class, thus making me stupid.

I answered, "Maybe just that they're not concentrating," showing polite tolerance. I didn't think it was proper to tell the professor I hated the guts of some of his disciples. Well, damn it, they were stupid, some of them. Their high school ambition and competitiveness had already changed to nerdliness and grossness, and they sat around the edge of the room, thinking about their own narrow interests or fantasizing, smirking at anyone who cared about anything as "trivial" as art.

This dim view, however, does not apply to everyone in the class. There were several who were interested in literature, or just nice people. Unfortunately, I couldn't find an audience among them either.

It was getting to be around the end of the term, and I handed in my major work for the term, a 20-page story about three high school kids wandering around the country. It was written in the first person, but the narrator ends up going to Berkeley, while the other two go to MIT. After three months of talking about writing, people in the class still called the narrator "you" in the discussion. ("Why did you kiss her?") No one cared too much about the story, but I had become resilient to that. By then, I was writing for myself, although I liked Joe and Ken to read my stuff.

I wrote on my Freshman Evaluation Form that 21.023 was the only class I took in which I learned anything "meaningful." Rather than teaching me something, it caused me to learn from myself. Although I did not think of myself as a good writer after the course, I didn't need to, because I had found that the most important effect of writing is on the writer. The course helped me mature into an observing, functioning human. I had learned a way of expression, a craft, a means of communication, even a weapon. I considered Joe and Ken to be friends.

Another result of my taking the course was my introduction to the MIT writing community, mainly through open readings. Many of the people at open readings could write beautifully and they were, in general, nice people. But they were always depressed, wrapped up in some unexplained sadness. Even though MIT was probably a lousy place for them, I felt that they were overlooking the humorous aspects of things.

I might mention that I won a prize for a story I wrote for the class, and I received a check and postcard at a luncheon they had. The postcard had a very nicely engraved picture of an old lady, Ellen King, for whom the prize was named. My "benefactress," Joe called her. On the way out, a writing professor looked at the card. She said the old lady looked like her urine would etch glass.

Free Writing in the Motor City

JEAN COLBURN

When I met Joe Brown in the summer of 1971 and heard about his writing classes at MIT, I had already been teaching at the Detroit Institute of Technology for two years. I had come to Cambridge with a group from my school to develop a new freshman program financed by an HEW grant for developing institutions, and my specific task was to work out a new freshman English course. When the DIT group learned that MIT gave only pass-fail marks to freshmen, we agreed to get rid of letter grades in our new program. This opened up for all of us possibilities of planning courses in which learning could be shared and cooperative rather than private and competitive.

In planning the new freshman English course, I liked Joe's ideas, but I had doubts about putting them into practice. I wanted to be realistic, and standards seemed a much more pressing concern at a small inner-city college like mine than at MIT. I looked at a first set of brief papers that a freshman class of Joe's had written. They were rather ordinary, but there were almost no sentence fragments, misspelled words, wrong verb tenses. (None lapsed into incoherence.) It was all very well to say there were more important things in writing—I certainly believed that. But how was I to help students solve problems with basic writing skills—ones that I knew would cause them difficulties in other classes and later in jobs—if I stopped pointing out these errors to them with my red pencil? Students at MIT, I thought, were going to make it regardless of the kind of instruction they received in freshman English. I had been hearing about their high SAT scores, and even an MIT drop-out has a certain cachet. DIT had some excellent students, but it also had many who had real difficulty with the reading and writing college courses demand. And what Joe was proposing didn't seem to provide any direct means to solve the problems presented by the freshman writing I knew.

I've heard these kinds of doubts voiced by other teachers. I still think they are based on valid concerns. But there were other concerns, too, and these ultimately influenced me to try something new, not just to re-package the standard, traditional course I had been teaching. I liked the DIT students, and, like most teachers, wanted to help them as much as I could. I identified with them because, like me, many were from working class families. They were a good mix of race and background and I liked their urban savvy, but I knew that ultimately this "smartness" would have little effect on their making it, and making it was important to them, for many saw college as a way to escape the assembly line or the unemployment line. I was convinced that much of the education these students had received and were continuing to receive fostered passiveness and lack of awareness about what they could or might be able to do. Moreover, the formal written assignments and class recitations were accomplishing far too little in giving them the verbal poise and agility that are important to making it.

Talking to Joe made me begin to see that these concerns I had about students were not incompatible with my concerns about their writing problems. Indeed, he argued, the two goals supported each other. I still didn't see quite how the mechanics of this would work in the actual classroom situation, but I—like, I suspected, many of my students—also didn't see the relevance of a good deal that I had been doing in the freshman English course, one taught from a departmental syllabus and based on the reading and discussion of anthologized essays with subsequent preparation by students of 500-word themes.

Part of my feeling about the lack of relevance was those 500-word themes. It had struck me during my own student days that those papers had no importance other than satisfying course requirements, that the genre was purely artificial. If the purpose was to get practice in writing clearly and coherently, then one could just as well practice by writing a short story or a business letter or whatever seemed important at the time. If the purpose was to develop analytical skills, then one could do this, at least in freshman courses, in a discussion where everyone's ideas were tested and argued at the moment. All of the writing in my freshman courses—to say nothing of the hours I spent "correcting"—left nothing more to show at the end of the semester than another drawer of "dead" files. Of course, most of the students learned something, but almost none were ever interested enough in the papers they wrote that either they—or I—ever wanted to look at them again. This seemed like little return for the labor involved. Especially for working class students—who seldom questioned the writing of these papers —it was another exercise in doing what you had to do, but with little sense of getting something out of it for yourself. As with assembly line work, the paycheck at the end of the week (or the grade at the end of the course) seemed disconnected from what was produced.

And the hours I spent grading these themes had gradually become nightmarish. I imagined amassing a huge collection of rubber stamps and arranging them on hooks. Then I could quickly scan each paper, pull down the appropriate stamps—"transition lacking," "watch sentence fragments" —finish a stack of themes in an hour and have Sunday for myself. But even the fantasy was depressing. I would be using the same stamps week after week on the same students' papers. And the whole futile exercise was slowly driving me up the wall, for I found myself reading student papers not so much for content as to point out errors—errors that were in fact often egregious.

I was also bothered that I alone was the audience for most of the writing students did. They saw me, at least in my role as corrector and grade-giver, as "the English teacher," and they were full of misinformation about what that meant, probably because many of them had little experience with really trying to communicate well. A student would sometimes complain that he had given me what I "wanted" on a paper, so why didn't I "like" it and give him something better than a C? If I pointed out that his arguments were illogical, his generalizations unsupported, his reply was that *I* after all had encouraged him to express his own ideas. The student was like the stereotyped used car salesman, convinced that only persuasion and a bit of bullying were needed to make the deal, that concern about the condition of the car (or the theme) was not only irrelevant but a positive distortion of the situation. This didn't happen often though; many students accepted C's in English as a fact of life.

Another aspect of the 500-word theme syndrome that troubled me was that I assigned the topics. These were related in some way to the assigned reading, and students were given several to choose from. It wasn't that my topics weren't good ones; I had often spent a good deal of time on them—watching especially that they required extreme ingenuity to plagiarize a paper on. But I knew that once I had the topics worked out I had already done an important part of the assignment for the students. My own experience was that often the hardest part of writing is figuring out what to write about and what approach to use. And though I tried hard to give topics that would appeal to students, I knew very well that often they didn't.

So that summer of 1971, with the help of Joe Brown, I planned a new first-semester English course for freshman, one that would attempt to resolve some of my dissatisfactions with the standard course. That initial plan was a fairly complex one, allowing students options and incorporating some of what seemed "essential" features of the old course, for example, assigned reading. Looking back, I see that I gave many options because I was uncertain of what would work. To change a course radically makes one question all the assumptions about requirements, but I at least find that some requirements are necessary. Like it or not, colleges are in the business of certification, and it is too late when faced with the final grade sheet to decide what a student should have done to earn credit hours. My concern was that a student by the end of the course be clearly at a point that he could have a decent chance of passing the next English course or any course in which there were essay exams. Moreover, it seemed to me that whatever requirements there were had to apply to all the students, that any other scheme would involve judgments on my part that would be difficult to interpret and defend. Shifting from one set of assumptions to another about requirements and what were necessary ingredients for the course took me some months and was very often a trial and error process in which students were involved. When in doubt, I tended to fall back on what I had done in the standard course, and the students invariably objected.

So the first week of the new course, instead of outlining for students what qualities I wanted them to strive for in their writing, I asked them to come up with a list of qualities that they wanted their own writing to have. Because many of the students in the program that first year had low grade point averages from inner-city Detroit high schools, I didn't expect much. But this is the list they worked out.

1. Good arrangement
2. The parts should be connected together to give meaning to the final version
3. The beginning should give the purpose
4. Important ideas should be expanded
5. Meaning should be clear
6. Spelling, punctuation, and grammar should be all right

It had never occurred to me as I read those terrible first papers I often got from students that even the weakest of them had a fair notion of what decent writing was. They had evidently picked this up from previous teachers and, I suspect, simply through the example of the reading they had done. They already knew the principles that I had been struggling so hard in the past to explain. The problem was that most of them had never seen much reason to practice them. But they knew that in this new course not only the teacher but their fellow students would be reading their work.

The first week of classes in 1971, I also told the students I expected them to hand in something, if only a paragraph, at least once a week. They strongly objected to this. If it was their own class and their responsibility, they should be allowed to work in their own way, including the setting of their own deadlines. They had many priorities—math classes, children to attend to, jobs, etc.—and to meet deadlines would often mean just writing anything to comply with my rules. I reluctantly gave in. Nearly all of them that year and nearly all of them since then finished the requirements by the end of the semester.

Later, students asked about finishing the class early. Most of them were in self-paced math classes, and they had begun to see the advantage of planning ahead so that they could squeeze out additional time for other things. That seemed like a good idea to me, too, because it would reduce the size of the group during the last part of the semester when some of the students needed extra help. So now, when the course requirements are completed, the student is finished with the course except for an in-class paper during the final week evaluating his own work. A few finish during the ninth or tenth week of the sixteen-week semester and a few more finish before the end of the term. There is usually a flurry of work at the end of the semester, however, as many students complete their work.

While the original plan I made for the new course focused on writing, there was also required reading. In a more open atmosphere, students were freer in voicing their opinions about the readings than they had been in the standard course, and it seemed that at least a few were always dissatisfied with any given reading assignment. For example, early in the new course, some students asked me to order *The Hobbit* for the group. But some of the black students (and one white student) objected to the book because, they said, it was frivolous and had no relevance to the life of the ghetto. Objections to specific readings were not always by race or religion, but it seemed more often than not that the readings caused unnecessary hostility over unresolvable issues, like bussing or simply an author's right to use unfamiliar vocabulary, in a group which I hoped would work cooperatively. Also, the discussion of readings often seemed unnecessarily to divert the attention of the group from the real purpose of the course, which was their writing. Currently, I assign no reading at all, but many students ask me about books to read and in some cases I suggest to a student a book or article which seems particularly relevant to his writing. One of the results of concentrating entirely on the writing has been that the reading students do (and some do none) is pretty much individualized. Another result, one that I did not anticipate, is that students' reading is often primarily for the purpose of finding writing techniques that they can make use of in their work and they often become surprisingly sophisticated about technique.

A second feature of the new course that was eventually abandoned was the option which allowed students to participate in a group writing project rather than working on an individual project. One such group project worked out well: three students put together a substantial book of their own poetry titled "The Life Book" and distributed copies to everyone in the program. These three formed the nucleus for a poetry workshop that has been running successfully now for three years and which holds public readings and gets out a collection of work done in the group at least once a year. Another group that first year, while finally producing a "book," was not so successful. The twelve students involved struggled for more than half the semester before anything substantial was completed, and many felt that the final product was disappointing. The lack of success was, I think, a result of the unwieldy size of the group and of forming the group before students got to know one another. Their interests were divergent, and some had apparently joined to avoid responsibility, planning to let others do most of the organization and writing. Three of these twelve, however, later banded together to complete a writing project for another English course. During the second year of the program, group writing projects were again offered as an option, but because I did not actively organize such groups and because of the negative experiences of some of the first-year students, no one elected the option. Thus, after the first year, all students worked on individual projects, and these became the major feature of the course.

The form of the new course, after the elimination of the less successful features, is quite simple, but it solved some of my dissatisfaction with the standard course by providing—in fact, demanding—that students take a decisive part in the class. The new course includes several kinds of writing, including ten minutes of free writing most class sessions. In this writing, the students write for themselves and I am only the reader. And while students write on anything they want, these brief, frequent exercises inevitably provide me with a good deal of feedback on how the class is going. The free writing also gives me a running account—and reminder—of the students' lives and concerns apart from school. Because most of the students have to hold jobs, work is a common subject. For example:

> Today is the first day of class at DIT and I'm already writing. Ten minutes to put down anything that I want. I guess it's so we'll learn to write spontaneous but it's kind of hard after no writing all summer. . . .
> I better keep writing even though I don't have nothing to say because I have to pass all my classes. This might not be a bad schedule if I can get out of here and to work by 1:00.

Another student wrote:

> Working can be such a problem; at least now it has become one. I can't remember what it's like not to be working. From the time I left the eighth grade, I've always held a job. Let me add that it has not been easy. Strangely, no undue amount of pressure has arisen until the

present time. The problem is clear—the desire to put in more hours than is practical.

Still another student commented in a piece of free writing:

> I work hard at everything I do. Working with people is very important in today's society if you want to succeed. Success is. . . . in how well you work with people and how well people work with you. Working is a good way to communicate and relate feelings to other people. There are different kinds of work that usually are not considered work. School is mental work and some physical work, but to some people it's just something that has to be done . . . If I work hard in school maybe all the work done then will pay off by having mental work instead of physical work when finished with school. Society has a stereotype set up where . . . people are not successful unless doing more mental work than physical work.

The second kind of writing students do for the course is for their personal writing project. This is the major assignment for the semester and the main focus of the course. The project grew out of my feeling that students should have something to show for their work besides a grade. I thought this could best be achieved by each of them writing and producing a long work, one for which they had chosen their own subjects and their own form. Writing a book is not an uncommon fantasy, and quite a few students it turned out had a book in the back of their mind, although most of them had never thought they would write at least a short version of it.

I find it helpful for both me and the students to establish early in the semester some basic rules for these long papers. They are to be about only those things which students have some direct personal experience with. Students may make use of books they have read. One student, for example, discussed aspects of *Walden* to begin each section of his paper, then contrasted Thoreau's values to his own and those of the urban Americans he saw daily. But straight library research papers are unacceptable. The papers must be long enough (40 to 50 typewritten pages) to justify three semester-hours of credit. Students may work on their papers in any way that suits them, but the final version (which is in effect published, with one copy becoming the property of the program) must be in acceptable form, that is, reasonably neat and well-written, with acceptable organization, grammar, punctuation, etc. This means the student will probably have to do some revising and correcting. While resources are available to students to help them achieve a good final version, the responsibility for doing so is theirs. For example, if a student asks one of the tutors or me to check over his manuscript, we go over only a couple of pages of it with him, explaining problems. We then try to give the student some written material on the problems to take with him. The student is told that when he has attempted to correct six or eight pages of manuscript himself, he can check back with us so that he can be sure that he understands and can apply what he has been told. We resist student attempts to get us to correct or edit a manuscript. Some students obtain needed help from family members or someone they know at work, explaining that they feel more comfortable getting help there than from student tutors, although tutors are chosen not only on the basis of their proficiency in English but also because they can work well with students. We openly acknowledge that mothers and girl friends sometimes are willing to do this kind of work and that indeed they may even teach the writer of the paper some basics in trying to help him. Some students decide that in the end too much of such help is not entirely without its penalties, for an overzealous mother can correct the humor and the flavor right out of a paper.

Students find a variety of ways to organize their material for the papers. Some divide them into chapters or sections and some write only one lengthy essay. Some include poetry and photographs and drawings. All are encouraged to experiment with different kinds of writing. Perhaps the best evidence that these projects are more than just an assignment to students is that many make extra copies for themselves and for family and friends. One student who completed a chronologically arranged autobiography for the course three years ago keeps his life story current and adds another section every few months to the copy owned by the program.

Thus, in the new course, students themselves are responsible for the quality of their papers, including the simple mechanics of writing. Besides help from the tutors and me and family and friends, students have other kinds of help available. One kind is the in-class themes on set topics (impromptus) that I give about once a month, correcting them in pretty much the traditional manner, although no grades are assigned. The marking of a few in-class papers grew out of the insistence of a number of students that they wanted work in "grammar," and the papers are a substitute for the "drill" sessions which I ran for a time for those who wanted to come. (More than half of the students did.) These impromptus are more traditional an assignment than used by most of the people writing here, but their use eases my conscience about identifying for students in writing grammatical errors, sentence structure and organization problems that they might be having. This also gives me a look at students' writing early in the semester so that I can see that they get additional help they might need from me and tutors. In their final evaluation of the course, some students say that they find the writing of these in-class papers helpful, while others say they do not.

The major help available to students, however, is the opportunity to hear what other students are doing and in turn to get the group's reaction to sections of their own papers during the course of the semester. Class sessions are planned one to two weeks in advance, and the reading of sections is on a volunteer basis. Some students obviously enjoy reading to the group, but even the shyer students read, probably, because they see it as an opportunity to gain experience before a group in an informal atmosphere as well as getting the group's reactions to their writing. Almost all the students seem to feel that as a member of the group they should participate in what is going on. After some three years and ten sections of the course, only a couple of students have chosen not to read their work to the group at all.

How do students get started on their long papers once they have the full responsibility of choosing their own subject and working in their own way? After the first semester, when I had long papers that had already been completed, I spent some of our early sessions in reading or having a tutor read sections from previous papers. This began to give some students ideas. Students also often come in and spend some time reading through papers that have been completed in earlier semesters.

I also ask students in the first week to begin to jot down ideas for their projects—what they might be writing about, what form they plan to give their material—and we discuss these in class. Some students know exactly what they are going to do almost from the outset, but others talk a lot about having nothing to write about. Their lives, they say, are dull and boring. Nothing of interest has ever happened to them. I ask them what kinds of things they like to read and then point out to them that these often seem to derive their appeal from the fact they recount experiences similar to their own. Everyone agrees that this is true and they begin to plan to write about their families, their school experiences, etc., and in the weeks that follow, the discussion of papers often includes remarks about similar experiences. Some students pick topics that seem unpromising to me, but the results are often surprisingly interesting. While some students begin work on their projects the first week, others get themselves started by volunteering to read a section to the class. With this obligation made, they then are sure to have a few pages. And once started, they find that the writing comes easier.

Students generally find helpful the reading of sections of the long project in class and the subsequent discussion to identify lack of clarity, lack of concreteness, etc., and they early begin to think about how to make their papers interesting to their audience. The reading and discussions also help to broaden students' experience. Blacks and whites see that they have more in common than they might have thought, but they also become clearer about what their differences are and what these differences mean. We have a few foreign students and their papers invariably lead to many questions about customs and daily life in another culture.

Are the class discussions of the papers always lively and interesting? No. But students feel much more responsibility to keep things moving than they did when I was physically and psychologically at the front of the room. Sometimes when a paper seems rather bland or the reader fails to speak directly enough to focus the attention of the group, the response to a paper is minimal. On one such occasion, after a series of three such papers, one of the quiet students suddenly exploded. No one, he said, had made any comment about the papers just read except that they were "all right." They definitely were not all right and people did not care enough about each other to try to say something that was of help to the writers, even though being critical was sometimes difficult. His vehemence startled everyone, but the classes got better.

There is some evidence by students' own statements that they feel the project has been helpful for sorting out goals and in increasing self-understanding. But perhaps the most concrete result when students write about personal problems is that both students and faculty in the program become aware of some of the hassles a student may be having and thus are able to deal with the individual with greater understanding.

Thus, my goals in the course are to increase the fluency and correctness of student writing by providing a situation where there is motivation for writing well. The increase in writing skill and the experience of having an audience and being an audience increases, I believe, the self-confidence and poise of students. I also hope that they get from the personal writing project a sense of having done something worthwhile for themselves and for others, and I believe that many of them discover that writing is a pleasure and a creative outlet. The final projects which the students turn in are not error-free but they are as a whole much more so than the papers were in the traditional course. And because the correcting and revising students have done is done on their own initiative, I believe they become increasingly aware of mechanics and good writing generally.

Student response to the course is largely favorable with almost everyone feeling that at least some aspects of the course were worthwhile. In the final week of the course, students are asked to write an in-class essay in which they provide answers to a series of questions about their personal writing projects and about the relationship of various aspects of the course to the project. This excerpt from one of these essays was chosen at random and is representative:

> Since an autobiography was suggested I decided to write one. Besides who knows more about yourself than you. I spent hours thinking about the things I had done . . . in school. . . . By reading it to the class, I observed their reactions to what I wrote. They seemed to like it and it held their attention. And by listening to them I criticized their mistakes so I wouldn't make them. . . . There were some places I had a lot of unnecessary words.
>
> The writing and correction of the impromptus helped me add some life to my paper and make less mistakes. I could express myself with the exact words I was looking for.
>
> The most helpful factor . . . was time. I had enough time to get it together. The least helpful factor was my third draft, even though it wasn't required.
>
> From writing the paper I learned that I was not as good as my parents and everybody thought I was. I was lucky I didn't end up in jail, on dope, or somewhere married. My paper wouldn't have been possible without the people in it. Today I see that some of these people were helpful in turning my life in the direction it's going. I didn't know I had skill, time, and patience to write a fifty-page paper.
>
> Now that my paper is finished I feel good like I really accomplished something. My paper is the true me. Other people might get to know me better and realize that my childhood wasn't easy. But I enjoyed it. I'm proud of it and where I came from, the ghetto. It might sound strange to you but never forget where you come from

no matter how high or important you get. You got to live with yourself.

If I was willing to try something new in freshman English with Joe Brown's encouragement in order to benefit students, I was also doing it for myself. What did I learn? I proved to my own satisfaction that students who were "remedial" did not necessarily have to be segregated into a special section. My few previous experiences with remedial English classes had been that they were frustrating because the students tended to re-enforce each other's worst habits. I encourage the scattering of students in the program who have been designated as "remedial" by the school's testing service to take a remedial English course concurrently with our freshman English and most of them do. The majority of these students complete both courses in one semester. I also learned that freshman English is a time-consuming endeavor no matter how it is taught. But as I became comfortable with the new course, I looked forward not only to the class sessions but to reading papers. If the time I spent with individual students increased, the time I spent "marking" was drastically reduced. How do I feel about it right now? I will be going on to other things, but like the students, I hope, I have a better sense of who I am and what I can accomplish in the classroom.

The Hammer and Nailers

ROBERT RATHBONE

This tale concerns the plight of those students in our high schools who do not follow a college preparatory curriculum. They have always constituted the majority of the secondary school population nationally, but when I taught high school English twenty years ago they were treated as second-class citizens, looked down upon by their college-bound schoolmates, and often neglected by administrators and teachers alike.

I realize that things have improved and that there were exceptions then. So what I have to say should not be taken as a blanket condemnation. However, I happen to have taught in two high schools where a rigid caste system predominated, and the inequities are still very clear in my mind.[1]

One of the many ways in which this depressive atmosphere affected the non-college group was to stifle any initiative they might once have had to improve their writing skills. The boys, in particular, couldn't have cared less. In the school I'll use to illustrate my points, they were known as the "Hammer and Nailers." Their joy was to use their hands to turn a wrench or saw a board, but not to write a composition.

I confess I began to dislike these boys intensely, almost immediately upon starting my job as an English teacher at this school. They always seemed to be the troublemakers: they were loud-mouthed, disruptive, were always late to homeroom, and, what was worse, showed no respect for my authority as a teacher and thus as a superior being. Since I taught only college preparatory English, I was able to avoid their indignities in the classroom. So life was tolerable.

One day I received a note from the principal asking me to come to his office. The outcome was that I was asked to exchange one of my college classes for a class of Hammer-and-Nailer seniors. I questioned the wisdom of this move, but my plea was denied.

The first week with this class was catastrophic; each day was worse than the one before. The crowning incident came on Friday when one student brought a water pistol to class and squirted it in my face. My first impulse was to take a swing at this wise guy; my second impulse was to do no such thing (he was much bigger than I). Anyway, I chickened out and put him on detention.

Over the weekend I was in deep despair. I thought very seriously about resigning and even quitting teaching entirely. What to do? After much

---

1. What you are about to read is true. It has been included in this book, first, because it illustrates that the approach to writing recommended by some of the other contributors can be adapted to meet all sorts of situations and, second, because the events it portrays gave me the encouragement and understanding I needed later on to help MIT engineering students improve their technical writing. [RR]

agony I decided to give it another try—at least for a week. I reasoned that if I could keep the class busy writing I might make it. So I scratched out a list of topics they could choose from:

What are you working on in the machine shop?
What have you built in the woodworking class?
How do you keep your tools in good repair?
Are you working at any job outside school?

When the class met on Monday I wrote these questions on the blackboard and asked them to choose one topic and to take the class period to write about it. In five minutes everyone was finished! The longest paper was two sentences. Here are some samples:

"I am repairing a Chevy engine. It needed to be repaired."

"Right now I am not working on anything special in woodworking class."

"I like working in the machine shop because I like working with machines and that's what I'm doing.

"Yes, I am working at a job outside school."

I certainly had asked for it and I got exactly what I deserved. (I thought, "You just don't hand out vague, stupid topics to these kids and expect them to write like Hemingway! For God's sake, be reasonable. At least motivate! Lead!")

The truth of this revelation told me that the best move to make was to say that they indeed had answered my questions and that now I was interested in having them give me some details orally. That did it. With the right questions ("I once had a Chevy. What model is yours?" "I've always liked to work with wood; even the smell of sawdust gets me. Can you work a lathe?") I was able to draw them out. As a matter of fact, they welcomed the chance to talk without being told to shut up! I believe they even showed genuine appreciation of the interest I had in what they were doing. But were they noisy—God, were they noisy! (I borrowed a tape recorder from the physics teacher one day and put it in my top drawer. During a Hammer-and-Nailer class the needle indicating volume went off scale at least ten times.)

The only complaint I heard during that first talkathon was that they could do a lot better at explaining things if they had the actual hardware at hand while they talked. Thus began a senior version of show-and-tell. I made arrangements with the shop teachers to let us hold a class "where the action was" and it was a *qualified* success. There was much noise (of all sorts), laughter and cat calls (of all sorts), and a torturing of the English language that would make any grade school grammar teacher wince. But there were good things, too. All the speakers were interested in what they were talking about. They showed pride; they were enthusiastic; they could be heard. They even laughed when they caught themselves making a mistake. Also, the audience made a positive contribution: they applauded and cheered each speaker; they let it be known that they were having a good time. And I must admit that I had a good time too.

So far, so good. It was Thursday and I had broken the ice with the group. But where to go now? They still hadn't produced any writing for me, and I realized this next step was critical. I was afraid I'd muff it. Fortunately, the solution was not long in coming and, as you will see, the students themselves provided it.

I was about to close up shop for the day when two of the boys appeared at the doorway. One of them was the character who had drawn a bead on me with the water pistol. His name was Douglas McDonald, but he was known in fashionable circles as "Champ." (I guess he got the nickname because he was always taking a swing at someone and seldom missed.) The other chap was called "Whitey." He was the oldest student in the class and, I am told, was greatly admired by his classmates for his expertise in disposing of raffle tickets. Together, these two could easily account for ninety percent of the action in any given classroom at any given time.

I was not overjoyed at their appearance because they immediately hit me where it hurt: in a loud voice that echoed down the corridor Whitey yelled, "Hi ya, Rathie! What's cookin'?" Champ then thumped Whitey on the back and they both laughed. I was embarrassed, angry, and nauseated by this demeaning exhibition. I felt myself shrink into a state of helplessness. My pride vanished altogether as they came into the room and Whitey perched himself on my desk. I began to mouth meaningless pleasantries, not really conscious of what I was saying or what they were replying. The numbness seemed to last an eternity.

Composure finally returned and I found myself asking why their class hated to write. Their answers amazed me, for I had pegged them as being nothing more than a cross between clown and bully, without a serious thought in their heads. I will try to recount the high points of what they said.

Their trouble started back in junior high. They were not physically separated from the college kids then, but segregation existed just the same. It was especially marked in the English courses. Their papers always had more red marks on them than those of the rest of the class. And when the teacher passed them back, the red was always clearly visible. They were never asked to read their compositions aloud to the class. If they asked a question, the college kids would laugh and make them feel stupid. Things did not improve when they reached high school. Except for homeroom, they were physically separated from everyone—even from the girls who were following the business course. They were in truth branded second-class. It wasn't that they didn't think it important to know how to write, they said, but that they hated doing something they were told they didn't do well.[2]

---

2. Engineering students have often been caricatured as poor writers. Many, like the Hammer and Nailers, carry on (at best) a peaceful coexistence with the English language because of the image thrust upon them by self-admiring literates. [RR]

They reminded me that no Hammer and Nailer had ever received a prize at graduation for his writing (much laughter) and that the school literary magazine and newspaper were monopolized by the college kids. I agreed with them that they indeed had reason to be bitter about the state of affairs and asked if the rest of the class felt the same way. They laughed and replied, "Even worse!"

I stated earlier that the students brought a solution to my problem of not getting the class to write. Actually, this discussion with Champ and Whitey gave me both a method and a subject. When I met with the class on Friday I had already put on the blackboard headings for two parallel columns: *Things I like about this school / Things I dislike about this school.* I asked the students to draw a line down the middle of a sheet of paper and to put these headings at the top. I said I wanted them to make a list in each column, that the entries did not have to be complete sentences, and that they shouldn't worry about grammar and spelling. When I saw some skeptical looks, I quickly added that I wanted them to be honest and to put down exactly how they felt. Someone asked if I was going to show the papers to the principal (they called him "old poop"). I assured them that I was not.

This time they spent about half the class period making their lists. When the last one had finished, I asked them to look over their entries and to put stars next to the items they thought were the most important to them. While they were doing this I peeked at the papers in the front row. Two things were obvious: all had more items in the "dislike" column than in the "like" column; stars were being attached to *all* the entries.

With ten minutes left in the period, I collected the papers and glanced at each one as it was handed to me. I could see that most of the students had taken the assignment seriously. One, however, had nothing in the "like" column; another had written "I don't have far to walk" as his quota of praise. I congratulated the class on doing a good job and explained the assignment for Monday. They were to do the same thing with two new topics: *Why I dislike to write / Why I like to write.* There was surprisingly little moaning following that announcement, I thought.

Over the weekend I examined the lists on liking and disliking the school. To be sure, there were some ridiculous entries—some just plain dirty, judged by yesterday's standards—but one serious complaint ran through all the papers. In sum, it said: "They don't give a damn about us." I must confess that my heart was bleeding just a bit by the time I finished their papers.

What I had thought would be the hardest feat to accomplish (getting the class to write a composition) actually followed the listmaking almost automatically. At the Monday class I passed back the lists and asked the boys to concentrate on the column "Things I dislike about this school." (I had correctly predicted their reaction; they favored the idea but first had to grab at each other's papers and read an entry aloud.) I then told them that what they had done with the lists was to produce the first draft of a composition. All I wanted them to do now was to expand their entries into a finished product. The room suddenly became silent. Before they could break it, I added that I had a surprise for them. I said that I would show them how easy this writing task could be. They looked skeptical but said nothing. I then asked Champ if he would go to Miss Fernald's room (typing and shorthand) and escort a visitor to the class. I added that Miss F. knew he would be coming and would take care of things. He returned in about five minutes escorting a young lady named Lillian. I knew that she would be coming; Miss F. had assured me that Lillian was her best student and was sure she would cooperate in the plot we had hatched.

I had thought their entrance would cause some commotion (Lillian was not unattractive) but I had underestimated the situation. Everyone stood up, some whistled, some applauded; cries of "Yeah, Lil!" and "How ya' doin', Champ?" could be heard as far away as the principal's office, I'm sure. I somehow managed to make myself heard above the din and restored a semblance of order. Thanking Champ for his gallantry, I asked Lillian to take a seat I had drawn up alongside my desk. When everyone finally was seated, I explained that Lillian was there to take dictation (puzzled looks), that I wanted one of them to talk on the subject "Things I dislike about this school," using his list as notes for the talk. (Surprise; they thought I was going to do the dictating.) Someone suggested that Whitey should do it, that he was the oldest and had more experience with women. I could see that Whitey was scared, but his bravado won out and he stepped forward to take my chair at the desk.

I will not cover the event blow by blow, although it was indeed an experience for me and for the class. Whitey stumbled and bumbled his way through dictation, was interrupted at the end of practically every sentence, and interjected "Oh, Jesus!" more times than I care to remember. But he did finish. I don't know how much of what he said Lillian took down. She was busy all the time, taking advantage of the interruptions to finish a previous sentence or to make a correction. Only once did she cause confusion by asking Whitey to repeat part of a sentence. He couldn't remember what he had said.

The next day everyone received a neat, typed copy of Whitey's dictation when they arrived in class. I had him read it aloud to the class and then we discussed it. By the end of the period, everyone seemed to be sharing Whitey's feeling of accomplishment.

From that point on the struggle to impart a small degree of writing skill to the Hammer and Nailers grew less difficult. As their hostilities decreased, so their interest and participation grew. It was not possible, of course, to let them all have a crack at giving dictation to Lillian. But they were quick to see that their solution to the problem of overcoming the psychological block about writing was to make a list (we never called it an outline) and using it, to talk their way through what they had to say to the class. It was the medium they knew best and they felt comfortable with it. They then found they could transcribe their thoughts into writing because they had been over the ground before. None of them won an English prize at the graduation exercises that June. However, they did give their English teacher a generous round of applause at the end of the last class. That made everyone feel good.

The Disaster Workshop*

NANCY DWORSKY

I had set up a class in lyric poetry with the expectation that we would read in class both "real" poems—that is, published poems—and poems we were writing. After a few weeks students weren't bringing in poems of their own, pleading that they just couldn't write right now. We decided, therefore, to bring in disasters, poems that we could not make work as we wanted them to—nor could we throw them away as total losses. To do this implies a number of things: (1) the author wants to change the work; (2) he has a real need for help in resolving the poem one way or another; (3) the most painful thing that can happen to him in a class is to have others agree with his judgment. A student, then, comes to class eager to benefit from criticism instead of being eager for praise. This differs from the usual situation where someone reads a work he feels finished with. There he wants it accepted, not torn up and handed back for reconstruction.

In a disaster workshop different people will, of course, work in different ways. One member got an idea about how to rework her poem that was totally unrelated to what others were saying about it. She was truly grateful to the student whose comment had triggered her thought because she had been unable to discover this idea by thinking alone. Not only did she learn something about her poem; she also learned something about the value of working with others. Then there was the student who said not a single word while his poem was being discussed, but took voluminous notes on everything said. And another who learned that an image he'd thought secondary actually carried the greatest effect to his readers, and hence decided he could go back to working on the poem, developing that image more sharply and simplifying the rest.

In every class I've taught there has always been at least one student who feels his words on paper are an inviolate extension of his soul. Such a student cannot bear to change what is once written, for it feels like a personal mutilation. He usually speaks of others' work only in terms of whether or not he can relate to it, and he rejects criticism of his own writing by falling back on the unbridgeable abyss between perceptions: "If you don't get it, it's too bad, but irremediable." It seems to me these students suffer greatly from criticism and use all the defensive techniques they can to protect themselves. Unfortunately, their armor fends off learning as well as pain. It turned out that an invitation to bring in a disaster was not more threatening to that student in my class, but provided him with extra protection and perhaps even the possibility of benefit. What he did was bring in, instead of a disaster, a poem he had clearly worked hard on and was pleased with. The first response he got from the class was everyone's assur-

*From *College English*, vol. 35, November 1973, pp. 194-195.

ance that it was not a disaster by any means, and then some reassurance that it was even comprehensible. When we then went on to discuss some things that perhaps could be improved he noted what we were saying and showed signs of accepting it.

The particular expertise that a teacher has to offer is most useful to a class under these conditions. What he knows better—or should know better —than the rest of the class involves the relation between what someone is trying to say and how they are saying it. In the more common situation, where a teacher is addressing a finished work, his critical ability tends to be useless. The exact point where the what of a statement is out of touch with the how is apt to be experienced by a writer in one of two ways. Either it is a passage that he is extremely pleased with and feels cannot under any circumstances be changed (which, in my own experience, is a sure sign of something amiss), or he's a little afraid that the passage doesn't quite work and hopes no one will notice it. In either case, when a teacher points to the offending part, the student feels attacked and rises to his own defense. When, on the other hand, he knows he is having difficulty and has presented his writing as needing improvement, he is most in a position to learn from the teacher's ability to pinpoint the problem.

I do not know whether approaching writing through disasters could work well with genres other than poetry. I'm quite sure there would be no difficulty with short stories, but I'm less sanguine about expository prose since so much of the work there necessarily turns on clarity of image, action or intention. Nevertheless, I think it would be worth trying with a class, perhaps as a writing workshop in conjunction with a lecture course. To the extent that analytic writing is intended to improve learning (rather than provide a means of evaluation) such a writing workshop might be highly useful. In any case, I hope there will be more experiments with Disaster Workshops. However counterintuitive it may be, I find it a hopeful road on which to move toward openness, trust, and serious discourse among students and teachers of writing.

ending

Scraps

SETH RACUSEN

Usually, we feed scraps to the dog. If he didn't already eat them. *These* scraps were taped together and ripped apart and stapled and underlined and crossed out and footnoted and inserted and. . . .

What really held them together were the comments of a few friends. (The night before they saw this, I had given up the hope of ever finishing, clinging to the idea that there'd be a *next book* this could go into). I might well have begun all over. You never know. Maybe I should have. And maybe I still will.

Writing this was a struggle. I've tried to leave some of that struggle in the piece; actually, I've had little say in the matter.

The draft before this began like this:

Somehow the agony of the writing process itself
always gets filtered out by the final draft.
Editing and rewriting and then polishing removes
the rough edges that might reveal the strain the
writer went through to put a piece of writing
together.

That might be the case with this piece of writing.
And that would be a shame: I've never struggled
this much with writing before.

One of the first titles was "Scraps From a Book of Agony." It began like this:

Every time I begin this piece, my voice is too
heavy. I sound like a missionary trying to convert
16th century natives into civilized Christians.

I'm not sure I will sound any different this time.
Maybe I should become a minister.

or something like this:

> Writing can never match the life it describes:
> and our lives can never match that life either.

like this:

> This society is one that alienates people. There
> are people who seem to operate well in this
> society: there certainly are some who profit
> from it. People are not the roots of this society.

or this:

> Writing and teaching writing are not activities
> isolated from the rest of what we do.

or even like this:

> I've been waiting for some time now to discover
> just what it is I have to say about writing,
> teaching writing, life on this planet, *something*
> that would belong in this book. I've written
> many scraps to myself: asking Questions,
> finding Answers, unearthing new Problems,
> understanding Failures, all trying to make some
> sense of it all.
>
> The scraps were all written in many different
> voices.
>
> I wrote all the different scraps.
>
> The purpose of this piece is to blend the voices
> and to connect those threads I always agonize
> over and then write scraps about.

And there were other beginnings: "Why live?"; a painful entry from one of my journals; a proclamation of my need to write in a clean room. Much of this has been written beneath a pile of papers.

And somehow this has emerged from that pile of papers. I really can't say anymore about cutting paper, taping it together and revising outlines and using multi-colored index cards with key ideas on them and the difference between typing and handwriting, especially when you can't type or read your own handwriting, or using a red pen or a black pen or lined papers vs. . . .

And here is another way this piece once began:

I often wonder what I am doing with my life: will any of what I do prove worthwhile; will any of it improve my life or anyone else's?

When I think of writing, or teaching at MIT or the Cambridge Pilot School, an alternative high school within a school, I question the value of my activities: will they prove worthwhile? What effect does writing have on people? Or talking about writing in a group? And what effect does a particular classroom style or educational system have on people?

I've spent whole days in bed, not wanting to
leave because there was no reason to.

I've spent hours at this typewriter, typing
endless strings of letters and syllables.

I've even written stories about meaninglessness.
The stories were meaningless.

When I've been depressed, nothing matters: the
people I know, the things I do. There is no
purpose to anything: work, play, good times,
bad times.

I remember writing that.

I also remember feeling that way. I still feel that way every now and
then. Usually, I don't get as dragged down as I used to. But I do remember
those long stretches of writing dull, boring stories; of feeling that nothing
was important, and that I had nothing to say. (And even when there was
something worthwhile, it wasn't worth writing about because I wanted to be
a "liver" and not a writer. If it was really worthwhile, I wanted to do it, and
not write about it.)

And I remember what kept me going through those bad times and
beyond: encouragement.

A lot of it.

Those who helped me through my writing blocks were encouraging.
They always managed to find some good points in my writing, and would
stress those in giving me any criticism.

And they were patient and understanding, and kind and consid-
erate . . .

They were teachers and students and friends and some of them are
authors of this book and some are elsewhere writing and some are. . .

Those people were important because I was reassured, knowing that
people I trusted and cared for believed in me.

And the writing classes I took were important because I had audiences who wanted to read my writing; they had liked some stuff I had written earlier.

I no longer write for those audiences. What I need to do now more
than anything is to take the time to write the two or three novels rolling
around my head. Three years ago I wouldn't have taken that thought very
seriously.

Slowly, you learn to talk about writing in those classes. Someone's
eyes light up when another person says, "You know, the main character in
your story reminds me of this dog I used to have . . ."

And someone disagrees, "No, he's no *dog*; he's Bogart! Don't you
see . . ."

And they argue. The author appreciatively takes it all in.

Slowly, you learn that whatever it is that you always hold inside and never say[1] is okay to say because you like hearing what everybody else has to say and like it best when others are being honest.

And you learn to respond not only to a piece of paper but also to a person. You learn to respond uniquely to each person, according to what you think would be most useful.[2] Honesty is always essential.

Some people are sure of their writing; some are not. We each are more confident about some pieces of writing; very tentative about others.

I try to respond to the writing on a gut level and gear my remarks so that they will be useful to the writer.

I've misjudged many people: there have been far too many instances when I've thought someone to be more sure of h/hself than s/he actually was or that person knew me well enough to take my comment as I thought I had intended it, instead of as a put-down. "Oh, so this isn't good enough" is how people usually react in that situation.

How do you get someone to reveal more: I always believe that writing has to be revealing for me to be interested in it. Often when I ask for more, I suspect I do it in a way that's forgetting just how supportive my friends 'were of me when I was in trouble and just how important they were.

There were times last spring when everyone I met seemed depressed except for one or two people who seemed happy. I couldn't understand how they could be happy at a time like that. They couldn't understand why everybody else was so depressed.

And then there are days I feel irrepressible. Anyone depressed would not want to be with me.

And when I'm depressed no one understands me.

And I never understand anyone else who's depressed.

I'm not surprised I've misjudged people in making remarks about their writing.

Just about nobody enjoys remarks about, "Oh yea, I saw the same story line in a Superman comic last week. Is that where you got it?"

Or: "You would have been better leaving out. . . ."

Some people can manage to say things that I, for one, can't. And every once in a while I slip in a line that someone else couldn't say. How you say what you say can be as important as what you say.

If the underlying message of a comment is "stop writing," the writer will hear that message and will get defensive, stop listening and/or stop writing. I've seen all three. As teacher, as friend, as a member of the class, whoever I might be, I've got to prevent a person from being buried. But usually by the time those words, "Ah, just, ah, why did you write this piece anyway?" are uttered, it's too late.

---

1. Because   (a)   it's-too-obvious-and-everybody-knows-it-anyway-so-why say-it; and (b) it might be *wrong*. [SR]

2. One recent suggestion that everyone write down at the beginning of a class what kinds of comments s/he wants makes a lot of sense. [SR]

The student teacher program began in September of 1972. We didn't know what it was at the time, either. The idea was this: students would team-teach a class with a teacher.

1. The student teacher, being closer to the other students in age and experience, is not as imposing as the teacher, and should make the other students feel more at ease in the classroom.

2. The student teacher would be more accessible to the students outside of the class, and would be more likely to get together informally; this, too, would put the class more at ease.

3. When students hear the two co-teachers arguing, they know it's okay to argue. When they hear them cut each other off, they know that's okay too. In short, the teachers and students shed their roles and become people.

The presence of students as teachers has usually broken down the traditional notion of authority that we all have. Occasionally, student teachers have been more authoritarian than the teachers. Overall, we've worked out pretty well.

As a student teacher, I felt responsible for what happened in the room. When there was a long silence after a reading, I would feel obliged to break the silence, and would do that more than before. And I held conferences with other students and I had to be understanding of them: I couldn't just not like them and be pissed at them like I normally would be. I was caught in all the binds that teachers are caught in: being torn between wanting to like all the students and simply not liking some[3]; interactions in the class are expressions of the feelings between people, good or bad, and a teacher is caught in a funny position, an unresolved one.

Sometimes I meet someone who seems lonely, in need of a friend or lover, and I realize that I can't be that friend or lover, that I can do nothing for that person.

Those persons can be students. I need to draw lines to protect myself from getting involved more than I want to. People usually use professionalism to insulate themselves. I turn icy cold. Aloofness can be a form of professionalism.

---

3. I keep wondering whether I am being dishonest in believing that I've never disliked any student (though some annoy me more or less sporadically) or whether I was just being namby-pamby. Some interest me more than others, certainly. But usually, in a writing class, people do try hard, and I keep seeing that, whatever that makes them do. I make it clear at the beginning that I will use every bit of power and responsibility and authority I possess to defend anyone who I think is being unjustly attacked; and I can do that honestly, I say, because I've never seen a piece of student writing that didn't have something interesting, some glimmer of a real possibility, in it. (I've seen lots of impossible writing in print, on the other hand.) The result is that people aren't mean to each other in my classes, and that's the only thing I could really dislike them for.

Digression: It used to be true that a second result of this statement was that many students, particularly freshmen, interpreted this to mean that they mustn't make any negative comments at all; with the result that when papers were read no one would say anything except me, burbling along, falsely cheery.

I think people are usually aware when I create walls, although we never talk about it; they, too, pull away. The real issues are usually too scary to deal with.

And too complicated: a mix of good and bad feelings must be added to the scenario. And my perception that, as far as I can tell, only I seem to be aware of the situation, which leaves me perplexed: we can't talk about a situation which undoubtedly will cause pain.

Sometimes I suffer, sometimes they suffer.

Sometimes whatever I do hurts.

Being a student teacher also made me learn more about talking about writing than I had learned before. I drew on past experiences and learned how to deal with people in different situations, how to be more useful for more writers.

I've always felt that what qualifies me the most to help others with their writing is that I've struggled so much with my own writing. That qualification is contingent on my memory of my struggles.

I, too, often forget the past: as we get older, we forget what caused us to be the way we were and we are often least understanding of those who do what we used to do:

I used to avoid my writing teacher when I wasn't writing much. I was embarrassed, would feel guilty whenever I saw her.

Two months ago one of my students was avoiding me. I was upset at the time: I couldn't understand what was happening.

Now, sitting at the typewriter, remembering the two events together, enables me to understand them both a little more.

I've learned something writing this chapter now.

Learning to talk about writing is not learning to be a literary critic; but is learning to talk with others to their faces about things that are important to them?[4] When you know them well, you might laugh with them about their problems and your own, but at the beginning, you tread water cautiously, hoping you're not blowing it.

Writing can communicate on many levels. When writing is read to a specific audience, it may speak to them in a way it would not speak to

---

But I still felt it was worth it, letting the writer know I was on his or her side, no matter what. Oddly enough, this kind of silence doesn't seem to happen anymore; when students have seriously negative comments, they keep an eye on me to see how far they can take them, knowing I'll intervene if necessary. And usually I don't have to; for one thing, other members of the class will usually rise to the author's defense in a more pertinent way than I can, and, for another, the critic remembers to be careful. Being very clear about my position on this has served to free, not stifle, the discussion. But it took me time to become that clear. [PC]

4. And about their writing. Literary critics primarily want to help other readers (and themselves) to a better understanding of an author's work. The purpose of a workshop is primarily to help the writer to a somewhat different understanding, one that will be of help to that author in accepting, clarifying, improving his or her own writing. [SWR]

others: MIT has few women; they are usually isolated in classes. A number of MIT women wrote stories in different classes last spring about their bodies being ugly, to which no one could adequately respond.

In those and many other similar instances, the writing ceases to be an artistic creation for the reader and becomes more of a direct communication to the reader, a request, a plea of a sort. Responding to a piece like that can be a delicate, elusive process, one that often leaves me feeling confused as to what's really going on. Rarely will a group dismiss that process.

Which leaves me now with the thought that those women might have gotten much more out of an all-women's writing class, group, or whatever, where they could discuss those feelings more freely and get more responses. I'm not at all sure if that's what they would have wanted either. But I have been in many classes which had one or more people who seemingly should have gone elsewhere with their writing and/or feelings for a more appreciative auditnce, if that is truly what they were looking for. And I think that they were.

Responding to a piece of writing is a struggle to understand another person.[5] Demonstrating both the struggle and the understanding is important. I need to feel understood; just knowing that someone is trying to understand me is rewarding.

The openness of the writing classes enables things to happen in these classes that should happen in school, but ordinarily don't.

The teacher does not pretend to know what is right and wrong, will not give assignments, will not tell students what s/he really wants; this is frustrating to those of us who are used to that other kind of teacher. That style forces us to look more closely at ourselves and each other; and to pay attention to what we each say. In a group of ten or fifteen, there's a fair chance that most people in the class will find some others who they will be interested in, and who will make the class worthwhile for them because of their interesting comments. The more traditional teacher keeps that from happening by stealing the whole show: either you get something out of that teacher or you don't. (The value that the opinions of class members are important nourishes the value that each member of the class is important, has something to say, and should write. Ta-da: *another* connection between a writer and h/h audience.)

Those writing classes spoiled me. I have never tolerated a class since that didn't allow real communication; a class in which the teacher was the major event; a class in which I didn't have the opportunity to learn from other students. Whenever I've run into a class like that, I've dropped it.

---

5. And to understand yourself. The main problem I've encountered in classes is silence; people just don't know what to say about a piece of writing. It is almost superfluous to add that writing classes are also reading classes, for much of their success depends on how well people are able to discover and express their own responses to a piece, to perceive and record the thoughts, sensations, emotions, images—reactions of any sort—that flowed through them while reading. [SWR]

In the beginning the classes are boring. Everyone is uneasy, putting h/h best foot forward. People reveal little of themselves in their writing: the class is afraid to talk about their writing.[6] Students are trying to find out what the teacher wants. The teacher is trying to find out why the students really are taking the course. Everyone is checking out everyone else.

This is a trying time, especially for teachers who agonize. Like Julie Olson, a student teacher:

> The greatest concern of mine right now in my class is the lack of contact, communication.
>
> There are people who are not coming to class. On one hand I realize that this is all right, that for many people the class isn't useful. Yet I worry. Many of the people haven't written anything and I don't want them to have to drop the course. Either I haven't created enough options or I have provided too many of them. I'm not sure. I don't want to pester people and call them up, yet I would like to know why they're not writing.
>
> My main fear is that I have been too frightening to members of the class. It's difficult for me to sit back and say, "Ho, Hum" in a writing class. I always want to challenge people, to push them a little further into their thoughts and experiences. And that is frightening, I think. It strains one mentally and physically and perhaps that is too much to ask of people who have other obligations, obligations that take priority over writing and humanities.
>
> I am taking out my frustrations with the structured university situation on the students in my class. I would like for scientists to have time for humanities, for writing and reading and knowing about themselves. Thus, I, in my own way, demand commitment.
>
> I look now at this piece that I wrote two weeks ago and the issues don't concern me as much anymore. There are still people who have written nothing, but I feel that there is little I can do in that matter. I will be meeting with these people to talk and either there will be some solution or there will not be one. I cannot pressure or prod, nor do I want to. Writing does not come from outside the writer.
>
> The doubts that I have had about the importance of running the class so loosely have in many ways been resolved. Many of the class members really liked it. They are producing more (and better) writing than ever and several people have told me that they are feeling happy about their writing.

---

6. It's natural that people become interested in each other's writing only after they become interested in each other. The first six to eight weeks of a course impose a structure, create a wall of writing for students to hide behind, to mask what's really going on: getting to know each other. A paradox: people need a purpose to get together naturally to know each other better and they need to know each other better to pursue the task. Writing is a goal for the group and a catalyst for the entire process. [SR]

Most of us attended schools to become a certified whatever-it-is. We take the courses we need to graduate; we fulfill the requirements a teacher demands to pass or get an A.

And we pass and we get our A's and we graduate. And we become certified whatever-we-ares.

That side of education exits in those writing courses.[7] We can't escape it. Another quality, much more important, saves them: people learn in the courses and actually enjoy them.

. . . I think I learned more about myself from this course than from any other I've ever taken. I enjoyed the format . . . I also liked writing and having it analyzed socially, morally, ethically, etc. (and technically once in a while) by my peers as well as by the instructors. . . .

. . . Doing the work and going to all the classes is really worth the time put in. I have found that it is possible for me to do creative writing, something I have never had much success at, because of this course.

. . . My biggest satisfaction arises from the fact of having been able to write what I desired on a social issue. After all, I can start considering the English language not only for technical expression, but also for written subjectivism. . . . [from a foreign student]

A great course . . . that allows the student to learn something about himself while fulfilling course requirements. Perhaps more time should have been spent on the way people write instead of what they write. I don't mean grammar and such, but more the approach taken and whether it keeps attention, says something or just words that anyone would say.

. . . The course also introduced me to questions concerning roles. . . . Who are the teachers? Who are the students? . . . Who are the doctors and who are the patients? Who assigns us our roles or are our roles taken on naturally at birth . . . or soon after. . . . Agee writes that "in every child who is born . . . the potentiality of the human race is born again." Does this mean that we actually don't take on specialized roles or does it mean that each of us takes on every role in the course of our lives? To me, both meanings are the same. I sincerely hope that Agee is right about this.

This class, ostensibly for writing, showed me a lot about people and myself.

---

7. But the freshman course was pass/fail. I think we've pretty much abrogated the certifying function. [PC]

8. Essentially, dope should not be made into another capitalistic venture. Risk, schmisk, most dope dealers are out to make money. [SR]

9. The other teacher. [SR]

10. Gary and I had taught with him the previous fall. [SR]

The class was titled, "Writing as Social Responsibility," which proved to be an albatross. I gave a lecture at the first class on the social responsibility of dope dealing.[8] There were three important reactions:

1. People thought they had to write on social responsibility. Everyone wrote at least one essay on social responsibility.

2. Someone tried to sell me a pound after class.

3. We got drunk the first four or five classes, enjoyed each other's company, did little writing after the initial surge of social responsibility essays, and gave each other limited feedback.

Gary[9] and I were upset at the way things were going. We had conferences with every student to say, "Let's talk about the writing more; let's be more serious." People took us seriously, mostly agreeing. One student offered his next writing as a guinea pig, saying, "We can cut mine up; I don't mind. Really."

Somehow, it happened: the class jelled. People began to write; stopped worrying about social responsibility and the reading list, and began to talk seriously about the writing.

Sandy[10] and I have spent many afternoons agonizing together, looking for ways to quicken that jelling process; we both decided it can't be done.

Yes, conferences help, and yes, some group activities help, and yes . . . yes . . . yes. But, people need time to get to know and trust each other, enough time to risk expressing themselves on paper and in class.

Our agonizing uncovered that, but we knew it all along. Always returning to what we suspected was true confirmed our belief in those truths. Which is probably what we set out to do, anyway.

One day a student read a piece about his friend who had attempted suicide. It was a piece on his feelings about a friend's suicide attempt: the sadness of realizing life wasn't worthwhile for a friend, and the anger and confusion of feeling inadequate for someone he cared for. His friend, another member of the class, was unaware that the piece was written, submitted, and xeroxed: he was not prepared to discuss the incident with the class or anyone else.

He was furious. We all were scared. We talked about suicide. We talked about anything else we could talk about. I remember asking for three shows of hands:

1. who had ever seriously thought about suicide
2. who had actually ever tried it
3. who had ever been successful

The third was considered in bad taste.

That others had also contemplated suicide and were extremely unhappy at MIT calmed his fury. That evening was an important one.

He eventually forgot about suicide; he even learned to stand MIT. He wrote this about the course:

This course was the only one this term that excited me and the only one I willingly work in. The classes are extremely interesting. I haven't done any creative writing in years, but this course has renewed my interest in it.

For him alone, it was all worth it.

Those who were most interested in doing the readings, who needed to be told what to do, when to do it, were most frustrated with us, with the course. We were also most frustrated with them.

> Sometimes, I get the feeling that the class lacks substance. . . . I can't get involved in the discussion. There are times when I feel that none of us are on the same beat. This is when Sandy and the two TAs should step in. I'm afraid that too often you people are out of touch with us and don't realize that we are losing direction and need help. [mid-term]
>
> . . . You didn't enforce us to do anything you lets us get away with murder. . . . If I had the class it would only meet 3 times a week and I think I would get more writings out of the people. . . . I would be more stritch than you was. [final, from a high school student]

The fear of not accomplishing much, not learning anything, is one that accompanies the fear of the lack of structure, direction. This student shared those fears; one of his comments below is a response to me saying, "Show us more of you."

> I don't think you have to go very deep into a topic to write about it. I also think that unless you are churning out TV programs, dirty paperbacks, comic books, fortunes for fortune cookies, or the like, you don't need to write for an audience. I think you should write mainly to please yourself. If your thoughts have any value to others, they can also read what you write if they wish. And if others don't wish to read what you write, so what? Who cares!
>
> This course was a very easy Freshman humanities option. It could have accomplished much more than it did if a list of books to read and a timetable (which would be kept to) were voted on the first day.

I believe it was a good experience for MIT students to struggle. I believe we all need to struggle with ourselves, but I am more fearful when I see

---

11. That we were able to attend meetings was the result of one student, Gary Woods, doing something that had never been done before, something that was unthinkable, something that would never have happened or have been sanctioned by "normal events." He sat in on a literature section meeting. They threw him out and then voted to allow students into future meetings. (I guess they must have had something important to say and thought that to be their last chance.) [SR]

12. A class analysis explains some of the difference between me as MIT student and the students at Pilot. I'm part of the alienated white middle class who reject materialism (we can take it for granted) in search for other "more important" things: a sense of being worthwhile. People from lower economic

people who are already downtrodden struggling than when I see people who have been told many times they were the cream of the crop struggling.

A few of us at MIT who were feeling particularly powerless tried to influence our academic fates. We began to attend literature section meetings[11]; we interviewed candidates for the two vacant positions; and played a major role in the selection process. Many of the faculty came into the final hiring meeting with their minds made up in favor of a candidate we could not tolerate. He was not hired; neither was our first choice; our second choice was. That evening was the height of student influence in the literature section.

Being active in classes led to being active in the literature section and to becoming student teachers. Being responsible for a class as a student teacher led to being more active in the literature section. Once I had taken that responsibility in the classroom, my perspective was changed: I never again could be an unknowingly apathetic student. Today, when I am apathetic, I am consciously apathetic.

Many college professors and their cronies speak of students and education in a way that they would not want others, especially students, to know about. Our presence changed the nature of meetings we attended.

But they were so tedious. We didn't do nearly enough of it.

In my year at Pilot School, I have never seen Pilot students act quite the way we did in classes, meetings of the literature section, etc. And although students played a major role in hiring, I was dismayed last spring when students withdrew their support of a candidate after some staff members favored another person. No student spoke or voted for the candidate most of them had liked in the final tally. That we at MIT are four years older, living away from home, are located in a more conducive educational climate, and were treated specially in schools are factors that could explain the difference.[12]

They have almost all been told they were stupid (ordinary, or worthless) along the way. For them to act in a way responsible for themselves, they would need to believe in themselves in a way they've been schooled not to.

---

classes are interested in that aspect of life, but usually achieve it within the context of what's more important for them: living decently, obtaining those material goods necessary and pleasurable for life.

School for them is mostly skill-oriented (and job-oriented), fun, and/or meaningless: writing can fit into any of those categories, but for me, writing seldom fits any. It took me quite a while to realize and accept that writing will be different things for different people.

And the student's feeling that the teacher knows what's right and wrong can only come from accepting the system's values, being put-down often by teachers and eventually by each other, from not taking themselves and each other seriously. That feeling is the one that drives me *crazy*, but, of course, keeps things together. [SR]

One student in my writing class in the spring had been told by a teacher that he couldn't write dialogue and that he shouldn't ever again. I told him that that was a lot of crap; that I was sure he could write just as I was sure he could talk; and that the only way something could improve was to work at it; that everybody could always improve h/h writing. He uses a lot of dialogue in his writing now; it sounds much more natural; his writing improved a lot over the term. What I feared at the end of the year was his decision to transfer to Cambridge High and Latin, one of the two "standard" high schools. Will some teacher there say something to him that will undo what he learned this spring? I tried to prepare him for that possibility so that he won't ever be hurt badly again.

Another student was informed before the start of the term that he didn't belong in another class that met the same period as the writing class I was teaching. The message he heard: You're not smart enough. He had been told that before.

He joined my class, still smarting from those words. I had set the page requirement for the term at 30 pages; his teacher told me he'd be lucky to do 10. The first month, he would write 5 lines and either rip it up or throw it out. He had heard me criticize a piece someone else had written and was convinced that his stuff wasn't good enough; that I'd make fun of him.[13] I realized he feared me, so I made a point of encouraging him; telling him that I knew he could write a whole page but also that whatever he did was fine. He wrote 5 pages in the first two months of the course; 25 in the last two months. I do hope that his next teacher is not judgmental; he also could be undone easily.

The students in my class had been judged their whole lives: the comments they got from teachers were judgmental; the comments they made to each other were cutting more than supportive. They often wanted to know how they were doing relative to each other.[14] At times they made fun of each other.[15]

They listened to me much more than they listened to each other. There were small groups in that class that grew to like each other; people within those groups paid attention to each other.

But as a group, the class flopped. They were uneasy at first to share their writing; they were uneasy all along to share their feelings on each other's writing. Class discussions of writing usually consisted of me giving feedback and asking questions of them.

---

13. My journal entry for that day was:

How do you get people to reveal more of themselves? _____'s immediate reaction—"Oh, so this isn't good enough." I must begin to accept anything _____ hands in. I must seem and feel pleased whenever he shows me anything. At this point, I will be pleased if he shows me anything. [SR]

14. "Did anyone else get an A+?" [SR]

15. Their feelings when they act that way are related to my feelings when I've felt meaningless; when people treat each other destructively, they are usually destroying themselves internally. [SR]

I saw some of them grow as writers and as people. The class failed as an audience in the sense I was used to at MIT: only written comments between students proved worthwhile.[16]

From their vantage, the class was one class out of many and I was one teacher out of many. Each term, they've learned to adapt to what the teacher wants. They eventually learned that I wanted them to write what they wanted to write; to try to experiment with their writing. I certainly mentioned my values: that writing be personal and engaging and. . . . But for them, my demands were one in a series of many conflicting demands. Next year, they'll have to put up with new ones.

We English teachers met several times (actually, *they* met quite a bit; I was at only a few of the meetings) trading assignments, most of which seemed interesting to me. Some worked; some didn't. The best assignment turned out to be no assignment at all.

I walked into class wearing shorts one day. Which prompted this:

> Well today I came into my teachers class. And he was wearing shorts. And the hairs on his legs were brownish black. And fuzzy like a thorn bush his knees were scabbey. And rinkled his feet were long. and dirty on the bottom. Just put it this way his legs are jamed. And his head you just want to spit on it to make it clean. Because it looks like a wet mop that has never been cleaned since it been there. His glasses looks like bi-focals. And his beard is kind of clean for a change. He has hairy armes that are like an ape and it is about time he changed his pants and shirt. And he was wearing these funny tongs on his feet that were ready to fall apart. And he had pimples on his face. And a heat rash all over his body from what I see.

Who would have guessed that wearing shorts would be the most provocative suggestion I gave that student all term?

They didn't learn to talk about writing in a group; to take responsibility for what happens in a room. They would ask me at the beginning of a period, "Hey, what are we gonna do today?" That question eventually drove me up a wall. How do you get people to be spontaneous?

I grew depressed with my role: telling them what they would have to do each day; sometimes my suggestions were useful; sometimes they weren't. I saw no reason I should come in and make those suggestions every day.[17]

---

16. I saw one student beaming the day after he and his parents received the report card in the mail. I included comments the students left in each other's folders on each evaluation. He had apparently never read their comments. He was surprised, pleased, flattered. Those comments changed his attitude about the class and himself. [SR]

17. A journal entry from then:

> I can't find what will be relevant for them. I can show them what's been relevant for me; what kinds of things attract me that I write about. I could get friends to come in and talk about similar topics (although writers, including me, are generally reticent to talk about

I eventually decided that *they* could do basically whatever they wanted to, related to writing: write, read each other's writing, think, talk, draw on days they were depressed, happy, etc. The one rule was that people should not interrupt others who were working.

If I were working with them over a longer period of time, I might have stayed with that. But their response to that over the next few weeks made me reassert the authority I was trying to shed and get them to sit down and write.[18] Some of them told me that that was what they had wanted me to do all along.

People acquire certain feelings when they are powerless:

1. the feeling that they've got nothing to say.

2. the stronger feeling that what they're saying doesn't matter; either nobody's listening or really cares, or nobody will act on what they say anyhow.

3. the feeling that nothing good can be done.

4. the feeling that the authorities (teachers) have the situation in hand; they have already made a decision, or they are the only ones who could make a decision, because of knowledge, etc., that they alone have.

I've heard frustrated students at the Pilot School express those sentiments after school meetings. I have heard parts of it before at MIT, at the high school I attended; the words are spoken in many places.[19]

I attended two all-student meetings at Pilot in the spring. I was disappointed. Students were not really listening to each other: I as the only staff member present felt obliged to remain quiet, hoping that somehow they would start to get themselves together. They didn't that time and from what I've seen at MIT, I doubt anything will come from what they did do.

Most Pilot School classes don't happen when the teacher doesn't show; most classes and activities in the school are dependent on teachers. That in part explains the failure of the all-student meetings. That they happened at all is a good sign, but not good enough.

Somehow, something is missing from the place. Perhaps it's the strength to be kooky and say something stupid in front of a group, or the strength to disagree with a large group. It could be the freedom we feel when we know we're doing something we want to. It's an intangible something that's missing. What's in its place is that feeling of destiny, that we all

---

the process of writing itself). What I've got to do is try and get them to share some of that with each other. Peers sharing experiences will help each other in ways someone else cannot. . . . The students communicate with each other—verbally. I must get them to try communicating on paper. [SR]

18. Some would read, write or draw regularly. Most would talk at least occasionally. Two would usually smoke cigarettes in the corner and look out the window. One would ride my bicycle; two would still ask what to do. I would talk with most of them at times. They mostly hung out in groups of two. [SR]

19. I speak them quite often. [SR]

go to school to prepare us for work we won't like either, because there's nothing else we can do. It's all been charted out. It's detestable, but others have lived through it. Our parents, for example.

Students enter Pilot School already accepting reality as it is taught to them; that most of them will not be a part of the rich, powerful elite of the society. They already feel ordinary, if not worthless. They hear what their teachers and textbooks say; they can see their parents' situations. They seem headed for more of the same.

The children of the rich are pressured by their parents to do well; they won't settle for less. Those children won't settle for the crap that usually gets dished out, are usually treated better by being put in private schools or "accelerated classes," as I was.

When I went to high school, I cut class for two months. I got suspended for three hours after others began cutting, too. I was "accelerated." They wouldn't dare do to me what they had done to others. They had already met my mother. She had defended me once earlier over a C+ progress report. The teacher involved never gave me another C+.

Just as their parents accept their fates, the children learn to accept their own fates, to learn to write for each successive teacher, to please when they are to succeed. They learn how much they are to succeed and how much they are not to succeed.[20]

Too many graduate from Pilot unable to read and write fluently, unable to express themselves clearly. I've seen too many people abused by a power who could read or talk quickly (landlord, employer, prosecutor, salesman, etc.). Who needs high rents, long hours, outlandish fines, encyclopedias?

Students must leave schools today able to express themselves verbally and on paper; able to question others; able to help themselves and others; able to have some control over their lives. They can if they're allowed to and encouraged to in school, if they learn to question the values that permeate this society, the schools, too many of the teachers, and most of the students by the time they reach Pilot.

That is the task of Pilot, of alternative education, of these writing classes: to undo what has been done, to free people to express themselves, to believe in themselves enough to risk themselves on paper in tricky situa-

---

20. I told one student at mid-term that I would be giving him an incomplete for the third quarter, but he could still get an A for the semester if he wrote a lot in the fourth quarter. He was worried about the incomplete; he said he couldn't show that to his mother. I told him I didn't know what to give him; he asked for a C+. I told him then that I'd give him a C+ for the third quarter and an A for the semester if he wrote a lot. He couldn't believe it; he wouldn't believe me; he had never received an A before; he always got B's for himself; this talk of an A was not credible to him. (He was the same student who wasn't "smart enough" for that other class that met third period. He left, very puzzled. He returned in the fourth quarter, as you know by now if you've been paying attention, and wrote a lot.) [SR]

tions, to help others they wish to help, to question those who must be questioned. People must learn to stick up for themselves and each other and regain some power over their own lives.

And what about me? I've got to live with a preachy ending; the realization that I didn't "blend the voices and connect those threads . . ."; the piles of paper in the still-cluttered room; and of course, I'm stuck with me.

I understand now what was missing at Pilot. The school has classes that are similar to the rigid social and economic classes that exist in society. The school seldom increases stratification, but does little or nothing to eliminate it.

Realizing this on paper is not enough, but I know I'll have a tough time conveying this stuff to others. It lies just below the surface to be denied by those who deny those sort of things and by those too innocent or oblivious to notice.

I know I will be at Pilot next year. But I do feel torn by various possible approaches, desires, personalities:

1. I want to write; I want to be a serious writer. I want to travel; I want to play guitar better. I want to get those things out of my system. I want to cultivate me; to think only of me, before considering anyone else or pursuing the other possibilities.

2. I want to become a "better person," more supportive and understanding of others.

3. I want to change others; to learn how to speak effectively to others to change them.

4. I must make time for my writing.

And somehow I must share what I've learned. I must pick a forum to share my view of life, of the Pilot school, to deal with those real issues that we don't normally deal with. All of us there must be willing to risk ourselves in many ways.

I'll run a writing class called "Writing and Living," or "Writing at Pilot," or maybe "Writing and Experience"; it really doesn't matter what it's called.

I'll begin the course by reading this piece.[21,22] They'd better say nice things after I read it.

And I'll tape the classes and keep a journal this time.

I'll keep one drawer empty for my scissors and my pens—the red one and the green one—for scotch tape and lined paper, for multi-colored index cards, for a stapler, for once-used typing paper, for . . . my scraps.

The dog will have to look after himself.

He always has.

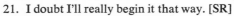

21. I doubt I'll really begin it that way. [SR]
22. Sure enough, I didn't. [SR]

appendices

Appendix I: Smarterbook

PETER ELBOW

The Smarterbook exercises are a more sophisticated form of free writing. Because they seem more structured, they appeal to some people more; they truly stretch people's thinking; and they liberate them. Not everyone wants to be free, though, and sometimes the exercises meet with resistance, at least at first. It is worth persevering with them, however. Free writing alone is usually interesting to the reader, but not always to the writer: Smarterbook often has the effect of convincing the writer as well that what has been said has imagination, uniqueness, energy, and voice. It has transformed some people's writing. "Those papers you gave us at the beginning—those were the best things in the whole class." Answering these questions can make you discover things you might never have dreamed possible.

The earliest Smarterbook exercises were devised by Peter Elbow and Dwight Payne. What follows is a small selection of exercises revised by Peter Elbow. A longer series will appear in a book on writing by Peter Elbow to be published by Oxford University Press. [PC]

1. THINK OF A PLACE YOU KNOW

Go to this place now in your mind. Look around and see everything there. See and feel the time of day, the time of year, the weather, the lights and the shadows, the quality of the air. Hear the sounds. Smell the smells. Dwell in the reality of it for a little while.

1. How has your mood been affected by being there?
2. Imagine being there for a whole year. Tell how it might make you better. And also how it might make you worse.
3. Imagine this place had never existed. What is there instead?
4. Imagine you are a tiny animal who has always lived there. Describe the things you notice from your animal point of view which humans usually don't notice. Then describe the things humans notice that you do not notice.
5. Name an animal your place makes you think of. (If you can't seem to think of one, put down the first animal that comes to mind right now.)
6. What color does your place make you think of?
7. What mode of transportation does your place make you think of (for example, roller skates, rocket ship)?
8. What person does it make you think of?
9. Imagine you are someone who thinks this place is very beautiful. Be this person and describe the place.
10. Imagine you are someone who thinks this place is ugly. Be this person and describe the place.
11. Imagine you are someone who thinks this place is boring. Be this person and describe the place.

170

12. Imagine that your body is the whole world. Where on your body is your place?
13. In what weather is your place most itself?

Take a pencil and paper and write without stopping for 10 minutes. Start with something about your place, but then just keep writing as fast as you can. Don't worry about or try to correct spelling, punctuation, etc. Don't stop for anything. If you slow down and don't know what to write, write anything, or write "I don't know what to write" as many times as you want. But don't stop, don't read over what you've written. Let the words take you where they want.

2. THINK OF ANOTHER PLACE

Close your eyes and take yourself to your place. Be there during a moment when it was important to you. See and feel everything there: the time of day, the time of year, the weather, the lights and shadows, the quality of the air. Hear sounds. Smell smells. Stay there silently a minute and let the experience fill you.

1. Imagine you have always been blind. Describe your place briefly.
2. Let the place describe you.
3. Your place is an animal. What animal is it?
4. Your place is a person. Who?
5. Name a story, a song and a movie your place reminds you of.
6. What is the first thing you think of that your place would never remind you of?
7. What other place does your place make you think of?
8. In what weather is your place most itself?
9. Some places have a proper name all to themselves—like "Chicago." Other places only have a general name they must share with similar places —like "bathroom." Give your place the opposite kind of name from the one it has.
10. How does this new name change things? (For example, how would your feelings be different? What things would you notice now? What would you *not* notice now? Would things happen differently there now?)
11. Find as many of your place's rhythms as you can. (For example, find things that happen there at regular intervals—whether they happen every second, every month, or every 1,000 years. Or any other sorts of rhythms you notice.)
12. Name as many things as you can that only happen there once. Are there any rhythms among any of them?
13. Think of your place as if it were old and near death. Now tell what place it was when it was only a child.
14. Think of your place as if it were a young child or young animal. Now tell what place it will grow up to be.
15. If "——————" stands for the regular name of your place, what does the following sentence mean: "If you do that again, I'm going to —————— you."

16. Imagine your place was the whole universe and you had always lived there. Tell how you and your neighbors explain the beginning of the universe. How do you folks think the universe is going to end?
17. Think of your place as if it is carefully planned in every detail. Now describe it briefly from this point of view.
18. Think of your place as if everything just happened by accident, chance, and luck. Describe it from this point of view.
19. Think of your place as if it is haunted. Tell about it (for example, how did it become haunted? What does it do to people it doesn't like?)
20. Imagine an anti-universe where everything is opposite or backwards from the way we know it. Describe your anti-place in this universe.
21. Take another sheet of paper and write whatever comes as fast as you can without pausing at all for ten minutes.

3. THINK OF A PERSON YOU KNOW

Think of an event in your person's life. Close your eyes and silently try to get into your person as this event is happening. Try to experience it in all its details and particularity. Make your five senses register. And your feelings.

1. Imagine that event is happening not to your person but to yourself . . . as yourself. What does that make you notice about yourself, your person, or the event that you hadn't noticed before?
2. Think of things your person possesses. Name the first three you thought of.
3. Tell how each is like your person or could symbolize him (her).
4. In what weather is your person most himself or herself? Do you know why?
5. Your person is an animal. What animal? Do you know why he is that animal?
6. Your person is a tree or plant. What tree or plant? Tell why if you wish, but you needn't.
7. Remember a particular occasion (different from the one above) when you were with your person. Go back and be there. Experience the details and the reality. Now switch to being your person and tell what things he would notice most.
8. Think of your person as a very good person and describe him briefly from this point of view.
9. Think of your person as a very bad person and describe him briefly.
10. Imagine something that would never happen to your person.
11. Imagine it happening to you. Try to have the opposite feelings about it from what you'd expect to have.
12. Think of your person as someone who can be well known and understood just by looking at him and reacting to his appearance: clothes, movements, posture, etc. Describe him from this point of view briefly.
13. Think of your person as able to be understood by looking at major changes in his life. Turnings. Describe him from this view.
14. Think of your person as able to be understood by seeing how he has never *really* changed at all; what look like changes are really just ways of remaining the same. Describe him.

15. Humans are fully free. They choose and cause what happens to them. Deep down they want it and are responsible. Describe your person in this light.
16. Humans are not free at all. They have no control over what happens or over the direction of their lives. Describe your person.
17. Find as many rhythms as you can in your person's life. (For example, events that repeat or recur whether the scale is in seconds or years.)
18. What events in your person's life occur only once? Any rhythms?
19. Tell a science-fiction story concerning your person.
20. Tell a riddle with your person in it.
21. Write for 10 minutes as fast as you can without stopping.

4. PICK A NUMBER BETWEEN 2 AND 15 THAT MEANS SOMETHING TO YOU

1. Can you think of an experience you had with this number (#) that might be the reason you chose it? If not, imagine an experience that might have had that effect. In either case, try to relive that experience fully. Have a hallucination for a minute or so.
2. Tell what dream you might have had if you fell asleep after that experience.
3. Name a few things you think # might make you think of.
4. Name a few things you think # might never make you think of. (Name at least 4 things.)
5. Numbers are always "going into" other numbers or "making" other numbers. (a) What numbers go into #? Name a few if there are lots. Are there any numbers you would make go into # if you had your way for a week or two? (b) What numbers does # go into? Are there any you wish? (c) Name a couple of numbers that make #. Any you wish?
6. What other things besides numbers go into # or are gone into by #? (Answer according to wish or reality.) What other things make or are made by #?
7. In each of the boxes below, place # dots. Whatever comes easily. Then connect the # dots with # lines to make a #-sided figure in each case.

8. "I'm going to count up to #, and if you don't start before I finish, I'm going to . . ." What scene comes to mind? Who is talking to whom about what?
9. Let the 5 boxes above somehow or other suggest to you 5 rhythms for beating out # beats on someone's back (or the table if you are alone).
10. Which rhythms seem most male; female; animal; vegetable; mineral; alive; dead; beautiful; ugly. (Write the words next to the boxes.) If each rhythm stands for one of the fingers of the hand, which is which?
11. Make the roman and arabic numeral for #. If each were a foot tall, describe the mode of locomotion of each.

12. Which part of the body does each resemble most?
13. Which everyday object does each resemble most?
14. Suppose both the roman and arabic numeral for # were busy being used for some different purpose: make up the most suitable roman and arabic numerals to take their place.
15. What activities would # people be ideal for? bad for?
16. Describe how things would be if there were # sexes.
17. If people had # fingers how would things be? What would we be good at and bad at?
18. Imagine there were a religion that worshipped #. Quickly make up a brief prayer those people would use.
19. How did that religion come about?
20. If # married another number, which would it be? What children would they have? Ditto, if it married a letter of the alphabet.
21. Go back to question 4 and see if your answer implies what you are thinking or feeling.
22. Write for 10 minutes as usual. Don't hurry, but don't stop.

5. THINK OF A THIRD PLACE

Go there in your mind. Choose a particular moment. Look around and see everything there. See and feel the time of day, year, weather, lights, shadows, air. Sounds, smells, textures. How your body is arranged. Stay there a minute.

1. If your place were a tree, what parts would be the roots? leaves? sap?
2. Imagine your body was the whole world. Where on your body would your place be?
3. Imagine the room you are now in is the whole world. Where in it would your place be?
4. If you fell in love while in some particular region of your place, what region would it be?
5. Who would you fall in love with while there?
6. If your place fell in love, what other place would it fall in love with?
7. Which of the two places would end up loving the other more? Would they stay in love?
8. What would these two places have for babies?
9. Imagine your place as a weapon. Tell how it works: what makes it go off? how does it hurt its victim(s)? who uses it? against whom? what weapon can overcome it?
10. If there were not only "french-kissing" but also "------kissing" what kind of kissing would that be? ("------" is the name of your place.)
11. Think of your place as an ecological system. *What goes into it?* i.e., what is input? what does it eat or breathe in?
12. *What comes out of your place?* What is output, what does it breathe out or sweat? what does it vomit, piss, or shit?
13. *What does your place go into?* for who or what or where is it input? what eats it or breathes it in?

14. *What does your place come out of?* What breathes it out or sweats it? what vomits, pisses or shits it?
15. Imagine your place as a disease. What does the disease attack? What are the symptoms? What is the treatment?
16. Imagine your place as medicine. What is it medicine for?
17. Who invented the medicine? How did he do it?
18. Imagine your place evolved from some place else. What place did it evolve from?
19. Imagine your place evolves into some other place. What place will it evolve into?
20. Make up a proverb that inhabitants of your place would use.
21. Think about your place and write without stopping for 10 minutes. As fast as you can. Write whatever comes.

Appendix II: Writing as an Agon or *How to Write an A Exam With a C's Worth of Knowledge*

NANCY DWORSKY

Not all writing is joyful, creative, and self-fulfilling. More often than we would like to think, writing is an agon.[1] Students are most familiar with this kind of writing, and it permeates other stations in life as well. Many letters, petitions, proposals, memoranda, recommendations, applications, etc. fall into this genre. As a separate genre it is characterized by a particular *tone*, that is, a particular implicit relationship between the writer and the reader. This is a hostile relationship. One in which the reader has power over the writer and is preparing to exercise that power, while the writer must depend on the written word, with no hope of success save the reader's good will—which the writer has every reason to doubt.

Under these conditions, the natural, fluent, and honest writer employs a tone of cringing subservience displaying with hopeless clarity his fear and helplessness. The reader, corrupted by power, as he necessarily is,[2] feels disdain for the specimen before him and judges him inferior, unworthy, wrong.

Even the most upright writer wishes to avoid this. He must consciously discover and adopt a tone more suitable to his ambitions. For this situation demands a tone of assurance rising from unquestionable authority —neither arrogant nor condescending (which is the tone most easy to slip into when you're trying to cover up anxiety. It's dangerous because it can make the hostile power that you're addressing quite vindictive.) True authority is free to be gracefully courteous, implicitly flattering to the audience by speaking to it as an equal. The writer must address his reader as friend and co-superior.

This is a hard stance to adopt when you're scared. It takes practice and it takes a sense of humor. Because as soon as you feel the seriousness of the situation, fear bubbles to the top. It is only reasonable that practice should be undertaken in school and the techniques mastered before entering the other world where the stakes are often greater than mere grades.[3] And it is useful to learn this tone through the writing of examinations for a number of reasons. First, in exam-taking there are some mechanical means that are always helpful, never fail, and can therefore be relied upon to pro-

---

1. What are you giving me, agon? I'm supposed to know agon? What do you want me to do, look it up? I can't look it up. My dictionary, it's ahere today, agon tomorrow. [KS]

2. Power corrupts; total power corrupts totally. Thucydides. [ND]

3. Grades don't feel so mere when you're in school, but they become that way from a postgraduate perspective. [ND]

4. Cf: Deeds cannot dream what dreams do. e.e. cummings. [ND]

vide a comfortable framework in which to practice writing with a confidence you lack. Second, the results are gratifying in themselves and provide positive reinforcement to an attitude of competence rather than helplessness in the world. (It could be argued that this attitude is unrealistic and hence should not be learned—except that claiming autonomy sometimes brings it about.)[4]

The third reason to learn to write an A exam with a C's worth of knowledge, and do it, and compare experiences with others who do it, is so important that it deserves its own paragraph: it makes you understand, deeply and sincerely, the differences between learning well and getting good grades. This is a difficult distinction to make, especially if you have been brought up to believe in justice, and your elders, and the institution of the university.[5] But grades and learning are not the same thing, and sometimes do not even speak to one another. And you do no honor to learning by confusing it with grading. When I was first in college the section man of a course I was taking was asked how the course was graded. He replied that he would grade the way he felt like grading. He added, after a stunned silence in the classroom, that he wanted to be fair, and he wanted to have his grading reflect the quality of learning that had gone on, but he was fallible, and other factors at times affect student performance; fairness might be an ideal, but it was not a reality. He told us we might as well learn from the beginning of our college careers that grading was ultimately subject to personal whim. His assessment was realistic, not cynical, and I have been thankful for it: it helped me value what was worthy in school and disregard what was not.

Recently, I found myself chatting with a group of unknown students about exam writing. I was admonished by a woman who declared that she preferred to take an A's worth of knowledge into an exam, and earn her grade. I recalled the first college exam I'd ever taken. It was in summer school and no one had told me anything about exam writing, so I wrote with a pencil, on both sides of the page and got a C on the exam. I was really surprised because I thought I'd done well. And upon comparing mine with an A exam I found that indeed the only real difference between our papers was the visual impression. The student who'd felt so superior to examsmanship shrugged her shoulders and said "well, of course . . . " And I imagine it was "of course." But that doesn't make it just and fair. If it is true that aesthetics makes the difference between an A and a C, then grading does not validly reflect the quality of learning, QED.

But the best way to learn is from your own experience. Once you have honestly and sincerely written an exam with a very little knowledge and

---

5. I love Nancy's cynicism so. So hard and clear—rings so clear. Admittedly she isn't "honest" either—she's pretending to be something different than she is—she puts a terrible spin on the ball—she hides warmth and affection and acceptance in very sneaky ways—double and triple ironies lying all over the place. But I think she puts lots of cues all around that acknowledge she's doing that—and that she's taking pleasure in putting spin on the ball and inviting the reader to join in the pleasure. [PE]

have gotten an A on it, then you will know for certain that good grades do not mean good students.[6] And then you are also in a position to use your own judgment on whether poor grades necessarily mean poor students.[7]

But now on to examination writing. Here are the rules:

1. The most important single aspect of exam writing is penmanship. If you happen to write legibly, you have an advantage, though not a decisive one. If you write illegibly, you must write on every other line to give the impression of trying to be as legible as possible. (You like the grader and want to help. All A students do.) Of course, ink and only one side of the page. But the most important aspect of penmanship is rarely mentioned: your handwriting should not vary from the beginning to the end of the exam. This is hard and takes practice, and care in timing since you will be writing more slowly after three hours if you're going to maintain an even hand, but it is well worth the effort. When the handwriting is smooth and even, no grader can believe that you're panicked, confused, and don't understand the questions, let alone the answers. The penmanship makes you seem so beautifully controlled.

2. The second most important factor that everyone can master is spacing. You must write the same amount for every question of the same length and you must do the questions in the order in which they appear on the exam. This is quantitative, not qualitative. If for every half-hour question you write five pages, then for every hour question you write ten pages; for every identification four lines or whatever. No exceptions. The reason for this is that when you write ten pages on one half-hour question that you know very well, and two and half pages on the next one, you do not demonstrate how well you know the first. Rather, you demonstrate how comparatively poorly you know the second, and an A student (which is the narrative voice in which you are writing) can answer all questions with equal ease and pleasure.

But how do you write equal amounts when you have unequal amounts to say? This is where you call upon your literary facility. When you have to squeeze a lot into too little space, you let your style break down, join points with dashes, even let sentences disappear. When you have nothing to say, the easy flow of friendly discourse takes over, e.g., "If this can be argued as valid, the question arises of whether there might also be any merit in the converse position?" Obviously it isn't always easy. Only experience can prove how vital spacing is. The impression that a well laid out exam gives the reader is that the student handles all questions with aplomb, is flustered by nothing, has the whole course under control. Under these circumstances, he is willing to forgive an oversight or two, believing that you really know whatever you omitted, but lacked time or were so interested in what you were writing that you forgot it by accident.

3. This brings up the most important substantive (as opposed to formal) piece of advice: never put your foot in your mouth. That is, never

---

6. Unless, of course, you manage to convince yourself that you're just more brilliant than you'd thought. But then honesty's gone out the window. [ND]

declare something as fact that you are not absolutely certain of.[8] This is difficult to follow when you have to cope with identifications—which is why identifications so often appear on exams. If you think you have an answer but are unsure, say so. Only identify positively those things you are absolutely certain of. If you misidentify something positively, you look like a fool and demonstrate your ignorance. If you admit uncertainty, there are two possibilities. Either you are right, in which case the grader sees that you really know the answer, but under the stress of the moment doubted your own knowledge; or you were wrong, in which case the reader sees that you aren't so far out of it, because you at least had an inkling that something was amiss. In either case, you demonstrate that you are in control of the situation. Obviously you are, if you're so at ease with your knowledge that you feel free to admit where it is incomplete.

(If you know very few or none of a whole series of identifications, it's hard to be graceful. You need a lot of chattiness, e.g., "This could be from N's Discourse on W, in which case it would appear when he is discussing Q. On the other hand, it might be R attacking N's position. I really am not at all sure where it's from." There are your four lines and you've said nothing incriminating.

4. There are a few less important rules that should be followed whenever possible. One is footnoting an exam. Provided you do it with a light touch, footnotes are very impressive. They should be references to things outside the course that you've read or thought of or someone has told you about, which in some way are laterally connected to what the exam question is about. Such footnotes provide a friendly touch, and make the exam pleasant to read.

Another rule: state the question you're answering at the beginning and the end of your essay. Don't copy it off the text, but paraphrase it. This shows that you know what you're supposed to be writing about at the beginning, and restating at the end suggests that it is just what you have been writing about. Together, the two statements suggest a clear organization to your essay that it may or may not have. And organization is highly valued in exams. If you are gifted with the ability to organize you need very little else, since organization often takes the place of content. This may sound snide, but still it's true. Because they are trying to squeeze a whole course into a couple of hours, exam questions often are so sweeping that there isn't time to write anything but an outline of what an answer might properly include. I remember a one hour question on an exam that said: "Discuss the relation between the New Economic Policy and Soviet Theory." There just happened to be on the reading list a 752-page book on this precise subject. While studying for the exam (see below) I had taken care to learn the chapter headings of the book, so I reproduced them on the exam, commenting that there was no time to discuss these things in detail, and citing the assigned text. That's all I put in the hour question. I got an

7. They don't, but that's another topic. [ND]
8. Cf: It does no good to tell more than you know, no, even if you do not know it. Gertrude Stein. [ND]

A. I don't think the grader was an idiot. It's just that the coolness and clarity with which I had gone about writing the table of contents convinced him that I really must know the substance of the book.[9]

A friendly tone, provided it does not become too familiar, is always appropriate. The reader does not expect it, and is impressed by it: you must feel very confident indeed if you can be so free and comfortable. My favorite example of this comes from my own experience with an economics course. I had not paid much attention to the course, in fact had missed all the quizzes and most of the classes, had studied desperately though minimally for the exam. When I saw the exam, I felt there was no hope. I scarcely understood the questions, and certainly was in no condition to answer them. But I was stuck for three hours, so I wrote along, chattering. As a leitmotif, I kept coming back to copper bottom frying pans in each question. (The specific reason for "copper bottom frying pans," rather than "pots" was that it took up more space, and I did need something to fill space with.) I left that exam feeling that I'd really made a mess, and hence was amazed (since I did not know then what I know now) when I got an A— on the exam. I had an opportunity to talk with the section man informally a week or so later, and I asked him how he had happened to grade as he did. He insisted that I had written a good exam—until he looked into it (for he still had the bluebooks in his office). And he declared with some disbelief, "You're right! It's nothing but bullshit. I was led astray by your literary talents." He was a pleasant chap, and aware that exam writing was an agon, so he didn't really mind being bested in the game.

Clearly, the grader was capable of more realistic judgment than he had shown. But he was not in a condition to read well when he was grading. The grader as powerful, ominiscient and wise is a fantasy conjured by the helpless student. He is, in his own way, as harried as the student. (I know it is true. I have been both people.) He is working against a strict deadline by which all grades must be in. He is, above all things, bored. He tends to be also irritated. There are many things he would rather be doing. He hates his work. It is two o'clock in the morning. He wants to go to bed but he has fifteen more exams to read before the nine o'clock deadline. He hates all the illiterate students who are trying to bullshit their way through the course, having learned nothing and being interested in nothing. He hates them for mixing up the questions so he can't read through a bluebook efficiently. He curses them for scrawling. He would like at least to tell them what he thinks of them, but the exams won't be returned so his only relief is marking down for every trivial error.

Into his airless study comes your exam. It is neat, controlled, friendly. It does not break down into a miserable scrawl, nor do answers go on forever when he least expects it. It is written in a human voice by a real person who demands and deserves respect. It was written by an A student.

I think a few words are in order on exactly what constitutes a C's worth of knowledge. And also, perhaps a defense of writing exams with this

---

9. I don't know if I believe this, Nancy, and if it's true I don't think I approve. But what the hell. [KS]

knowledge instead of with an A's worth. The fact is that you will never be able to write a whole A's worth of knowledge into one exam. Knowing too much, or thinking too clearly and deeply, may interfere with writing properly. If you have learned a great deal in a course, have enjoyed it and worked on it and feel satisfied, that's well and good. However, when it comes to writing the examination, you are best advised to forget all that, and settle down to studying for the *exam*, and for nothing else. (I used to knit while doing this studying. It left me with something to show for exam period which otherwise would have been a total waste, since one doesn't learn much that stays long.)

How to study:

1. Get hold of an excellent set of lecture notes, one that preserves every one of the lecturer's favorite thoughts and insights. It is a good idea to pool notes with other members of the class and go over them together. Whatever the reading list covers, whatever a section teacher's personal emphases might be, the exam will focus on the professor's favorite topics. You may feel perfectly free to disagree with what he has said (A students often take that liberty) but you must first reproduce it accurately. The better you know these notes, the better off you are. There may be an opportunity to refer to an anecdote that Professor X told—or you may need it for padding.

2. Read selectively from the reading list (you don't have the time or the energy to read it all), concentrating on conclusions to chapters and final chapters. The table of contents can be a good outline if it's trying to be informative rather than enticing. Try to grasp whether the book you're reading supports or conflicts with your professor's opinion. This is a useful thing to mention on the exam. Again, working with other people can be a help, though in this case you will learn more by telling someone who has not looked at the book what it is about than you will by trying to get information from others. Telling is a way of learning. Listening is more apt to be a service. (Ask teachers; they're almost sure to tell you they never learned as much in a class as they have teaching it.)

College outline books are useful if handled with care: They have been written, by and large, by hungry professors who are basically loyal to their brethren and hence hostile to students. For this reason, they often include gross errors which, if repeated on the exam, indicate immediately to the reader that you have not read the material. I know this is true. I have caught students doing this and have responded mercilessly.

It is a good idea to read something from the "Suggested Reading" list, even if, or especially if, you have not read the whole required reading list. It gives you something to refer to, if only in a footnote. It suggests that, like a real A student, you have been so interested in the material that you have gone beyond requirements. And it is often easier and more pleasant reading than anything in the list of required texts.

Read over those lecture notes again.[10]

---

10. I also have lectured to classes about the very similar techniques a friend of mine used to pass exams in college. He and a group of friends would

When I lectured on this topic to my classes at Harvard, I was often greeted with disbelief. That is, my classes felt that I wasn't really giving useful advice, but just ego-tripping, telling how great I was in beating the system. I began to beg for testimonials from people who had tried the method, as well as suggestions from anyone who'd come upon new and useful techniques. And I did get testimonials. One was from a student I didn't know who stopped me in the yard one spring day. (I had been pointed out to her by a student I did know.) She told me that she had been running a D+ going in the final of Soc. Sci. 1, and rather than knock herself out to get a B on the final and a C for the course she had just forgotten the whole thing until the night before the final. . . . There she was with time running out and she panicked. Her roommate had notes on my exam writing lecture, and she felt she had no time to try anything else. So she studied the lecture notes and followed my rules. And sure enough, the exam came back with an A— and a B for the course. She stopped me in the yard to thank me. I was equally grateful to her. It made me warm and happy to know that I had been of some use in the world, especially knowing that I had sowed the seeds of proper disrespect. Teaching is a fundamentally subversive occupation.

---

get together a few nights before the exam with a complete set of lecture notes, a complete set of texts, and selections from the assigned bibliography. They worked very hard. They outlined the lectures and the books (using chapter headings and introductory and concluding paragraphs); they memorized key dates and theories, and the spelling of all important names (this is very important—about 3 a.m., a student who has not bothered to learn to spell the name of a central figure in a course can drive a grader to give up on human nature forever). In other words, they organized, and came to understand a vast amount of material so that they could summarize it and present it concisely. It was intelligent and efficient, and it is genuinely a good skill to have—politicians, for instance, and executives, must have it in order to operate well.

I saw my friend recently, at our 20th reunion, and I told him I had told my students about his method. He was surprised, and then he looked sad. "But I feel bad about that," he said. And so did my students when I told them. In a business situation it's OK, but in college it feels like cheating. It feels like a betrayal of what college is all about—learning. Even if, for one reason or another, some, or most, courses fail to live up to that ideal, it is real, it is one of the things that has produced this book. And we are willing to seem sloppy or naive or scared and receive C's so as not to betray it. We don't want to get away scot-free with not-learning (even though the kind of studying you describe *is* learning).

Nancy, I agree, but with bitterness and despair. The President is not supposed to lie, and college is not supposed to teach me to do what feels like lying, and give me an A for it, either. And you can't tell me to accept and cope with all the injustice there is in the world—especially not at exam time. Listen, I've got all those books—*important books*—to read and remember. All those ideas. I've been lazy, I fell in love, my roommate has had a rough time this term and has needed help. But I wanted to find out about these things when I signed up for the course, and I still do. They're important. Not for the exam. For me. [PC]

Appendix III: Other Suggestions on Writing as an Agon

PATRICIA CUMMING

There are other situations besides examinations when you are pretty sure you are writing for someone who doesn't like you and/or what you are going to say. There are times when you must write it in a language that is not your own, that seems foreign, rhetorical, dishonest. There are times when you must communicate material you do not even want to think about, let alone work out sentences which explain it neatly. At these times self-discipline, obedience, necessity, and will can flail or quail. The suggestions that follow cannot make anyone doing this kind of writing enjoy it; we hope, though, that they may help at least to get it done.

1. Drop the course or get another job.

2. Ask an objective friend to write it . . . or edit it . . . or rewrite it . . . or type it . . . ; and especially proofread it. When you are out of college you can pay someone to do this.

3. Write it with a group of similar beleaguered souls (friends, not a committee). Bring beer, wine, food. Also pencils and paper.[1] Talk a lot, and bring a tape recorder too, if possible. A separate room with a typewriter is also useful.

4. Sometimes you can adopt a persona and pretend you are writing a play; the report is something a character in it would write (your professor or your boss or Erle Stanley Gardner). Write the piece as if you were writing a monologue in his or her voice.

5. It often seems necessary, particularly at the beginning or the end of these pieces, to say something eloquent, sweeping, profound, or rhetorical. This is hard, even or especially if you believe in what you are saying, because these sentiments have usually been expressed thousands of times before. It is hard to say anything arresting about the function of the university in America, for instance, or the need for values. In these cases, *quote.* Even if you have to spend half a day in the library finding a properly prestigious person who has said what you want to say, you will save time in the end.

6. Write about why you don't want to write the piece. Or free write about anything that comes to mind. Or try a Smarterbook exercise. Anything that gets you writing at all will help.

---

1. A number of authors of this book had to turn out a proposal at one of our meetings; although we were well supplied with things to eat and drink we found we had only one writing implement between us—Joe Brown's special pen —plus a two-inch pencil stub. And the only lined paper we had was the similarly sacrosanct pad on which Joe was completing a short story. At two critical points we had to turn what we thought was the next-to-final draft over to friends who put it in shape for us. [PC]

7. Read your piece to a writing group. Form one if necessary. Tell the other people in it what your deadline is. It is possible to hand in something late to a supervisor or a professor and accept the consequences of your misdeed, but it is harder to disappoint a group of friends who are counting on you to finish.

8. Even one other person who is sympathetic and concerned about your progress helps. One friend demanded to see two pages (of any kind of writing) every day of a thesis-that-was-not-being written. People who feel guilty about not writing often get angry at the person who is trying to help (make) them write. Sometimes that anger frees them to get to work. But you should both be prepared for this.

Also, be sure your friend reads the section on "Responding to Writing."

9. *Be sure* to get someone who can spell and punctuate to proofread the final copy. In this situation you are virtually certain to make mistakes.